PRAISE FOR
PULLED BY THE ROOT

"*Pulled by the Root* by Heidi Marble and Alysa Zalma, MD, is a fascinating and compelling exploration of the complications of being adopted and how adopted people struggle to navigate the relationships adoption creates and also legally extinguishes. With Dr. Zalma's psychiatric analysis of Marble's challenges to maintain a complex web of relationships, the book becomes a tag-team effort to provide context to what we all struggle with as adopted people: meaning."

—GREG D. LUCE, Founder of Adoptee Rights Law Center, Executive Director of Adoptees United Inc.

"I've know Heidi as one of my most popular breast-cancer-survivor speakers for fifteen years. Knowing how she's touched the hearts and minds with her sometimes brutal honesty and yet magical storytelling (with notes of ironic humor), I was not at all surprised by the frankness, beauty, and grace of her words in the memoirs. Along with psychiatrist Alysa Zalma's perspective, they blend each chapter with lived experience and psychological understanding. Among Heidi's many intimate revelations, she shares the gifts she inherited from both of her mothers. I was struck immediately by these words she wrote about her adopted mom: 'you used words like paintbrushes.' You will find her story engrossing, heart wrenching, and revealing in the depths of emotion of mother–daughter love, complicated by the torn-up roots that mark every adoption."

—BARBARA CHRISTENSON, Owner,
Speak Well Being Group

"Like Heidi, I've traversed the intricate terrain of reunion with both sides of my biological family, navigating through a myriad of complex emotions. Despite the diversity of our experiences, the common thread is a profound need to unravel the roots of our existence.

"*Pulled by the Root* is a delicate balance between Heidi's vivid recollections and feelings on her riveting journey of self-discovery and the insightful analysis of her experiences provided by Dr. Zalma. The harmonious convergence of the two voices creates a narrative that is both heart wrenching and heartwarming."

—CHARLES RAGINS, Two-Time Emmy Award–Winning Animation Designer, *The Simpsons*; Fine Artist, Writer, Adoptee

"The adoptee experience is often one of isolation. This book provides the chance to be connected through shared experiences and emotions that are based in both science and spirit. It creates a space for introspection that feels raw yet safe. A space for vulnerability, courage, and ultimately healing."

—MOLLY WASHINGTON, JD, Attorney at Law, N'dee/Apachee Adoptee

"Heidi Marble tells her adoption story of relinquishment with deep-felt emotions, depth, and rawness. Dr. Alysa Zalma's chapter analysis weaves in the science of how the body and mind experiences trauma, which gives the reader a deeper understanding of the complexities of the adoptee experience. It is an essential read that touches the heart."

—JANET NORDINE MS, LMFT, RPT-S, Adoptee

"Heidi Marble and Alysa Zalma have written a remarkable book that sheds tremendous light on the experiences of adopted children as they navigate their lives. *Pulled by the Root: An Adoptee's Healing Journey from Trauma, Shame, and Loss* tells the very personal story of Heidi's experiences with both her adopted family and, later, with members of her biological family who she discovers as an adult. She also explores how her experiences as an adopted child impacted her relationships later in life. Each of Heidi's chapters is followed by a chapter by Alysa Zalma, a board-certified psychiatrist and therapist, discussing the remarkable psychological challenges experienced not only by adoptees but also by family members in both adopted and biological families. I read this book from several perspectives: as a neuroscientist who is interested in how life events can impact our behaviors and personalities; as a science communicator who is passionately interested in communicating the science underlying human experiences; and as an adoptee who, like Heidi, has experienced growing up with one family and then discovering an entire other family as an adult. To be sure, not all adoption experiences are the same, and some of the discussions in the text may not apply to everyone. But I learned so much from the combination of personal stories and the concise and clear analyses proved by Dr. Zalma that I will carry with me throughout my own journey as an adoptee. The book also provides remarkable insights that will help everyone, from any background, understand both the joys and the challenges of adopting a child and of being an adopted child."

—**LARRY S. SHERMAN**, Author, Public Speaker, Professor of Neuroscience, Oregon Health & Science University, and President, Oregon and Southwest Washington Chapter, Society for Neuroscience

PULLED BY THE ROOT

Pulled by the Root: An Adoptee's Healing Journey From Trauma, Shame, and Loss

by Heidi Marble and Alysa Zalma, MD

© Copyright 2024 Heidi Marble and Alysa Zalma, MD

ISBN 979-8-88824-099-1

All rights reserved. No part of this publication may be reproduced, stored in a retrieval system, or transmitted in any form or by any means—electronic, mechanical, photocopy, recording, or any other—except for brief quotations in printed reviews, without the prior written permission of the author.

Published by

köehlerbooks™

3705 Shore Drive
Virginia Beach, VA 23455
800-435-4811
www.koehlerbooks.com

PULLED BY THE ROOT

An Adoptee's Healing Journey from
Trauma, Shame, and Loss

HEIDI MARBLE AND
ALYSA ZALMA MD

VIRGINIA BEACH
CAPE CHARLES

DEDICATION

To those who have been pulled by the root, may you find ground to stand on.

Maybe you are searching amongst the branches for what only appears in the roots.
—Rumi

To be rooted is perhaps the most important and least recognized need of the human soul.
—Simone Weil

AUTHOR'S NOTE

Please note that letters, emails, and journal entries have been edited for clarity and *Chicago Manual of Style* guidelines, but the authenticity of the pieces have remained.

TABLE OF CONTENTS

Foreword 1

A Note 3

Introduction 5

Preface 7

Chapter 1: I Chose the Blue One 9

Chapter 2: Finding Marty Jo 30

Chapter 3: Stuck at Thirty-Five Mph 58

Chapter 4: True Grit—The Cowboy Way 69

Chapter 5: Bugs and Windshields 90

Chapter 6: My Queen, My Wongee, My Grandma 109

Chapter 7: Uncle Smack... 134

Chapter 8: Weezy 151

Chapter 9: Love Can Build a Bridge 168

Chapter 10: Simple Kind of Man 204

Chapter 11: Sun-Te-Uh (Sontia), the Quiet Finnish Queenx 221

Chapter 12: A Boy Named Amy...................................... 234

Chapter 13: Counsel 248

Acknowledgments: 263

Bibliography 265

FOREWORD
by Jennifer Utley
Director of Research at Ancestry®

As a family historian and storyteller, I've discovered amazing stories in countless family trees. And I've learned something that is undoubtedly true: *being human is messy.*

It was true for our ancestors. It is true for our families today. It is true for each of us.

Finding ways to cope and navigate the mess has become essential. And for those who face the additional complexities of adoption, there isn't just one path, and the path is often unclear.

The lessons shared here in *Pulled by the Root* could be one of those ways to find healing. Heidi Marble and Dr. Zalma offer a heartfelt look at Heidi's personal journey and point out not only ways to identify the trauma but also how to work through it.

Pulled by the Root explores adoption from the heart, mind, and soul, offering lessons learned from each perspective. The book is a delicate dance between memoir and therapy session, examining what it means to be a child, woman, daughter, sister, niece, wife, mother, mother-in-law, and chosen family. Through archetypes and personal stories, the reader is invited to traverse the landscapes of forgiveness, permission, and healing.

I am neither an adoptee nor a therapist. But through my work, I've witnessed firsthand the unfolding of countless adoption stories. Some reunions are beautiful, fostering healing experiences that bridge the gaps of time and circumstance. But some, sadly, are not. Which is okay. Sometimes, just knowing the truth is enough. Like a family tree, each story is unique, with its own twists, turns, and intricacies.

Through AncestryDNA, I unexpectedly found myself on the receiving end of a long-lost cousin's adoption revelation, experiencing the gamut of emotions—shock, excitement, fear, and an alarmingly strong instinctive desire to protect family. This journey has afforded me a personal entry into the complex, multifaceted nature of adoption and the profound impact it has on individuals and families.

As you follow along with Heidi's journey, remember to be kind. Acknowledge the multiple sides of every story and find a way to embrace and accept the emotional responses of others. The waters of adoption are tricky, and we've all made our share of blunders. It is in our hearts that we find the capacity to give people the grace they deserve and to take, as Heidi says, "better care of our hearts."

So, find yourself your own blue chair (see chapter 13). May the outpouring contained within this book serve as a guiding light—inspiring understanding, compassion, and resilience on our own messy path of exploration and healing.

A NOTE
from Jim Newcomer, PhD

When Heidi asked me to review her memoir, I had no idea how deeply it would affect me. Only when I accepted her offer and started reading her manuscript did I get a glimmer of her genius, her ability to use a breathless style to probe deep corners of her own and others' psyches. Like a tightrope walker, she can balance the wind of emotion against the weight of experience and use the combination to hold your attention, breathless and terrified, and then reach the other end with triumph.

Why would you want to read this book? I could say why you ought to read it, but there's no ought in this book. Just delight—and pathos, fear, celebration, loss, victory, and coming home. So that's why.

Heidi experiences the trials of growing up the same as the rest of us, except more intensely. She was unsure whether she was the only person going through that type of trial or if the experience was universal; she could never shake the "what if"—what if she had been in her biological family? What if she didn't have to experience this cruelty? What if this shortcoming was an inherited trait that her family of origin would consider normal?

In these pages, Heidi introduces her adopted family—and then her biological family, character by character, one to a chapter, each adding something vital to her story; each one is so vivid that you'll think you're living with them. She begins with her adoptive mother and carries readers to her abusive adoptive father—a sadistic police officer—her sadly optimistic and tragic (and also adoptive) brother, and then to her meeting with her biological mother, the sister who turns out to be nearly a twin, and her husband and son—a real family to count on to be her own.

Heidi's poem about her biological mother provides a breathless example of her penetrative power of description that makes readers fall in love with a character, flaws and all.

Is it any wonder that, when she found and contacted this wild and free woman, her adoptive mother turned her back on Heidi and retreated into anger?

In addition to Heidi's deeply human and moving descriptions of her intimate life with these real, breathing, emotionally trying, and tragic people, the chapters are interspersed with analytic commentary on the universal issues of child development by psychiatrist Alysa Zalma, MD.

Heidi's intimate and moving story, combined with academic analysis, outlines the adopted person's acute uncertainty and longing in the context of universal child development issues—and points out how the experience of adoption concentrates/intensifies that uncertainty and how it mixes with loss and the search for identity. As a result, readers get both a moving presentation of tragically flawed people—doing their best but often falling short—and an academic harvest of the universal, dramatic themes. Readers will uncover the textbook on adoption and childhood development.

I recommend you dive right in at the beginning—there's no shallow end to this pool, and swim as fast as you like through the length of it. I predict that you have never read anything like it—a combination of moving portraits, a deep story that emerges from the portraits, and an analysis that reveals the universal structure of Heidi's search for a home and family of her own.

Jim Newcomer, PhD (initial editor of the book),
founder of NewcomerEdits

INTRODUCTION
by Heidi Marble

Sitting face-to-face with my husband's office printer, I literally had soul cramps. With sweating brow and bloated anticipation, I pulled up a chair and found myself gazing into the dark orifice of the machine, watching the first page crown. Pages stacked high were born into my hands, the warm ink omitting a damp, earthly smell. For the first time, I held the weight of my truth, and the title rolled across my tongue, *Pulled by the Root*. The root is where everything starts—the umbilical cord that connects the very core of our being.

Pulled by the Root digs into the ground, where this life journey began, my relinquishment through adoption. Now, at fifty-seven, I am unearthing the reality of what that abandonment means, the significance of that loss, and how it has informed every step of my journey. This is an inquiry into how we can come to terms with our past and the consequences that accompany it. The tangled mess I find myself in now has everything to do with never feeling grounded. This book is an endeavor to take root in the truth, with every dirty, gritty inch of it, to dig so deeply that everything is exposed and understood. Without planting our story and sinking deep, we are destined to be tossed about, yanked, transplanted, and perhaps even consumed.

The only hope is to rely on the fertile ground of facing ourselves and others with compassion, to understand that all things regarding growth live in our truth and the truth of others. I wish for you to develop thick, hearty roots, that those roots are sunk into abundantly nourished soil, that you are blessed with warm rain and sunny days, and when the storms come (as they will), their mighty strength anchors you.

PREFACE
by Alysa Zalma, MD

Our book's healing story and novelty come from our relationship—Heidi's and mine. It is our interweaving of Heidi's personal story as an adoptee and my psychiatric perspective on the psychology of adoption. My perspective is based on my knowledge as a clinician psychiatrist and the research completed through our work together. I wanted to offer relevant psychiatric literature and sources that would provide more breadth, heterogeneity, and connection from a multidisciplinary perspective. Heidi and I share a desire to deeply understand trauma and create a healing story broad enough to help a large group of people. We combined our talents with the intention to reach a wide audience.

We include the "first" (biological) families of adopted children, the adoptive families of adopted children, the foster care families, the education communities and schools that teach and nurture them, and the mental health communities and practitioners who treat them. Because of this, many people may read our book on multiple levels.

To heal a trauma from the adoption experience requires going beyond one's narrative. This is what we hope to explain through the novelty of our work. In each chapter, we unearth Heidi's personal narrative, followed by my commentary, delving into many realms of psychiatry, psychology, twenty-first-century shamanism and energy medicine, and more—to highlight relational traumas and healing most specific to the adoption experience.

This book can be read in many ways. Readers can read it as intended, in order, with Heidi's narrative first, followed by my commentary, addressing themes relevant to the chapter. Readers can also read each author's work in full, coming back to gain a deeper understanding of the narrative or commentary. However it is read, it is our hope that our readers will be able to create their own personal healing stories from their individual traumas.

CHAPTER 1
I CHOSE THE BLUE ONE

"In another woman's womb, I was knitted of bone and blood, born to her, raised by you. Losing both of my mothers while they were still alive is the empty place I carry."
—Heidi Marble

THE BLACK BOX

The black box waits on a cold granite kitchen counter, an upright rectangular container, 8" x 10", with a small, printed label on the upper right corner. A tiny digital clock on the oven reminds me it is too early to wake. Trickling sounds from our way-too-expensive coffee maker ride the air as liquid fills an egg-speckled mug. A glug of cream mixes under the current of my bent spoon, swirling a design into a caffeinated galaxy. The warm mug now clasped tightly in my hands, I take my first sip, tempering the heat on the roof of my mouth. I struggle with my overly puffy, black winter coat until I am finally enclosed safely in its polyester marshmallow of warmth. I use my toes to anchor my slippers on my chilled feet while attempting to tame my long, tangled hair. Rotating beams of light shimmer through the low branches of towering, snow-dusted pines beyond the white-paned windows of our kitchen. I feel conviction set in.

TODAY IS THE DAY

The black box has been at my side for a week—a constant companion. I know today is the day it must be opened. I walk around the box like a cat preparing to pounce on its prey, sidestepping to make myself look bigger (which isn't hard given my coat and hair). Bristled up, tail twice the size, claws out, dancing back and forth, and coming closer only to retreat quickly, it's a tango of alternating courage and fear. The circling—going high, going low, and peeking around corners—continues for a long time. With trepidation and a low guttural growl, I approach it—*the black box*. My coffee-warmed hands land softly on the top, and I begin to lift the flaps when, suddenly, everything stops. My eyes fall shut on a memory; a few small tears weave through my bottom lashes. I see her. I feel her. My adoptive mother. Not a detail of the scene is lost. Even two years of space can't fade what I remember.

I am there again, hanging clothes in her new assisted-living apartment at Mallard Landing, better known as the "Duck Pond." A blazing sun makes sure the whole damn room is aggressively lit. My eyes squint, and guilt bears down on me with unrelenting force. My head is hanging in shame as I avoid eye contact.

My mother, Joy, sits posed in her charcoal-black faux leather recliner. A Tiffany lamp with huge coral flowers leans on a bent iron stand. There are old photographs still wanky from my hurried hanging. I hand myself over for manipulation, the rod and strings of guilt animated by her direction—a puppet in her hands, a marionette with a chipped, painted smile, lifted, pulled, and twisted.

Repulsed by the smell of cigarette smoke, expired perfume, and cheap laundry soap, I try to untangle the mounds of clothes heaped on the bed, feeling the pull of every string. I am acting out the ungrateful daughter performance with each verbal yank. I untangle hangers while internally screaming, "Why do they have so many @#%*&! varieties of hangers?" Most are thick plastic in horrible colors of pink, others are wire, and some are wooden. I am utterly convinced that these hangers were designed specifically to torture daughters who move their mothers into care homes.

Scooping up heavy stacks of fashion from all decades, my back hyperextends. I commence repeated trips to the closet. I anchor as many hangers as I can in one action, trying to get it over with. All the while, her clothing is fighting me like a ninja warrior—twisting, tripping, and choking without mercy.

The strings being pulled between us tighten; I sense the uncontrolled movement of my tense limbs. My hinged jaw opens and shuts, trying to find words; my painted eyes are wide and fixed. Frantic, I collect the fallen clothing from the ground while pieces of me clank together in her glare.

A familiar sound alerts my ears—the grinding wheel of a plastic cigarette lighter. My mother's chin slowly sinks toward her chest, the whites of her eyes rising like two half-moons. Her brows lift, one higher than the other, and a freshly lit cigarette dangles precariously between her dry lips.

She inhales a deep serving of cigarette smoke as I yell, "Mother, you can't smoke in here!"

She slowly replies, "Oh, yes, I can."

The smoke pouring from her nostrils and mouth adds shape to her words.

Another helping of smoke later, she points with her shaking hand. "Heidi, do you see those two dresses? The floral chiffon and the indigo blue? Bring them here."

I bring them toward her. On a stage of flat beige carpet, I stand in a cloud of Marlboro smoke, a dress dangling from each hand. Her glowing cigarette holds a wilted column of ash, and the moons in her eyes are now full.

Then, her audible exhale. "You choose."

"Choose? What are we doing here, Mother?"

She repeats, "You choose—the one you want to bury me in." Smoke slips out of the pursed slit in her lips. The ash column falls on her food-stained polyester pants. She flicks it off, leaving a hot dusting of gray. The thickest string, the one tied to my core, cinches tighter. "You choose because what I want doesn't matter."

My chin falls to my chest, the moons of my eyes rise, and I say, "I am sorry you feel that way. If you want me to pick, I will—but it won't be today."

A week before, I had found her collapsed in her apartment next to our house. She was bleeding, bruised, and surrounded by the acrid smell of urine and cigarette smoke, with a half-eaten piece of toast and spilled coffee next to her head. On the floor, a low fog crawled out from under her chair. Perplexed, I slid the chair back and discovered a live cigarette. I muttered the words, "I can't do this anymore." The culmination of our war had come to a head. Psychological blood was everywhere—splattering, pooling, and streaking down the walls. This battle—the battle to keep her here, to ease my guilt—was now over.

For nine years, I had struggled with a revolving door of caregivers, most of whom had left crying without notice. She wanted *me*—only *me*—to care for her. Caregivers were my placeholders, my salvation, my armor, a space between us so necessary that when they would leave, I felt like I couldn't breathe.

Being alone with my mother was dangerous. She knew my naked soul—every curve, scar, and weak spot. A look, word, or suggestion had its way with me every time. I did not possess the skills to be healthy, to snip the strings of control. Perhaps my action was cowardly? I still struggle with that idea. It feels much better to say that I did what I had to do to survive, that I felt an obligation to be controlled and punished for what I did, and that I readily gave her control over my strings to extract from me the payments on my guilt.

PUPPETEER

Controlled from above,
Hinged mouth hangs open,
Fixed facial expression,
Strings pull me up.
Head, back, and center,
An unsteady collection of pieces.
Words not my own,
Your breath fills me.
You know just what to move,
The way to make me fall.
I am not me.
I am me-with-you.
The us that has become,
Under and over,
Tangled,
Heavy,
Pulled in all directions.
Shame doesn't have a backbone;
Shame only takes direction.

THREE MONTHS BEFORE HER DEATH

I remember the very moment I decided to talk to my mother about her final wishes, the ones that needed to be updated, the plans that would need to change because everything else had. She wanted to be buried next to my adopted brother in Tucson, Arizona, thousands of miles away. No one is left there now, only a few scattered relatives and friends without the strength to travel. In a short time, she will pass away in Washington, the state she has called home for almost a decade.

Hospice prompted me to plan and ask hard questions. So, I began the disturbing job of calling funeral homes to look into dealing with such matters. At this point, I was so empty that I could barely function. I just needed something to be easy. Three choices appeared before me, none of which included, "It's okay to run and hide." The first choice was to have her body flown to Arizona and continue with a formal burial. The second choice was to opt for cremation. The last choice was to transport her body myself! *WHAT? People can do that?* Apparently, you can with the right certificate. Since that would never happen, I decided to discuss the idea of the second choice, cremation instead of burial.

Deep breath, stiff drink (never mind; that will have to wait until I get back home). As I have hundreds of times before, I sit in the driveway, psyching myself up to go inside the residential care home where she has lived for two years. So much hurt has happened in this place. It's like entering a den of rattlesnakes hissing and striking. Her room is off to the left of a small living room with a despicable floral couch.

I see her from the side, fiddling with a Kleenex. She hears my greeting and says, "Oh, hi, darlin'."

Her mood seems giddy, almost childlike. I sink into her recliner, adjusting the absorbent pad on the seat, considering that I might need it before our visit is over. I pull her chair close to me so we are face-to-face. "Mother, I need to ask you something important." Her eyes widen, her chin goes down, and the whites of her eyes rise.

"Mom, so much has changed, and I want to make sure we discuss your final wishes and come up with a plan."

I could not say the word *cremation*. Instead, I said, "What if you could be with both of your kids after you pass?"

My mother was very smart. Even inside, with all her illnesses, she figured out the innuendo. Her brow crinkled, and she tilted her head slightly to one side. A peaceful smile crossed her face. Then she said, "Okay, I like that idea."

"Are you sure, Mom?"

"Yes, I am sure. Now, can we talk about something else?" Yes, we can definitely talk about something else.

SEVEN DAYS BEFORE MY MOTHERS DEATH

I make this journal entry:

> Mom, I woke up on the edge of morning, wondering how I could bear another day of watching you die. Exhaustion, frustration, and confusion swirling my insides, I drove in a storm, snowflakes melting like angel wings on the windshield, hanging on the steering wheel like the edge of a cliff. It has been twenty days since you took your last bite of food and eighteen days beyond your predicted passing. I have pounded my fists and been on my knees, begging God to help. What is the point of this suffering? Witnessing your skin draped like wax over your bones, the suppleness of your body gone, watching you waste away, the brutality of it all. Your eyes glossed over, hanging half shut, mouth open, and begging for air. Your once olive skin now gray-tinged and pale.
>
> Your death is stubborn. I am breaking into pieces. When I walked into your room today, the heater was on full blast. Your body lifted slightly with pillows so you could see out the window. The flowers I had brought yesterday already bent in repose. You did not wake until I whispered, "I love you." Then your eyes

stretched to open, and your smile followed. You looked at me with a stare—no blinking—you looked into my soul. I have never been looked at like that before.

For the last twenty years, you have looked at me with such hatred. Not this time; this was different. Tears drenched my face, wetting your chest. Your hand began to move under the covers. At this point, you hadn't moved on your own for days; there was no strength available. I pulled the sheet back and watched in amazement. Your eyes never leaving mine, you began to lift your shaking hand, lifting it only by the force of will. Softly, your open palm touched my cheek, your smooth, trembling fingers touching my tears, wiping them away. My heart burst through my well-crafted walls and crumbled to smithereens.

I put my ear to your heart and wept while it beat weakly. Your other hand found the center of my back, and you gave me a few tiny pats. All my resistance dissolved, every last bit of it. Everything fell away; our souls overlapped, an eclipse that blotted out any doubt. I drank in the feeling, and I know you did too: the missing, the regret, the forgiveness, the reconnection. Now I understood why you had stayed, why you had clung so fiercely to life. It was so we could see into each other's hearts one more time.

We laid there together for hours, on the edge of heaven. A long goodbye orchestrated by the angels. In our shared suffering and grief, we found a way back to our original bond. The bond that had seemed severed for so long remained after all.

These days, these beautiful moments were our healing, Mom. Thank you for telling me everything I needed to hear without speaking a word. Now we were two—two women who loved each other deeply, who had shared fifty-four years of life. Two women with broken hearts. Two women wishing we could have loved each other better.

THE CALL COMES

February 11, 2019. The digital clock on my oven tells me it's once again too early to be awake. Sleep seems elusive, and when it comes, nightmares fill my head. I am walking around in a coma of grief and fatigue—my fuzzy black robe hanging open, pockets full of crumpled, used tissues, the tie nearly dragging on the floor like a dog's tail of shame. Remembering the night before when I had wrapped my mother in my grandma's bluebird quilt and combed her tufts of thin, gray hair, I think of how hollow she felt as I carefully swaddled her.

Finally dressed, I take a long sip of coffee and whisper, "Shit," when the cup is empty. The phone breaks the silence. I move toward the counter in slow motion. My heart already knows. The numbers on the screen confirm it. It is Michelle from the care home. I answer, and she says, "I am sorry, Heidi. She is gone. Your mother died in her sleep."

All my pieces fell to the floor; the strings had snapped. I am a pile of contorted pain with no one to pull me up.

Two weeks earlier, in the thick of her dying process, I had known the time had come, the time I was dreading. It was time to choose. In the farthest left corner of my closet, out of view, were my mother's two dresses: indigo blue and floral chiffon. I pulled them out and touched the fabric, remembering so clearly the last time I held them at the care home, that day still so tightly woven into my memory, the feeling stored deep. Now I had to choose. I chose the blue one, folding it neatly into a small hot-pink gift bag.

I drove my husband's overly masculine truck through unmerciful traffic to the care home—the dress next to me in the passenger seat. When I arrived, the hospice nurse and two caregivers, Anna and Michelle, were whispering in the kitchen. The hot-pink bag in my hand matched the color of my cried-out eyes. I explained how much it would mean to me to have my mother leave this world in her blue dress—the blue dress that had been intended for only special occasions, the dress that had swirled as she danced and billowed in the winds of foreign lands, the dress that had traveled with her for over twenty years, the dress that made her feel beautiful. I handed them the bag for safekeeping.

Now . . . *she is gone.*

I can't.

I can't see her dead.

I can't.

I can't move.

I can't drive.

I can't.

I just can't.

My head is so full of devastating images from the last month, I cannot add this final image; I cannot feel her cold. I thought I could, but I can't. I can't dress her. I can't. My soul slips out of my body.

A few hours pass, and I receive a text message from Anna, one of the caregivers I adored. She told me that she and the hospice nurse had dressed my mother in her indigo-blue dress. They remembered my final wish and wanted to do that for us. They did what I could not do.

I crumpled to the floor, weeping. Sounds rose from the deepest bottom of my being, sounds that howled and moaned, convulsing out of me violently as I heaved gulps of air. Then, Anna sent another message: *Can I send you a picture of her?*

Silence. I stopped my rabid panting. My face was hot, slathered in burning tears. I sat on the floor, cupping the phone in my hands; my robe spread open. I shut my eyes and heard the ding of the photo arriving. Shuddering in a deep breath, I slowly opened my swollen eyes and looked at my phone. A gasp flowed. There was my mother on crisp white sheets. Head on a flat pillow, toes pointed like a ballerina, and her white hair combed off her face. The indigo-blue dress an ocean of color surrounding her—the image so small, her death so large.

TIME TO OPEN THE BOX

My fingers carefully open the flaps on the lid; a twist-tied clear bag sits inside. How can this be all that's left of her and left of me? I carefully remove the contents and place them gently on the dark granite counter. I say, "Hi, Mom."

Today is the day. I will spread half of her remains, and I am alone. My mind races back to the first time I held the black box a week before. How strange it was to have the funeral director say, "Here is your mother."

I picked up the clear bag containing my mom's ashes. Leaving the black box behind, I turned the front doorknob, trying not to have a disaster. Outside, I slowly carried her remains to the dormant dogwood tree, the tree that we planted to honor my grandmother, the tree that blooms hundreds of gorgeous, pale-pink blossoms every May. It's the tree we planted next to the apartment we built for them so many years ago—the one my son now lives in. I place the bag on the ground and untwist the tie. Breath rolling from my mouth, I lift out a handful of ashes.

I'm stunned by their beauty. They're an aggregate of tiny white shapes. I thought they would be gray and dusty, but they are beautiful. With a whispered blessing, I toss the ashes as high in the air as I can. The sun glints on her remains as they shower down, half of my mother now scattered in ribbons of white on the wintery ground. I stand, shivering, wiping tears with my soiled hands.

BACK WHERE WE STARTED

March 13, 2019, one month later, it is sunset at East Lawn Cemetery in the Arizona desert, on the edge of spring. The last time I stood here, we buried my thirty-one-year-old adopted brother, Justin. I feel like a body without a soul. A double his-and-her rose quartz headstone sits amongst a patchwork of grass that is more yellow than green. A small oval frame with a pitted rim holds his faded, smiling photograph. The desert rains have stained the engraved words with dry streaks. The other side of the headstone is smooth, waiting for her name.

Her final wish to be buried next to her adopted son, who never married or had children—the tragedy impales me. I am shaking inside my gray patchwork coat as it opens like wings. A storm has rolled in, a violent storm, the kind only the desert knows how to act out. A storm that I am sure was sent by my mother. Three crisp, typewritten pages twist in my cold hands.

Freshly scattered dirt tossed about our feet looks like coffee grounds where they buried the second half of her cremated remains. They buried the woman who adopted me. They buried my mother. This final goodbye is now up to me. I am all that is left of us. My husband steps behind me as I try to collect myself. I feel the comforting strength of his hand on my shoulder. My son, Blake, and his girlfriend, Sontia, were wrapped in each other's arms, braced against the cold.

The wind moves the clouds; they darken, push, pull, and billow. Gray shadows animate their pillowy shapes on the ground. I put a choke hold on the pages that seemed determined to escape my grip. I blink away the blurring tears that evaporate into lines of salt across my face—a strange, unapologetic relief that it's finally over.

The torment of the last twenty years has come to a close. I don't have to try to make things right anymore. It's a sense of awe that I am still alive, wondering how I have survived all this. Awe is mixed with cutting emotions of exhaustion, regret, and shame. I was completely unaware of how much suffering was yet to come. Not realizing that my mother's voice will never leave—it is as much a part of me as my bones.

LETTER AT THE GRAVE

The wind further intensifies, and under the sullen sky, I read this letter as the wind rips the pages:

Dear Mom,
It seems fitting that we would end where we began in Tucson, Arizona, embraced by the Foothill Mountains as the desert sky paints pastel pictures around us, the air filled with spring and the

heady scent of mesquite. It was in this high desert that our lives intersected; you wanted to be a mother, and I needed a mother. Your stories of our first few days always filled my head. Your accounts of how the nurses would hold my tiny body close to the nursery glass, how you waited five days before you could hold me. We were destiny, a kaleidoscope of decision, indecision, and fate. One baby, one biological mother, and one adoptive mother, changing the course of each other's lives forever.

It is not lost on me that, without you, I would not have my husband, Troy, my son, Blake, or his girlfriend, Sontia. God understood how we needed each other, and it is my honor to bring you back home. I have brought you back to where half of your heart is already buried. Justin was too young to die, and I watched as grief suffocated you. The image of your body wilted over his casket will be chiseled in my memory for eternity. I am so sorry you had to endure that unimaginable loss. Now you and he can rest together, as you wished, both of your souls free of this world, your bodies given back to the earth.

You were stunning, Mother. Your beauty stopped men in their tracks, the kind of beauty that you didn't even understand, the kind of beauty that made women want to be you. Your eyes gold like a lioness, your olive skin highlighting your stunning features, you deserved so much more than you ever received. Your intelligence was as gorgeous as your beauty. You were well traveled and well-read, and you used words like paintbrushes. Conversations were artistic, full of color and depth. Your voice could soothe, sing, or sear.

You knew how to listen—not just hear—listen. You took the time to care for so many and always gave sound advice, advice that had substance and helped untangle many painful situations. You never allowed me to brood on my troubles. Thank you for this gift.

You were an artist; watercolor, acrylic, ceramics, and

sculpture creations were your breath. You had a way of making even the mundane beautiful. You taught me the power of glue guns and the soul-healing power of creativity. Thank you for these gifts.

Shall we discuss manners and decorum? You insisted on ladylike behavior at all times: legs crossed, perfect posture, elbows off the table, chewing with your mouth shut—just to name a few. A bar of soap and the sink became my companions, as I often had to wash away the sins of my tongue. Time out became a familiar place to consider the consequences of rude behavior. Thank you for these gifts.

Watching you suffer an abusive marriage and still find joy astonished me. I always wanted you to leave; the few times we did, you always came back riding on the fumes of hope. A better tomorrow held enough light for you to try to make your marriage work. You were determined not to break apart our family. You felt that the pain of a divorce would far outweigh whatever pain we were enduring behind closed doors. It felt as if you picked your poison and drank it from a crystal glass. When Dad was at work, music would play, laughter would rise, and joy would be ours. Watching you fight so hard for the happy family you wanted, although the happiness didn't happen, it still resonates. Thank you for this gift.

Education was paramount, and going to college was a required rite of passage. You wanted to empower us so that we could become independent and steady. Your insight into the importance of autonomy is grounded in every success I have ever achieved. Thank you for this gift.

You encouraged our dreams no matter how far-fetched or high-flung. If they fizzled or caught fire, you were there to comfort or console. You set no limits. Thank you for this gift.

I loved you so completely. I could not figure out where I ended and you began. When our relationship hit major turbulence, it was my life's greatest heartbreak. That heartbreak allowed illness to establish itself in me. That heartbreak broke all of me, including my body. A wall grew so thick and so tall, I would never be able to knock it down. I am sorry for the hurt I caused you.

Watching you die slowly twisted my insides and exhausted the very core of my being. There are regrets–regrets that we wasted so much time doubting the other. I can't do a damn thing about that now. What I can choose to do is honor what you did so well.

May you finally find the peace this world wasn't able to give you. May God hold you in his loving arms. May your worries dissolve at our Holy Father's feet. Until we meet again, I hope you know, YOU MATTERED TO ME. YOU ALWAYS MATTERED.

WHERE THE SOUL MEETS THE BONE

I fold what is left of my letter, and everyone goes to the car to give me a moment alone; I can no longer stand. My soul meets the bone of grief. An emotional skeleton, I collapse on the grave. I am both dead and alive, wanting only to be one or the other.

1936-2019

You mattered.
Your life mattered.
Your touch,
Your words mattered.
Your hopes,
Your dreams mattered.
Your pain,
Your suffering mattered.
Your talent, beauty, and grace mattered.
Everything about you mattered to me . . .

—Your daughter, always, Heidi

CHAPTER 1
CHOOSE THE BLUE ONE
THEME 1: FORGIVENESS AND SOUL RETRIEVAL
Alysa Zalma, MD

Recently, one of my patients who survived a traumatic cult experience asked me, "How can I heal from this [trauma]?" Retrospectively, after having abruptly left the cult, he felt "brainwashed." The cult involved many people, including his parents and siblings. He notes that he felt betrayed by his mother, but he now also misses her and is unclear about his sense of self without her. Much like Heidi, he mourns the relationship with his mother that was, as well as what it was not. He did not have the chance of reconciliation that Heidi describes in this chapter.

> **Everything fell away; our souls overlapped, an eclipse that blotted out any doubt . . . the regret, the forgiveness, the reconnection.**

Melanie Klein, a child psychoanalyst, arguably did some of her most important work on discovering one's capacity for love and reparation (Greenberg and Mitchell 1983, 127).

These are themes that are explored with careful optimism. Klein's earlier work on infant development laid the foundation for this ability for love and reparation. As a preamble, Klein discusses that much of one's behavior, relational experience, and core sense of self originates from the infant's first year of life, when fantasies of the "good" and "bad" mother originate (Klein 1975, 262, 266).

However, according to Klein, the capacity for love and reparation is formed slightly later in development, when the infant "understands" the concept of one mother, who has good and bad traits. She theorizes that in the second quarter of their first year, the infant becomes able to "understand" that, indeed, there are not two mothers (as previously experienced by the infant as "split-off" experiences of their mother, each piece either "good" or "bad"), but there is only one mother, who houses both good and bad features of herself (Greenburg and Mitchell 1983, 125). This integration is a significant accomplishment of normal infant development. The preverbal fantasy of "two mothers" at this age is gone, and integration of the infant's mother becomes a reality. The child now has only one mother. Any fantasies moving forward about how rageful or grateful the child is toward his mother are directed at one person.

Klein states that love and reparation are the rewards for the ability to forgive, which is also a central theme of this chapter. Klein states, "If we have become able, deep in our unconscious minds, to clear our feelings . . . toward our parents of grievances, and have forgiven them for the frustrations we had to bear, then we can be at peace with ourselves and are able to love others in the true sense of the word" (Klein 1975, 343).

The concept of forgiveness has been heavily researched, demonstrating positive correlations to mental and physical health. Studies in medical literature show potential physiological correlations between overall health and the ability to forgive (Hulett and Heiney 2021; Worthington E. et al 2005). Additional studies also show a positive correlation between forgiveness and improved mental health (Toussaint 2016, 727). There is also literature primarily devoted to self-forgiveness and mental health (Maynard 2023, 265), which is a central theme of this chapter and the book as a whole.

There is a poignant interplay between Heidi and her mother, Joy, which holds the promise that Heidi's trauma related to her relationship with her adoptive mother can be fully healed and traversed. Heidi may be able to let go of her resentments and forgive Joy for her transgressions. She may also be able to let go of her guilt and forgive herself for her role in the interpersonal triangle created between her adoptive mother, her biological mother, and herself. This is a common yet tragic triangle that many children of adoption will recognize. It is also one that "first" and adoptive mothers may resonate with.

How is she going to be able to do that?

The title of this chapter, "I Chose the Blue One," speaks to this question, as the color blue becomes a significant theme throughout the book, a symbolic and metaphorical vehicle toward accomplishing the ability to forgive, love, repair, and heal from trauma.

The blue dress was the one Heidi's adoptive mother wore in her younger life when she was more "alive," more beautiful, and more adventurous. This dress was the dress of her mother's past.

The dress . . . swirled as she danced and billowed in the winds of foreign lands, the dress that had traveled with her for over twenty years.

This dress was symbolic of the essence of Heidi's adoptive mother before her traumas, when she still had these pieces of self/soul intrinsic to her. Her trauma had not yet taken or "stolen" pieces from her. From a shamanic perspective, the essence of one's self is sometimes "stolen" from a "soul thief." This is one of the means through which "soul loss" may occur (Ingerman 1991, 12).

Sometimes, this "thief" is a parent who may consciously or unconsciously want pieces of their child, perhaps having been a victim of soul "thievery" themselves (Ingerman 1991, 99).

Choosing the blue dress is a beautiful symbolic gesture by Heidi. She wishes to return the lost soul pieces to her mother and allow more access to her soul pieces that were "stolen" from her mother's transgenerational "thievery."

From a shamanic perspective, the answer to my patient's question above—and subsequently to Heidi's and many adopted children's—is that when the pieces of self/soul that existed before the trauma are returned to the person, the trauma (the thing that took these pieces away) is no longer part of the person's story in the same way. To symbolically and metaphorically receive these precious pieces of self/soul back is at the crux of healing from the trauma.

Heidi has two mothers, as do all children of adoption. For some adoptees who meet and know both mothers/caregivers, the fantasized "good" mother and the reality "bad" mother may switch roles multiple times in their lives. For many adoptees, as with Heidi, these two mothers may remain in their psyche their entire lives and inform much of their early development and adult life and how their physical body reacts to these conflicts.

One of the many conflicts/dilemmas of adoption is forgiveness. The adoptee wishes for forgiveness for wanting to know who they are. For the adoptee, wanting to know their biological roots may create fears of betrayal and guilt.

Heidi also discloses how she felt betrayed by her biological mother and wanted to know why she was given up/relinquished, fearing she was defective or not good enough to keep.

Part of the key to unlocking healing is forgiveness.

The answer to *who am I has crucial links to the traumas of adoption.*

The interpersonal triangle of daughter, adoptive mother, and biological mother is transgenerational and involves all three women at varying levels of soul loss. All three women share the experience of betrayal and "relinquishment" from different perspectives. They have all experienced some traumas that are ultimately related. From a shamanic perspective, many co-experienced and co-created traumas are related to transgenerational soul loss. All three women have "arrived" at that place, speaking more to their similarities than their differences. A transgenerational soul loss may be more fully understood by biology and experience.

Heidi wished for permission to ask who she was, where she came from, and who her biological parents were. She wanted to know why she was given up.

Her birth mother and adoptive mother wanted to know the answers to their own *who am I* questions about themselves. Had Joy allowed Heidi to raise these questions, their love likely would have increased. Collective healing through permission and forgiveness in this adoption triad may help break the cycle of transgenerational trauma.

Many women and mothers who have forsaken their permission to know who they are become envious when their daughters (or other women) search for who they are. The mother-daughter relationship for adoptees magnifies this intrinsic tension. This may have occurred between Heidi and Joy as another example of transgenerational soul "thievery."

In their attempt to retrieve their essences, daughters, adoptive mothers, and biological mothers ask, "Please tell me who I am." Perhaps this shared question seeks to know, "How do we belong together?" and "How can we be separate and different and still feel safe together?" The answers to these questions and the retrieval of the collective and transgenerational lost essences of soul/self are this book's theses and the healing journey.

CHAPTER 2
FINDING MARTY JO

"I can grieve you now, which feels alive in the deadness that has gripped my soul in the horror of your absence."
—Heidi Marble

"There are two great days in a person's life—the day that we were born and the day we discover why."
—William Barclay

"Neither society nor the adopter who holds the child wants to confront the agony of the mother from whose arms that child was taken."
—Margaret McDonald Lawrence

HAUTE COUTURE

Describing my birth mother is like designing a high-fashion garment, confronted with zillions of different bolts of fabric, spools of thread, and unending possibilities. Her life was a variety of patterns strewn about, feathers lofting under her swish. Marty Jo was one of a kind, a brocade of rich, ornate colors loosely hemmed. Conforming and pleasing never appealed to her; Marty's survival breathed her truth. She fashioned her life to fit her will, never bothered by what others thought about her choices. She was real in all the ways that scare people who conform. Marty walked the runway of authenticity, smashing any hisses under the point of her high-heeled boots.

DOUBLE TROUBLE

My mothers could not have been more opposite or complex. Yet they shared a few fundamental aspects—courage and rebellion. However, those characteristics played out in them in different ways. My biological mother was outward and obvious in her pushback; my adoptive mother was more refined and cunning. Each had the same velocity, intensity, and strength when navigating life's upheavals. My biological mother was a runner, not willing to be imprisoned. My adoptive mother chained herself to obligations even when they didn't serve her. Both were potent and unforgettable women; both threaded through me in ways I cannot deny.

LOVE IS A BATTLEFIELD

Finding my birth mother became an obsession after I gave birth to my son. The primal urge to seek increased until it was a reconnaissance mission. I became a tank pushing through uncharted terrain. I trudged onward, digging heavy tracks in sacred ground. I did not respect the emotional landscape I trampled on. I was ravenous to find out whatever I could. I regret how I handled myself with reckless abandon, battling for what I wanted, shooting in the dark at any target. The unnecessary hurt I caused still haunts me. I wish I had taken better care of our hearts.

PACK WISELY

When you embark on the journey of finding your family of origin, you need to be prepared. You must address the needs of all parties in the adoption scenario. Adoptive parents should understand their child's specific needs regarding their relinquishment. Every adoptee, orphan, or abandoned person has an individual response to their circumstances, which must be carefully considered. Parents giving up their children need tenderness and understanding during the emotional storms of discovery. Adopted people need to understand that collateral damage can happen if careful steps aren't taken. This is high-stakes emotional warfare. It can be catastrophic.

I wish I had approached my situation with more compassion, taking more time to understand the threat that my adoptive mother felt, taking more time to appreciate my biological mother for welcoming me, appreciating her for peeling open old wounds, and taking more time to help my adoptive mother adjust.

Instead, I became a warrior determined to place a flag in the ground of my history, to finally secure a deed to my past and erect a foundation. It upset me deeply that my adoptive mother appeared selfish in her nonsupport of this fundamental need I was experiencing. It felt as if the unconditional love she had professed throughout my entire life was becoming conditional. For the first time, I fully rebelled. Had I not decided to meet my birth family, I would have resented my adoptive mother eternally.

I was caught in a vice, a no-win situation. This was a spiritual journey I had to take. I wanted my adoptive mother to trust me and believe in the resilience of our connection. I was naively soldiering on in defense of my birthright. A part of me still wishes my mothers could have met face-to-face. I still want to believe that had they looked into each other's eyes, everything would have been different. But my adoptive mother would never agree to meet Marty, even when Marty had a terminal cancer diagnosis. I had to respect her and accept her decision. I "accepted" it as resentment grew like a powder keg.

BACK TO MARTY JO

Her name was nearly longer than her life. When trying to capture her persona, I wrote a bouncy poem. It darts between images and ideas, both told and seen. Hopefully, it paints a picture of her rapturous and complex spirit.

SHE WAS

SHE WAS Marty Jo Fleck, Pochyba, Pochyba (yes, they married twice), Sawick, Fleck
She was the first kick off the one strap church shoes girl
Run in bare feet, grow her hair long girl
Uncrossed legs, see-through clothes, smoking pot kind of girl
Strong liquor in the afternoon girl
She was the truth of nature, wild and free girl
Burn your bra, find your groove girl
Bell-bottoms, tan skin girl
Saying "yes" when others said "no" girl
Feet on the dash, hand out the window girl
She was your tie-dye, denim overalls, picking herbs and wildflowers girl
Birthed children, couldn't stay put girl
Made no apologies, stood by her choices kind of girl
No use for folded wings, all-out flight girl
Carried a broken heart while smiling kind of girl
Lost her Daddy at five girl
Nobody took care of her heart girl
Would not be tied down to anyone girl
Would give you everything and nothing girl
Held you or maybe you held her girl
Intoxicated you with her intelligence girl
Spoke the world into pictures kind of girl
Hurt too much, died too soon girl
Was too big for this earth, needed the heavens girl
Left a trail for others to follow girl
Never conformed, showed her spirit girl
Brave and bold like thunder girl
Split the night open, spilled the stars on her skin girl
Always forgave you girl

Your sins didn't matter to her girl
The woman who birthed me girl
I wish I could be that kind of girl . . .

WILD CHILD

Marty personified freedom in captivity—captive by circumstances never short on trauma. Her long-horned demons could never be completely outrun. Trapped by health problems, financial strain, and a string of broken relationships, she still found a way to extract beauty from every situation. She was not held down by the gravity of her pain. Marty used her misfortune as an incentive to live without compromise. Her vision was big picture; the minutia of daily living never interested her. It was outside the lines where she felt most alive. Although her fertility was robust, she was not able to sit in the seat of conventional motherhood.

How we were reunited is a story worth telling. In our discovery of each other, questions were answered, wounds were opened, and wounds were healed. A collision of two souls who needed to reunite. She gave me everything I asked for and expected nothing in return. I wish I could have allowed myself to love her more. I wish I had been brave enough to pull her closer. Secretly, I resented her for giving me up, for denying me the chance to be with her, my siblings, and my large extended family. To think I came close to never knowing Marty sends shivers down my spine. Our lives merged only because of my adoptive grandma's love for me. Without my grandmother's letter, I would have missed meeting this kind of girl.

THE COLOR PURPLE

Wongee, my sweet wongee—yes, that is what I named my adoptive grandma. No one could ever figure out how I was able to come up with such a name. At two years old, I was intent on calling her Wongee. Despite all efforts to correct my pronunciation, the name started to stick; she became everyone's Wongee. She was my person and deservedly has her own chapter in this book. My adoptive mother defined my womanhood, but Wongee defined my soul. She was a force of nature—a red-headed German hurricane of boldness and daring.

Wongee loved to write letters and often sent newspaper clippings, magazine articles, and a few crisp dollar bills so I could buy myself a Dilly Bar at Dairy Queen. Occasionally, she would squirt a few spritzes of her heady white shoulders perfume on the paper, making the ink bleed into blurred dots. Hints of her petal-pink lip prints lingered on the envelope where she licked it shut.

I was thirty-three years old, a new mother with a one-year-old baby boy named Blake. My mail, amongst other chores, had a way of building up. One fall afternoon, I made my way to an overstuffed mailbox. The purple letter slipped out as the rambunctious pile spilled from my hands. Suddenly, my state of being lifted; my heart smiled. It was a letter from my wongee. Risking a lethal paper cut, I reached inside the bulging envelope and pulled out the contents.

A perfectly folded newspaper page from *The Arizona Republic*, three handwritten pages, and two crisp dollar bills emerged. I knew the article must be important; a robust collection of blue-inked circles surrounded the headline. I gathered my Dairy Queen money, stuffed it in my purse, and plopped down on our uncomfortable, rose-patterned tapestry sofa. The sun was streaming beams of light, making the dust in the air shimmer like glitter. I began to read, my heart pounding a noticeable beat.

The article was about private adoptions and how adoptees could access their files only via an intermediary. There was a contact number for the Supreme Court of Arizona. The weight of what I was about to do went through every part of my body and soul; gravity pulled me into stillness. All I knew was that I had to try to find my biological mother, the urge as intense as breathing. The only way was forward; nothing else was under consideration. I ran to my desk and grabbed the phone. I held the lit keypad, pressing each number with intention. The phone rang three times before the intermediary answered; there was no turning back.

SIX MONTHS LATER

The intermediary who began working on my case warned me that I might never find answers. If both of my biological parents were dead, they could do nothing about it. My files would stay sealed. As months passed without news, my hope began to evaporate. I talked myself into being okay with never knowing the where, what, when, why, and how of my existence.

It was deep winter in New England, the landscape quiet, white, and frozen. Trees were shrouded in thick ice, and shards of frozen water hung from their branches like fringe. December was just ending in an exhausting slump. This time of year always brought a sense of dread to my heart. Everything felt empty, less joyful. I never liked stripping the house of Christmas I. I spent weeks missing the smell of pine, colorful twinkling lights, and beautifully wrapped presents.

It was time for a party to perk up my dull mood. A New Year was waiting, and it deserved some sparkle and celebration. Our guests started arriving under an abundantly star-studded sky. The house was filled with twenty-some people. Sparklers, pointed paper hats with silver pompons, and freshly wiped champagne glasses were ready to go. The fireplace was dancing with warm ribbons of fire as we prepared to welcome the New Year. I was completely unaware that these would be the last few moments of life as I knew it.

The phone rang, but I ignored the interruption. Before I could speak my mind, my husband Troy answered the phone. I flung him a wide-eyed look: "Why are you answering the phone when we have guests?" He slipped around the corner to avoid any further eye contact. Not a second later, he reappeared, eyes wide; I was scared. His hand over the speaker, he whispered in my ear, "It's the intermediary calling from Arizona regarding your adoption." My breath stalled. I grabbed the phone and excused myself.

Working my way up the slippery oak stairs to our master bedroom was no small feat in my high heels; the phone clutched in my hand as

I tried not to slip. I aggressively shut the bedroom door to muffle the noise below. My heart pounded like a drum, my head reverberated, and my thoughts changed like cymbals in an orchestra of angst. I sat half on and half off the edge of the bed. My sweaty hands removed from the speaker; I lifted the phone to my ear. With one deep breath, I found the courage to speak. "Hello, this is Heidi."

A clean, smooth voice responded, "Hi, Heidi. This is the intermediary working on your private adoption case. Sorry to call on a holiday, but I felt this news could not wait." I held my breath like a seasoned diver. "We found your biological mother, Heidi. I have good news and bad news. Can I share what I found out with you?"

I didn't care—I wanted it all. Without a pause, I firmly said, "Yes."

"Let's start with the good news. Your biological mother is alive, and her name is Marty Jo Fleck. She is so excited that you found her; she has been waiting for you. Marty is from a small Victorian town in Central Pennsylvania called Bellefonte, next to Pennsylvania State University. She wants you to know that she was just diagnosed with breast cancer and will begin treatment soon. She became pregnant with you at seventeen and wants to answer any questions you may have. Marty has always wanted to meet you and hopes that can happen."

MY BIRTH MOTHER? CANCER? MEET? TALK? Whoa! My body separated into categories of every emotion possible. I scrambled for a piece of paper and a pen, taking down my biological mother's phone number. I gingerly thanked the intermediary for her hard work and hung up. There I sat, on the edge of the bed, on the edge of a decision that would change everything. My feet dangling over a cliff of uncertainty, phone in hand, I decided, I chose, to call.

YOU'RE A GIRL?

Two rings, *brrring, brrring*. Marty answers with a shaky voice. "Hello?" And I say, "This is your daughter, Heidi."

With a breathy giggle, she says, "You're a girl!"

Her nervous laugh follows as my life re-collides with hers. She had no idea I was a girl until the intermediary had revealed my orientation earlier that day. She always assumed that I was a boy. Perplexed, I asked how she could not know I was a girl; it was pretty obvious to me. But Marty explained that "they" did not want her to know the sex of her baby. The nurses held up a bedsheet as they took me away. It might have created a bond with me if she had known. They also didn't want her to touch or look at me for the same reasons.

All she recalled were my ear-piercing screams fading behind our thin white barrier. They gave her a spinal block during labor and delivery to further desensitize her connection. All to make it easier to let me go, an attempt to sever an already established, primal connection. My birth had been long and difficult, requiring forceps. She had to push on command without the urge. The doctor pulled me from the womb so forcefully that my cheek was cut to the bone. The wound laid my upper right cheek wide open. To this day, if the light is exactly right, you can see the scar.

Marty explained that she was so solid in her decision; she never shed a tear (that hurt even though she didn't mean it that way). I suppose I had the idea that she would be grabbing for me and screaming, "Don't take my baby!" A movie scene of regret, doubt, and angst. That was not the case; she had already worked through giving me up by the time she birthed me. She had to be strong to endure my father's death and having a baby too young. There was no way it would work out for us to be together. Her determination to bring me into this world was accomplished.

EDGY

No longer on the bed's edge, I shifted toward the headboard to get more comfortable. I snuggled deep inside a collection of 1990s pastel-colored pillows under the soft light of a burgundy-shaded lamp. Our conversation reached a level of ease and flow. The phone, smashed between my shoulder and ear, captured every nuance. Her words were slightly shaky, raspy, tossed with the frequent pull of cigarette smoke. Questions volleyed back and forth between us as we filled in the blanks.

I felt the "occupied" sign in my heart click on.

Her tone changed as she eased me into the present. The reality of her breast cancer diagnosis had to be addressed. She would have to undergo a lumpectomy, chemotherapy, radiation, and hormonal therapy. Her voice grew thin, morose, and low. Quiet tears rolled down my face as I imagined what she would endure—imagining that what I had just found might be lost again.

I had been so focused on the discovery of my biological mother that I didn't consider I might have other family or even a father for that matter. Surprise! Marty revealed that I have a half brother, Jeff (Pangy), and a half sister, Jennifer (Weezy). She told me I came from a huge family who always knew about me. I was not a secret.

A sister? A brother? A big family? My brain could not process what I was hearing. When I hung up the phone, the conversation spun through me—the truth of my existence colored in. It was time for another phone call to my adoptive mom, Joy—a phone call that would permanently destroy our relationship.

NO TURNING BACK

My adoptive mother knew I was looking for my biological family. At the onset, she had given me a hesitant blessing. There was no doubt in my mind that our love would tolerate this disruption. But I had not grasped the significance of what was about to happen.

Back to teetering on the edge of the bed, I anchored myself, feet shoulder-width apart, a straight shot to the bathroom in case I needed to vomit. The telephone lit up the keypad under my sweaty fingertips. I dialed, pushing each number deliberately. *Brrrng, brrrng.* The tambour of my adoptive mother's voice answered with a lyrical tone, "Happy New Year, darlin'." That would be the last time I had her full affection.

When I told her that I had news about my adoption, the air sank. I told her they had found my biological mother, and she was sick with cancer. My fantasy of her saying, "I am so happy for you! Can I meet her too?" was soon squelched. Her response was below-zero cold.

"Oh, so are you going to meet her?"

She questioned my need to meet her, and I tried to be reassuring. But as I grew more frantic and concerned, her voice grew icier.

The days of her sweetness toward me had ended forever. My nerves went into overdrive. I verbally plowed my way through sentences, trying different word choices to plead my case. In between my words, the silence was broken by a few clicks of her cigarette lighter. She then gave me a blow to the gut.

"Go ahead and do what you have to do."

I heard the familiar pull of her breath as she inhaled helpings of smoke. My heart uncomfortable, dense with nervousness, I hung up the phone. I was shivering. In one phone call, I had lost my mother, my safe place, my best friend, my first love. I would never feel the warmth of her love again. Without warning, my mother had made a decision about me. I had become the ungrateful daughter with my "unfaithfulness."

At that moment, I was not insightful or mature enough to understand that this could be permanent. Although guilt gripped me instantaneously, I was convinced that we could make it through this. After all, being adopted was part of who I was, right? She always said that she loved all of me. She had told me she would love me no matter what, and I had believed her with every ounce of my being. If anyone had told me what was to come, I would have called them a liar. There is no way my mother would ever, ever turn on me. This was just temporary.

TWO WEEKS LATER

Thinking that my biological family was just three hours away was exciting. Marty Jo decided to postpone her cancer surgery until our reunion. I began preparing. I gathered photos, wrote down questions, and started picking out my wardrobe. At the same time, I called my adoptive mother daily to comfort, explain, and fill her in on our plans. It seemed crucial to me to be totally upfront and transparent. I invited her to come. I invited her to talk to Marty. She refused it all. Her chilled voice repeated the same mantra, "Do what you have to do."

After two weeks of getting nowhere in our communication, my anger rose above my guilt. A sense of entitlement reared its ugly head as I force-fed my opinions. I used tactical weapons like guilt bombs, reminding her of Marty's cancer, reminding her that this may be my only chance to understand the circumstances of my adoption. But my adoptive mother was having none of it; I felt her cold shoulder as she covered her ears to my desperation. Nonetheless, I persevered with complete faith that nothing could ever break our bond. Conversations became more strained and intense as the meeting day approached. I decided to go anyway. I decided to go, even though she didn't want me to. I did do what I had to do.

Why would we decide to leave in a snowstorm in January with a one-year-old? Because that's how hell-bent I was. Everything was arranged, and I was certain our four-wheel drive Excursion would do everything the advertising said. I thought we could go off-road, in twelve feet of snow, at the top of a 14,000-foot mountain if necessary. Halfway between Boston and PA, the road became so treacherous that traffic stopped. No Expedition, Excursion, or Path Finder could help us now. People were getting in and out of their cars, semis half on and off the road. There were no trees, bushes, or rest stops for those of us with full bladders. Desperation kicked in, and I found a new use for my son's diapers (use your imagination). Finally, after hours at a complete standstill, the traffic slowly began to move.

It seemed like we were trapped inside a snow globe, dancing with fluffy snowflakes. Our windshield wipers made arches of melting streaks. Smudged orange streaks of sun began kissing away gray clouds, valleys of snow turning pink. Fleetwood Mac was on the radio as we crossed the state line into Pennsylvania, where we were greeted by massive dinosaur-backed rolling hills, Amish farms, hardwood trees, frozen lakes, and roads of iced-over rivers. A strange knowing gripped me; something in me recognized this place.

We had a reservation at the Toftrees Resort in State College next to

Pennsylvania State University. A small amount of daylight was left, and Blake was happy to be out of the car. Sunlight ignited his blond hair as I unpacked and prepared to meet Marty for the first time. A large clock in the room kept time with a loud *tick tock, tick tock*. Time felt suspended and unmovable. The woman I only knew in my imagination would be here in an hour.

I must have checked myself in the mirror a zillion times, trying to make myself abandon-proof. I decided on high-waisted, dark blue jeans and a floral top. My hair was a bouncy mess of hot roller curls, stiff from hairspray. I added more perfume, deodorant, and lipstick. I was so nervous. I could not hold still, getting up and down from the low, pearl-colored couch as if it were on fire. I wanted her to be proud of the woman I had become.

PEEPHOLE

I heard her footsteps. I approached the door and looked through the peephole. All I could see was the top of her blond head. A mutual pause followed by her strong knock, my sweating hand slipped over the shiny gold knob, a door the only thing between me and my past. Then . . .

There she stood, my birth mother, all 5'4" of her.

We embraced immediately, and I welcomed her in. She excitedly met my husband, Troy, and her grandson, Blake. Marty sat close to the sliding-glass window, the last bits of sun backlighting her perfectly bobbed hair. Her eyes were like mine, green and blue, with hints of gray, her brows thick, her nose sharp and refined. Her expressions animated, her laughter melodic and frequent, and her sense of humor and wit on full display, I studied her every move, every expression, to see if I could discover any part of myself. There we were, after all this time, woman to woman. Of course, I wanted to start from the beginning.

JOE AND I DECIDED THIS COURSE

It was now dark in our room, and the window behind Marty reflected the scene inside. She was a contradiction of strength and fragility, my history, our history, waiting on her tongue. Marty reached into her oversized purse and pulled out a letter. She read it to me.

Dear Heidi,

I became pregnant sometime in January in the front seat of a 1965 baby-blue Chevy Impala. We really loved each other, but we weren't ready for a baby. Your father was in a motorcycle accident. It was April 1965, and he suffered a devastating injury. He was in a coma from the time his head hit the ground. He was coming from State College, Pennsylvania, on his way to see me in Bellefonte, the next town over. We had just had an argument on the phone.

A few weeks prior, when the pregnancy was confirmed, both families had a meeting at my house in Bellefonte. Joe and I had already decided we should put you up for adoption. I was seventeen years old, in my senior year of high school. Your father, Joe, had just started his first year of college playing basketball for Penn State University.

Shortly after the motorcycle accident, Joe was taken from our local hospital to Geisinger due to the severity of his head injury. That was the first and last time I saw him. He was never the same, and he remained comatose and paralyzed until his death. Now you are growing inside of me, and I am watching him die.

My mother and stepfather traveled to Tucson, Arizona, in May to make arrangements for a private adoption. Her sister, Bertha, and niece, Bettie Lou, both lived there, and I could be with family. I could also get away from the increasing pressure from Joe's family to keep you. But Joe and I had decided to give you up, and I was determined to follow that agreement.

I was five months pregnant when I arrived in Tucson in June 1965. Joe was still comatose in Geisinger Hospital. The day I left Pittsburgh, it was cold and raining, not pleasant. When I arrived that day, it was like deplaning into a furnace. The tarmac was a long distance from the terminal, and I thought I was in Hell. I didn't know what my aunt and cousin looked like. They had left Bellefonte in the early 1950s when I was just seven.

It was all prearranged that I would wear a specific maternity dress to help them recognize me. The dress was white, with pink nickel-sized polka dots and pleats. I wore frosted-pink lipstick and pink nail polish. You in my belly, now we were safe, or so I thought.

I went to live with my aunt and her shit-head husband in a run-down trailer park. They were major drinkers. I had a tiny room, very little cooling, and a tiny picture of Joe. I just kept telling myself that this was the best choice. That Joe and I had decided on this course.

GETTING GOOD AT GOODBYE

I have known Marty for ten years. Soon after meeting her, Troy, Blake, and I moved to California. I saw her less and less as I attempted to heal the relationship with my adopted mother. My birth sister, Jennifer (more about her soon), kept me posted on Marty's health. It soon became evident that a final goodbye was coming. When it did, it was early spring 2013; by then, we were living in Washington. I made my third trip back east to say goodbye. Marty outlived every prediction, but this time would indeed be the last. Marty's cancer had found its way to other parts of her body. She said she was tired and didn't want to endure treatment.

My sister planned all the details of my surprise visit. The anticipation and excitement were dampened by the pending reality.

I arrived haggard on an early morning flight directly into State College. I quickly unpacked and got on the road to surprise her. Marty's tiny house was directly off a winding Pennsylvania highway outside Bellefonte. Within thirty minutes, the click of the blinker in my sister's car sounded. The smooth pavement gave way to the sound of gravel. The car rocked on the rough driveway. We decided to park across from her house, next to an industrial building, the back of our car facing her home so she would not notice us. My heart pounding with anticipation, I shut the car door gently. Her caregiver, Tammy, made sure she didn't see us walk up.

On her small porch, the peeling paint was dropping like tree bark. A few colorful pots and garden decorations were arranged beside her door. Marty had a degree in horticulture. Sadly, these plants lacked her energy—dry and as crisp as bacon. I braced myself to see her. I wasn't sure what to expect. Would she look like a wisp of herself? Had the cancer taken her beauty and vigor? We knocked, and she opened the door holding a bowl of steaming macaroni and cheese, her blond hair wavy and ribboned with gray, her eyes still glimmering with feistiness. Her joy, greetings, hugs, and laughter danced in the air.

We all made our way to the kitchen, where her green and glorious plants were flourishing, still enjoying her touch. There were ferns, vines, and things I didn't recognize growing wild and free under her care. Her fat, long-haired gray cat jumped on the kitchen table. He turned on the purring and focused his gold eyes on us. Marty opened her old fridge door and offered us cranberry juice. A Mr. Coffee held some leftover brew. The air tingled with the smell of pasta and Folgers. She pulled up a chair and sat across from us, smiling and holding a thick white mug. Her wide smile was as big as the moment we found ourselves in.

SIDE MIRROR

As the visit ended, we found ourselves melancholy from the wild ride of emotions. The warmth of the coffee maker emanated against my arm. Happiness faded slowly as we neared our final goodbye. I held her thin, frail body against mine—her soft, damp hair against my cheek, the edge of her glasses pressing into my skin, her hand on the center of my back. I wanted to memorize everything about her. I whispered my gratitude, regret, and pain in her ear. I held her tighter, but my grip could not make her stay. Her voice responded in whispers. I told her how much I would miss her; she assured me she would still be around. Then I blurted out, "Is this really goodbye? You know, we have done this a few times already."

Once again, our laughter was filling the room. The front door creaked open, and we found ourselves on the peeling-paint porch with the brittle plants. Marty Jo commented on not having the energy to garden, pointing out one lone blossom on the bush in front of us. That blossom, which I would never have noticed, she saw it in all its glory. She had a way of finding beauty in her circumstances.

I stepped off the deck; the stairs wobbled under my feet. My body felt as if it had no bones. My stride was thick, labored, and unstructured. Everything seemed heightened and irritating. This time, the leaving was for good, and my soul was caving in. Our paths would separate forever.

Part of me wanted to run back and collapse at her feet. The car engine started, the air conditioner blasting on high, when I took notice of Marty's reflection in the side mirror. There she was, standing on her porch, in a loose, long-sleeved white linen shirt over a pair of light blue jeans, the gray cat weaving in and out of her legs. Wavy silver hair aglow as she waved goodbye like a pageant queen, the lone blossom in front of her—a pop of color in the pain. We turn onto the smooth pavement; I stare into the side mirror, a reflection of trees and road. I will never see Marty Jo again.

SHE'S GONE

It was Valentine's Day 2014 when I got the news. Marty Jo had died in her home, my sister by her side, as she flew away. The effect of her death . . . a permanent hollow spot. Her spirit is never far, and I know her strength runs through my veins. I am proud of the rebellious women in our family—all of us a collection of walking, talking contradictions. We can sweet talk, cuss like sailors, decorate anything, destroy anything, cook amazing food, love hard, leave hard, fiercely defend our babies, believe equally in God and the Devil, and outlive any odds, blazing a trail sprinkled with hard liquor and glitter. We won't take no for an answer, and we always find a way to get what we want. We will give you everything and take it back if you betray us. Some of us pout (me), some of us rage, but you will know us, and you sure won't forget who we are. You will know we're here because we live aloud, scattering our hearts. We are wildly spirited—here and beyond. Thank you, Marty, for giving me a beginning and loving me the best you could. I will always try to see the lone blossom.

CHAPTER 2
FINDING MARTY JO

THEME 2: NATURE VS. NURTURE
Alysa Zalma, MD

"The child's ambivalence is met and matched by the ambivalence of his parents. For children are never unmixed blessings; they are always competitors as well as heirs" (Brinich 1990, 44).

Like virtually all adopted children, Heidi fantasized about having a real birth mother. Then, suddenly, the mother she had fantasized about was given to her as a New Year's gift, and just as swiftly, her adoptive mother was taken away—all on that day.

"All on that day" are the last four words of the chorus of the folk song "Sinnerman," which enjoyed popularity during the 1960s. Many folk groups, including The Weavers, sing about a man who cannot escape his sins, no matter where he runs or what he does. Such is the plight of the adopted child, who always "sins" by yearning for their fantasized biological "other" mother, burdened with much guilt in this process. To "atone" for such a "sin," many experiences of guilt are universal to the adopted child (Brodzinsky 1990, 9).

According to psychoanalytic theory, all infants have preverbal internal experiences of "good" and "bad" objects, where, when they experience frustration, anger, and other complex emotions, it creates a dichotomy of the "bad" mother/parent and the "good" mother/parent (Greenberg and Mitchell 1983, 125). In later childhood, these earlier preverbal experiences may be expressed in personae found in many universal fairytales, such as the "bad" parent becoming a wicked stepmother or witch and the "good" parent becoming the fairy godmother or the benevolent king. The child does this in part to keep themselves "safer" from fantasized retribution/retaliation from the "bad" parent and the guilt they may feel from the intensity of their rage toward this "bad" parent.

The "good"/idealized parent is the one the child fantasizes about after having sad, angry, and otherwise complicated feelings toward their actual parent. For Heidi, the "good/idealized" parent is her biological parent, Marty Jo, and her "actual" parent is her adoptive parent, Joy. This "imaginary/good/idealized" parent is the one who will satisfy all their desires, demand no psychic payment, and extort no psychic retribution for any of the desires the child has. The ability to "split off" (separate) both good and unacceptable aspects of one's parents in fantasy life is protective and part of normal development. In this way, the child learns to incorporate all elements of internal objects (representations of pieces of mother/parent) in ways that feel safe and will not "annihilate" or destroy the child. This normal process becomes complicated by adoption when a child learns that there are two mothers/parents, and the idealized parent and the actual parent are not the same person.

By having a safe place to feel the intensities of these emotions and assign them characters, the child can better incorporate the notion that "good" and "bad" aspects may exist in one parent, in all people, and in themselves. This is the "material" of which fairy tales are made, and the archetypes of pieces of the personality become personified in the tale. This is perhaps why fairy tales are so omnipresent and why they have become so ubiquitous and part of the thread of common human experience. One may extrapolate from Heidi's or any other adopted child's story why this phase of normal childhood development becomes much more complex.

Thus, by using an unconscious stage to play out their emotions, the child can come to terms with them and universally see "good" and "bad" aspects of people. They "see" this unconscious "story" in a fairy tale, the main vehicle by which the unconscious becomes conscious. This is the other main reason why fairy tales are sought after by children and adults alike; they are the universal stories that make their unconscious internal "battles" conscious in actual story form so that one can derive meaning and even a sense of wonder (Bettelheim 1977, 19).

The adopted child has a unique situation where they already have two actual mothers.

This child is "banished" to their unconscious and subconscious underworld, not only to experience what non-adopted children experience but also to feel that they may be "punished" for their own desires for their "real" mother.

When the birth mother/parent is found and the adoptee and biological mother/parent have made contact, new betrayals become more explicit, as is seen when Heidi talks for the first time to her biological mother and then immediately calls her adoptive mother.

Marty Jo, the biological mother she fantasized about all those years, instantly became Heidi's forbidden object. The fantasy became a reality and created a complex triangulated relationship among the three women. Marty Jo was also a forbidden object to Joy; Joy did not want a rival to displace her in her mother-daughter relationship with Heidi. The term "forbidden" in psychoanalytic theory usually refers to a drive or relationship that is not held in conscious thought but later may surface from the unconscious or subconscious (Freud 1923, 17-18).

Marty Jo may have desired more of an heir than a competitor at the stage of her life when Heidi actually meets her. This may have increased the notion that the two mothers were competing, and unconditional love was fragile. Joy had more to lose, and Marty Jo had more to gain. As Heidi so poignantly divulged, this is a potentially impossible moment for any adoptee.

Heidi created the interpersonal triangle between actual/present parent, Joy, the fantasied/biological parent, Marty Jo, and herself. From that moment, the good and bad parent split became more defined and real, especially between (adoptive) mother and child.

This "good-bad" parent occurs to the infant in the earliest stages of the infant's life as actual split-off pieces of the mother (Klein 1975, 262, 266). Later in the infant's development, both pieces are understood as actually one person, with the mother (parent) having both "good" and "bad" attributes. Klein posits that moving forward, defense mechanisms develop to protect the infant against further dangers of "the loss of the loved object" i.e., the mother/parent (Klein, 267-9). The danger of the loss of the loved object(s) becomes more real at this juncture as Heidi seems to have to "choose" between mothers in the triangle created among herself, Joy, and Marty Jo.

With adopted children, this triangle is different and potentially more dangerous. As they mature, many experience a central injury of adoption, with the knowledge that their adopted parent and biological parent are two different people.

How does a child choose between two mothers?

This scenario happens intra-psychically in normal childhood development when children feel anger, sadness, abandonment, etc., toward a parent. They may create fantasies of disowning the "bad" mother and merging with the "good" mother, but they may then fear retribution and feel guilt for their internal anger at their mother. Fairy tales pay homage to this internal struggle of children and often hinge on the tension between the child's "good" mother and "bad" mother, who are embodied in two separate figures, such as a fairy godmother and the evil witch or the real mother who dies and the cruel stepmother who succeeds her.

The universal tales of *Cinderella*, *Little Red Riding Hood*, and *The Wizard of Oz* illustrate the use of these story elements; they assign separate characters to the universal, internal experiences of children. Plots turn up the reconciliation or violent tension through escape, the rescue and destruction of an evil mother, or the discovery of a child's missing elements incorporated through growth (heart, soul, and courage). This is explained in psychologist and author Bruno Bettelheim's account of this phenomenon in his famous work, *The*

Uses of Enchantment, where he explains that "all the child's wishful thinking gets embodied in a good fairy; all his destructive wishes in an evil witch. . . . Once this starts, the child will be less and less engulfed by unmanageable chaos" (Bettelheim 1977, 66).

The "unmanageable chaos" that Bettelheim discusses may be the conflicts the ego must traverse between the unconscious desires of the child's id and the wrathful and fated destruction of those forbidden urges by the superego.

Heidi did not initially anticipate having to choose between her two mothers; as an adult, she failed to see one as the "good" and one as the "bad." Joy felt threatened, which forced Heidi to feel like she was choosing. This seemed to unleash Joy's feelings of rivalry, betrayal, and abandonment. In response to this, Heidi experienced anxiety and guilt. Before speaking to Joy, Heidi experienced previously unknown happiness and excitement from her first contact with Marty Jo.

Joy's "iciness," as Heidi describes, thrusts her into the fairy tale role of wicked stepmother. Heidi was unexpectedly caught in the jealousy of the older stepmother towards her daughter's beauty, youth, and competence. This universal phenomena embodies the powerful and universal features present in every parent-child relationship as the parent ages and the child matures. As the women in such an adoption triad come to understand that they all have worth and value in this relationship, their rivalries and conflicts may be processed and addressed. Unfortunately, for many such adoption triads, this may not be the initial experience.

Heidi experiences the rift immediately. Joy, who had been Heidi's mother, became her "stepmother."

The icy "do what you have to do" is a comment on Joy's jealousies; Heidi is doing what Joy could not do, attempting to ask, "Please tell me who I am." In being unable to have a biological child, trying to tolerate an abusive marriage, and feeling Heidi's betrayal to find her "real" mother, Marty Jo became a feared and hated rival to Joy.

Joy may have always wanted to be the "Run in bare feet, grow her hair long girl . . . feet on the dash, hand out the window girl." In this case, unbeknownst to both daughter and adoptive mother, Heidi is the woman the adoptive mother always wanted to be and the woman the biological mother was.

Joy's jealousy of Marty Jo becomes transparent. The knowledge and truth of biology (Heidi is not her "true" daughter; thus, they are not like each other) have fully been exposed. The contact with Heidi's biological mother instilled fear in Joy: the mother-daughter relationship would be severed, and Heidi would discover that they are not alike in the fundamental ways a biological mother and daughter are.

Heidi discovers that she would like to be more like the "Run in bare feet, grow her hair long girl" she found in Marty Jo. In Heidi's discovery of Marty Jo, Joy (as many adoptive mothers may conclude) may have feared that Heidi would no longer want her to be her mother. Joy may have feared that what she gave Heidi (nurture vs. nature) was not enough for her. This may have been a huge rejection for Joy.

Heidi tried to mitigate Joy's sense of betrayal, but what had been done could not be undone.

As with every adoptee, one of the main quests is the truth of their biology. They, understandably more than non-adopted children and adults, seek to understand this combination of nature and nurture more intently. With more than ordinary intensity, Heidi grappled with the combination from both her mothers.

As for all of us, Heidi is a product of her DNA (nature) and her environment (nurture). Children of adoption understand how their environment shapes them, but they always wonder how their DNA creates them. They also wonder about the many "what-ifs" beyond their genetics. *What if I were not adopted? Then, I would know my genetics and would have had a different environment than I do now.*

The combination of how environment and DNA informs whether certain heritable traits are expressed is part of the quest of "who am I" for adoptees. During their first conversation, Heidi learned of Marty Jo's terminal illness and that she was in the midst of treatment for breast cancer. Heidi became more aware of how her genetics could affect her.

With the knowledge of both mothers, Heidi was able to reflect on her life and wonder who she was with more detail. She more deeply understood her experience of self and how the split between nature and nurture informed this.

Both of my mothers could not have been more opposite or complex. Yet they shared a few fundamental aspects—courage and rebellion. However, those characteristics played out in them in different ways. My biological mother was outward and obvious in her pushback; my adoptive mother was more refined and cunning. Each had the same velocity, intensity, and strength when navigating life's upheavals. My biological mother was a runner, not willing to be imprisoned. My adoptive mother chained herself to obligations even when they didn't serve her. Both were potent and unforgettable women; both threaded through me in ways I cannot deny.

Heidi understood that she is a product of both, but could her adoptive mother leave such an "imprint" on her that has actually modified her DNA? This is the study of epigenetics, the environmental experiences and stressors that may "turn on" already present genes and "express" certain markers on them. That this phenomenon occurs is the subject of epigenetics (Center for Disease Control and Prevention Genomics and Precision Health 2020).

The phenomena of nature vs. nurture, of the penetrance of DNA and epigenetics, is of continual intrigue and study. It attempts to answer the question, "Am I doomed to live out and repeat my genetics (set variable, DNA), or is there something else I can do (changeable variable, environment)?"

The answer to this question continues to intrigue adoptees. What happens when twins/siblings are separated at birth? Will they still be products of their DNA, or does the environment matter? Much scholarly research addresses these very personal questions. Some research reveals the inevitability of one's genetics, and some predictably argue that environment plays a pivotal role in how one's genes are expressed (epigenetics).

Within psychiatric literature, many twin studies show the inevitability of one's genetics. Much of this research looks at studies in which twins were either raised together or separated at birth and adopted into separate families. The famous Maudsley studies within psychiatric literature discuss various cases of twins, separated at birth and raised in separate households, who still develop the same severe mental illnesses (Cardno et al,1999, 162).

However, other studies speak to the combination of both genetics and environment and how, although certain genetics have more of a likely "penetrance" (i.e., more likely to be expressed no matter what the environment is, like the Maudsley twin studies), much of "who we are" is a combination of both.

Jane Brody, columnist for *The New York Times*, writes about this very topic and offers a personal account of her twin sons. When her sons grew up, one of them also became a journalist. He notes, "Genes confer a potential, but the environment often determines whether that potential is [or is not] expressed" (Brody 2018).

So, when Heidi describes herself as "double trouble," she is right. Her genetics are essentially "immutable," as Brody puts it, but what she incorporated into her personhood/character/sense of self was deeply influenced by her environment and her relationship with her adoptive family, whether they brought her nurturance or trauma. These experiences influenced her behaviors and participated in her genome expression that went beyond her original DNA bestowed to her by her biological parents. Essentially, these environmental factors, known as epigenetic differences, can turn the genetic expression of various genes "on" or "off." It is intriguing to learn that we have some control over certain "instructions" overlayed on our genetics. These "instructions" turn "on" or "off" certain genes that are intimately related to disease states, such as breast cancer, colorectal cancer, and lung function during smoking and after cessation of smoking. These expressions may even persist into future generations (Tang et al. 2016; Johnson et al. 2014; McCartney 2018).

In her desire to discover who she is and where she came from, Heidi writes "She Was," a poem for and about her birth mother, a tribute. Embedded in the poem are two wishes. The first is Heidi's wish to see more of herself in her birth mother. The second wish is that she might be forgiven for her adopted mother's feelings of betrayal and be healed. She sees within Marty Jo an uncanny ability to forgive.

To choose one mother over the other is an impossible choice. It is one of the most traumatic dilemmas for an adoptee to face. The fact that Heidi did not understand that she "chose" Marty Jo over Joy set off feelings of betrayal and anger for Joy, which Heidi initially did not understand. This changed Heidi's (and Joy's) life inextricably and permanently.

The awareness of potential feelings such as these in their children may be helpful to adoptive parents so when the universal question of "who am I" inevitably surfaces, they can meet their children with openness and permission to explore these questions. If this uncovers feelings of betrayal, rivalry, and jealousy, this may open opportunities for the adoptive parents to connect with their community and/or with a mental health professional to explore their own personal growth.

The fear of having to choose one parent over the other may hinder many adoptees from pursuing their birth parents. They may remain consciously ignorant to avoid wounding their adoptive parents, who might view the choice as a betrayal.

Marty Jo seemed to have an easier time making decisions that affected her life despite potential repercussions and seemed so capable of forgiveness. This was alluring to Heidi, who evermore longed for the love lost from Joy due to her decision of "choosing" Marty Jo over her.

Never conformed, showed her spirit girl
Brave and bold like thunder girl

Split the night open, spilled the stars on her skin girl
Always forgave you girl
Your sins didn't matter to her girl
The woman who birthed me girl

In all her longing to be more like her biological mother, the story of Heidi's life deeply echoes Marty Jo's. She has escaped neither her genetics nor her environment, which is what she wished for. Having more say in who one is provides much hope for any adoptee who wonders about losing out on any of their lineage, whether it be from their genetics or environment. While we may think we cannot control our genetics, we can have more impact than we previously realized. When we interface with our environment, this can inform our genetics, one of the central themes of this chapter. Knowing this and using it to our advantage to better understand who we are may change our perceptions, environment, and genetics.

I wish I could be that kind of girl . . .

CHAPTER 3
STUCK AT THIRTY-FIVE MPH

MY FIRST FATHER, JOSEPH ELWOOD EGLI

"I'm sorry we never met, that both of us had to leave. The tragedy is that we missed both our hello and our goodbye."
—Heidi Marble

THIRTY-FIVE MPH

Under a canopy of quivering late summer leaves, the smell of gasoline and blood rises from the hot pavement, where John Egli kneels beside his dying nineteen-year-old son, the red speedometer needle stuck at thirty-five mph; my father's motorcycle was a twisted knot of metal. Machine and man lie on a bed of shattered glass that glints under the high sun. Paramedics gather his body as his blood disappears inauspiciously into the asphalt. Sirens wail out their distinct warning. A blur of red and blue strobing lights flash as they rush Joseph's body away. It's 100 miles to the nearest trauma center. The debris field is quickly swept up so traffic can move again. Cars roll over fresh oil and my father's drying blood.

He will never open his eyes again. His tall, 6'4" frame will never stand. His hazel eyes will never open. His basketball shoes will never squeak across the maple plank floor. He will never wear his #21 jersey or feel the glory of standing in a cool stream while fly-fishing. He will never hold my mother. I will never meet him, and he will never meet me.

A ventilator bellows air into his lungs. My grandparents drive 200 miles roundtrip a day to see their son until hope is driven out of them, until there is no more life to support. On a hot summer afternoon, they sign permission for his death. A sheet pulled over the life they had, a toe tag placed on a life stopped short. In the late day, with humidity only the East Coast can offer, they drive 100 miles back home as their son's body grows cold—the pavement as dark and scorching as their grief. Yet, inside this tragedy, something unexpected happened: a part of their son is growing inside the womb of his seventeen-year-old girlfriend; Marty Jo Fleck is five months pregnant with me.

ZONE DEFENSE

It was 1965. My biological grandfather was the head basketball coach (1955-1968); even today, he still holds the record for the most victories at PSU. He was inducted into the Penn State Hall of Fame in 1993. He lived and breathed basketball. It wasn't just a way of life; it was their religion. College athletes made his home a sanctuary, where my grandfather preached the gospel of zone defense to a congregation of giants who had to bend over to get through the door, their size fourteen to eighteen shoes parked like thick white boats at the dock. His first-born child, my aunt Bonnie, married Ron Avillion, a key player on her dad's team. They had tall, beautiful babies and decades of love. My grandfather was kind and gentle, with a sprinkle of sass. He often repeated this classic comment: "The Penn State football team could beat us—in basketball."

Imagine that you are the head basketball coach of a major college, have three children—Bonnie, Carol, and Joe—and two children, Joe and Carol, are simultaneously dealing with unwed pregnancies in the 1960s in small-town America. Now your only son is dead, and you are trying to persuade the birth mother and her family to allow you and your family to raise your grandchild instead of giving her (me) up for adoption. How do you rebound off the backboard of that situation?

SIDELINED

My grandparents knew plenty about being sidelined; abandonment had ricocheted through generations before them. At four years old, my grandfather, John, was orphaned when his father fell from a tree and died from a punctured lung. His mother, unable to care for two young boys, relinquished them to a "war mother's home" (a.k.a. orphanage). A few years later, an aunt rescued the boys and raised them until my grandfather's athleticism caught the eye of the local high school football coach. Soon, my grandfather was proving his worth under the illumination of stadium lights. The head coach took him into his home and raised him during high school, guiding him into a full college football scholarship. During my grandfather's first year of college, he met a blue-eyed, blond, wavy-haired, button-nosed beauty named Nathel ("Nate"). She came from a difficult history. She was known as the "bastard" child of incest. Her mother was a mighty and spirited woman who loved her well. Together, they formed a coalition to overcome the shame. They put a finger and a fist up to anyone brave enough to judge their situation.

Nate and John married. He left her and my two-year-old aunt Bonnie behind to fight in World War II. In combat at the Battle of Bastogne, my grandfather was shot. The bullet passed 1.5 inches from his heart and exited cleanly through his back. He was transferred to a hospital in France to fight for his life. Nate was informed of his death and spent two weeks grieving—until she learned he was still alive. Upon his return, he was given a Purple Heart for bravery.

This extraordinary couple, who had risen above so much, built a warm, loving family with three children and a home welcoming many. Their hearts and lives grew wider because of their experiences with abandonment. Now, in an unimaginable double tragedy, they are on the court of trauma that they knew so well—facing off first with the death of their son and then with the fight to keep his child; there was no game plan or playbook for that contest.

THE POWERS THAT BE

Before the 1970s, fathers had no rights to their unborn children—and certainly, dead fathers didn't have any. My grandparents' rights were nonexistent. My grandparents did what they could to persuade my biological mother and her family to let them raise me, but after many back-and-forth meetings between the two families, it was evident that would never happen. Nate was devastated by the loss of her son and his baby. John continued to coach basketball for a few years before retiring, only to die of cancer at sixty-one. How I wish I could have known them and given them something back. I will never get that chance. My grandparents left this earth before I could find them.

OUR SON

One somber winter day, when I was thirty-three years old, my aunt Bonnie took me to the Center County Cemetery in Happy Valley, where all three were laid to rest. The details of that day will never leave me: the angst of seeing their names etched in stone, the two dead roses, the winter cold, the wisps of pine branches carved on their gravestones, and finally, the permanence of it all.

The cemetery held the deep hush of January. A few leftover fall leaves curled in the swift breaths of the wind. It was time to see my father's grave. We wove in and out of a staggering number of headstones. The rolling, snow-dusted Pennsylvania hills stood in the distance. My breath was visible as I pulled my hands out of thick, knit gloves.

I see his name and press my knees into the icy winter ground; my bones grind as I trace the patina copper letters that say, *OUR SON*.

It was as if they had run out of strength to say more. I shut my eyes. I need to feel this, not just see it. My hands—my fingertips—run over the cold numbers like I am reading Braille. My words feel like coarse gravel as I tell my father, "You have a grandson. I am horrible at basketball. I am sorry we never met. I never had the chance to feel your arms. I never looked into your eyes. Your voice never filled my ears. I'm sorry we never got to say either our hello or our goodbye." I stand up in my wet-kneed jeans when a rush of knowing warms me, and I am made aware of how important this moment is—for both of us.

CHAPTER 3
STUCK AT THIRTY-FIVE MPH
THEME 3: THE MULTIVERSE/PARALLEL UNIVERSE AND BENDING TIME
Alysa Zalma, MD

My father's death took me to a place I had never been and a place I had never left in his absence. I'm sorry we never met, that both of us had to leave. The tragedy is that we missed both our hello and our goodbye.

The universal core themes of adoption include all the what-ifs adoptees often experience. What if it could have been different? What if I wasn't adopted? What if (the events) that led to my adoption didn't happen? Who would I be? These questions can all be answered using the paradigm of the multiverse, within which other parallel universes exist, and the discussion of quantum physics (Tegmark 2003, 41-51).

This chapter discusses the possibility and the probability of occurrences that happen beyond what is explainable and possible in linear human existence. Both abandonment and intergenerational loss—as well as hope—belie the predictable and explainable.

It may be considered that Heidi tacitly wonders about the multiverse and parallel universes when she juxtaposes the death of her nineteen-year-old father and her own five-month gestation.

The famous English theoretical physicist, cosmologist, and author Stephen Hawking highlights the idea of the multiverse, the idea that many universes exist side by side. The idea of the multiverse was first contemplated as part of quantum physics by the American physicist Hugh Everett, who proposed it in 1957 (Byrne 2008).

In trying to better understand the concept of the multiverse, *Scientific American* authors Vilenkin and Tegmark found it useful to distinguish between four different levels of understanding. They discuss, "Level I, other regions far away in space where the apparent laws of physics are the same, but where history played out differently because things started out differently), Level II (regions of space where even the apparent laws of physics are different), Level III (parallel worlds elsewhere in the so-called Hilbert space where quantum reality plays out), and Level IV (totally disconnected realities governed by different mathematical equations)" (Vilenkin and Tegmark 2011).

In Heidi's depiction of linear reality, her father dies in a motorcycle accident while she is gestating in her birth mother. Joseph, Heidi's biological father, and she were never to be in the same human timeline in this linear universe. Yet, and because of this, his absence had brought her to a "place she never left." This was a suspended animation space for Heidi. Why did she "never leave"? Or, to consider the multiverse, *what else was simultaneously happening?*

In Heidi's linear life, being "stuck at thirty-five mph" was her father's accident and subsequent death. At his gravesite, she returns to the place she never left in this linear universe/reality.

The cemetery held the deep hush of January. A few leftover fall leaves curled in the swift breaths of the wind. It was time to see my father's grave.

In the multiverse, Heidi continues to live many parallel existences in the place she "never left." In her linear timeline, she wonders what would have happened had her biological father lived. And, if he did die, what would have happened if his biological parents would have adopted her? And, if he had lived, would her biological parents have raised her? Would she still have been adopted and met her biological father later?

What if, within the multiverse, her father does not have his motorcycle accident. To make it more unbelievable from a linear reality standpoint, what if Heidi is her own daughter and is also the daughter of Joseph, the father who did not have the motorcycle accident? These are just some examples of the possibilities in the multiverse.

In the last scene of the 1978 *Superman* movie starring Christopher Reeve, Superman/Clark Kent's love interest, Lois Lane (played by Margot Kidder), is killed in a car accident as a result of an earthquake. The duality of Clark Kent and Superman may be considered an example of the multiverse where two men live parallel lives. This may also be understood as two men with the same consciousness, and one being a different self of the same person living a parallel life. In the film, from the perspective of the linear universe, Superman does not save Lois Lane from the earthquake. If only he had gotten to the scene of the accident a few minutes earlier.

In the movie's penultimate scene, many interpretations are possible concerning Superman's ability to save Lois Lane even though an earthquake kills her in one reality. One interpretation is that Superman turns back time (time travel) and can find Lane before the earthquake strikes. Another interpretation that is more central to the theme of this chapter is that Superman enters into the multiverse where many outcomes for many parallel lifetimes are possible. This interpretation affords adoptees more answers to their "what if" questions.

As Superman is either turning back time or entering into the multiverse, he hears the voice of Jor-El, his father, say to him, "It is forbidden . . . is forbidden . . . to interfere in the course of human events." That it was forbidden would assume one linear reality only, the one where Lois Lane dies in the earthquake. One interpretation is that Superman rebels against a solely linear reality, where only one outcome is possible.

And this changes everything.

Superman instead finds his entrance (portal) into a space where the multiverse is possible. The film shows the earth in space spinning backward. After Superman enters the portal of the multiverse, he can move freely between the parallel universes.

The next scene of the film is (arguably) in a simultaneous parallel universe, where Superman greets Lane "back in time," and the earthquake did not happen/will not happen/may or may not happen or hasn't happened yet. They are about to embrace before they are interrupted by a junior member of Lane's journalism staff. Superman leaves the scene, confident that the earthquake will not come to overturn her car and kill her. The audience is "stuck." We are unsure of what will occur "now." Will the earthquake still happen? Why does Superman leave the scene, not there (again) to save her if needed?

Anything is possible in this space—both in the film and Heidi's story.

That trauma repeats itself is a linear reality phenomenon.

As we see in this chapter (and will see in subsequent chapters), adoption traumas repeat within one linear lifetime and also transgenerationally. In the multiverse, traumas are not replayed. They, in fact, did not happen.

There is nothing to replay. From the energy medicine perspective, it cannot be replayed if the trauma/event did not happen. In twenty-first-century shamanic history and teachings, the Egyptian Forgiveness Cord Cutting Ceremony is a powerful and fantastic portal to the multiverse (Jan Engels-Smith, Soul Retrieval Class, Lightsong School of 21st Shamanism and Energy Medicine 2021). In this sacred ceremony, one travels energetically back in time to a person, place, or event. The "cords" to this person, place, or event are energetically "cut." This releases all that has come after the "trauma" associated with the person, place, or event, and many transgenerational cords are cut and released. This provides the portal and entrance needed to the parallel universes that, energetically speaking, already exist. They are already happening. The person who has not yet cut these cords continues to live in their linear reality, "stuck" with the repetitions of the trauma.

In this ceremony, one must, in contemporary shamanic terminology, "go before the grievance," the grievance being the actual person, place, or event. To break the cycle of the stuck-ness of her adoption traumas discussed in this chapter, Heidi must go *before the grievance* of the event of her father's motorcycle accident. In twenty-first-century shamanic terms, the word "grievance" is somewhat synonymous but fundamentally different from our modern definition of the word "forgiveness." During this ceremony, energetic cords are cut, and by "going before the grievance," one has energetically traveled before the trauma(s) have occurred, so there is nothing to forgive (Jan Engels-Smith, Soul Retrieval Class, Lightsong School of 21st Shamanism and Energy Medicine 2021).

During this ceremony, Heidi would "go before the grievance," which means she would energetically travel back to the motorcycle accident and stand in front of it, using an energetic or symbolic laser (such as a sharp rock) to "cut" the cords. She would then cut the cords twice, once after she said, "the motorcycle accident" (the event) and once after she said, "I go before the grievance." This signifies that the cords are being cut before the event happened in this linear reality.

Then she would say, "*I am free.*"

Subsequently, she would be released from this linear reality, and all parallel universes within the multiverse would be available to her. In the actual ceremony, the participant would say as many people, places, and events as they could think of to "go before the grievance" and cut the cords.

In the multiverse, the space that Heidi had never been and never left, she now wakes up one parallel morning and looks in the mirror. She does not recognize herself. It is another version of herself in another universe. She is not in her house. She has gone before the grievance of her father's motorcycle accident. All feels quiet. All the cords are shriveling and becoming strands of confetti as if left over from a New Year's Eve party. There are many grains of rice, as if there had been a wedding. After the ceremony, many images may come to the participant. Perhaps the grains of rice turn colors and become other entities.

The grains of rice are very beautiful. Grain one is a deep purple and spans most of the southern hemisphere. Grain two is fissured and then starts to become whole, a ruby-red color, spanning the distance between the seas of the southern and northern hemispheres. Grain three is a lake, cobalt blue. All the colors change as Heidi is swirled around this space; she takes on the temperatures and colors. They were molten hot, and now they are cold, wet, and full of rain. She turns into the rain, first as a storm; then she changes colors, yellows and greens. As this space goes from south to north, the rainstorm (Heidi) changes to water droplets and pure light. All is quiet again.

The realities before the trauma of her father's motorcycle accident are back because, from an energy medicine perspective, the trauma now did not happen,

Heidi is her own daughter. She is her own mother. She is also her own father.

All at once, simultaneously, in parallel universes.

She is an eight-year-old, a beautiful, energetic girl in a farmhouse, with the sun streaming in on a summer's day, playing with her mother's lipsticks.

She is a thirty-five-year-old beautiful woman, so full of life and energy, laughing with glee, looking at her eight-year-old daughter, who has pink, red, and melon lipsticks painted across her face.

She is a forty-one-year-old muscular, strong man who does not own a motorcycle, who is so proud and thrilled with his wife and daughter, brimming with joy because of his full life and connection to family.

She is in the multiverse. She had never left. Many of her are now in all of these lives. She is also simultaneously in her "original" linear life.

She knows him now. They have met. She is living her dream because she is his dream. He has a grandson. She has a daughter. She is his daughter.

CHAPTER 4
TRUE GRIT — THE COWBOY WAY
COWBOY WISDOM

"Real cowboys never run; they just ride away."
—Cowboy proverb

"Courage is to be scared to death and saddle up anyway."
—John Wayne

GOTTA RIDE

My adopted father, Ellis Dwayne Hamilton, was my greatest adversary, and you know what they say about adversaries. He taught me a lot, much of which I wish I never had to learn. His strength was beyond anything I have ever known. He knew how to suffer and make everything around him suffer, too. His pain was electric with its unpredictability. He taught me about danger, survival, and courage—taught me the cowboy way—that you always gotta ride it out.

His one-sided smile, wavy charcoal hair, and hazel eyes set deep in a face carved with lines. His chiseled good looks made people notice—leathered skin a road map of his tough life. He was 6'1" and had swagger—serious knock-'em-dead swagger. Oddly enough, a bout with polio left one of his legs more rigid than the other, making his glide even more appealing. His posture was perfect, and he knew how to move his body in ways that could lure and intimidate. Veins spread like roots across his lean muscles; not an ounce of fat could be found on his frame. Years of brute force made him formidable when it came to physical strength. He knew he was good-looking and used that to leverage all sorts of favors.

There wasn't a mirror he didn't introduce himself to. A reflective surface, whether a store window or lake, became a place for him to admire himself. He religiously hand-steamed his Stetson hats, molding them like clay. He ironed his Wrangler jeans meticulously so that a crease would run perfectly down the middle of each leg. He spent countless hours polishing belt buckles, guns, and cowboy boots. He was freshly shaved every day, and he liberally doused his palms with Old Spice shaker cologne, slapping his cheeks with punishment. The spicy smell made its way to you before he did. Each hair on his head had a place and was secured by my mother's potent Aqua Net hairspray. It was a rare occasion that I saw him disheveled.

Ellis was born to wrangle cattle, brand, castrate, ride bulls and broncos, and rope anything with horns. His birth father died of polio when he was two years old, and his death set the trajectory toward the hardening of his heart. His interior life still remains a mystery to me.

I was always looking for clues to understand his tyrannical ways. Ellis's mother, Dorothy, had seemed hell-bent on not being alone with a young child, and being a widow hadn't lasted long. Within a few months, she married her second husband, Bud Hamilton. He was a crusty rancher who looked like he walked straight out of a John Wayne movie—legs so bowed you could drive a small car through them. He always had on a raggedy cowboy hat and jeans covered in pale dust. Bud's cowboying skills were unmatched; he could make a rawhide rope dance like a silk ribbon.

Grandpa Bud would spend hours trying to teach me to use a rope like a proper cowgirl. Because my skills were so horrible, he fashioned a sawhorse with horns for me to practice. But even this unmovable makeshift cow didn't help. We would start our sessions with Bud tangoing with the rope. He would make it spin, dip, and fly. I would giggle and hold my arms flat against my legs, and he would swirl the rope up and down my body without making contact. I could feel only air touching my skin.

As he would pass the rope to my hands, it would instantaneously turn into a tangled mess of rigid fibers. My tiny hands would fumble to bring the rope to life under the shadow of his hat brim. The rope was unforgiving and seemed to stiffen just to spite me, the rough bristles turning my arms red and his bowlegged shadow overlapping mine as I fumbled endlessly. These roping lessons were something I had to tolerate if I wanted to eat Grandma Dorothy's food. And that was worth the price I paid.

I preferred being at the hem of Grandma Dorothy's flowing skirts in the kitchen, watching Bud roll cigarettes while she cooked. He always sat in the same chair with the split-open cushion on the right side of the table, the table itself piled high with scattered newspapers. While waiting to be served his meal, he would dump ripe tobacco from a tiny drawstring bag. The pungent smell intermingled with whatever was cooking on the stove. He wet his thumb and forefinger on his tongue to help him separate the thin rolling papers. He would tap a river of tobacco down the middle of each paper with great care, looking under the rim of his glasses. Without stopping, he would roll, lick, and twist until a dozen cigarettes were stacked. The last one was always ceremoniously placed between his chapped, split lips and lit. The cigarette bobbing up and down, he would talk about his day as smoke softened him.

His bone-colored cowboy hat, a brown wave of sweat stains running along the brim, always tilted slightly to one side. Bud did not have the grooming priorities that my father had. He always smelled of earth, horses, salt, and smoke. His face bristled with gray whiskers, his eyebrows wild and wooly. Hair grew lush out of his ears and nose, and that never seemed to bother him. He had at least six pairs of worn-in cowboy boots lined up beside his bed and a blue plaid robe that should have been thrown out ten years prior. His best friend, Jim Beam, was hidden in paper bags stuffed under his truck seat. My grandmother would often ask me to see how many hidden bags I could find and bring to her. It was impressive how clever he was in his sneakiness. No matter, I loved the challenge, and I often came to her with arms full of primarily empty bottles covered in ragged skirts of paper bags.

Bud was an authentic cowboy; he could wrangle, brand, and birth any living creature. My own father's cruelty was learned through his example. It doesn't take a genius to figure out that the solidification of my father's heart started with Bud's abuse and Dorothy's allowing it.

I would perch on the second rung of the fence, watching my father and grandfather bring the cows home before the sun dropped from the sky. Bud's silhouette was distinct—a sturdy horse between his legs, feet anchored in the stirrups, his rope circling the wind as the herding dogs darted back and forth. Nervous, wide-eyed cattle mooed and moaned under his yaays, yips, and whistles.

Noisy, ten-foot gates would swing open as sweaty cattle rushed in, the sun pulling color out of the sky behind us. He could dismount a horse like he was floating. After, the horse would stand obediently by with her bridle hanging. You could hear the distant clank of his spurs, the whisper of his leather chaps, and the thud of his cowboy boots under tired steps. He would lead his horse to the barn to be wiped down, undressed, and fed.

On our walk back to the ranch house, you could always see my grandmother through the rippled windowpanes, cooking. She was plump and lovely, her gray hair tinged with hints of purple, perfectly coiffed, her skin creamy, her lips small and perfect, Maybelline red. She looked particularly grand in her printed lavender dresses with the rounded lace collars. A well-worn apron would be tied about her waist, and her chubby hands would be covered in flour. With ease, she would place bowls of comfort food on a stained daisy tablecloth. Rung out cowboys blotted their brows and stuffed paper towels into the tops of their shirts and then began eating ravenously until plates, bowls, and bones were dry.

UNBEARABLE

My days on the ranch were full of great comfort and searing fear. Always having an affinity for animals, I felt the unbearable cruelty. There was no horse whispering. The cowboys would make a wood fire in the middle of the arena for branding cattle. It would blaze and then die down into hell-red coals into which the branding irons were sunk deep.

The cattle would be forced to the ground with a prod, a rope, and sheer cowboy force. It often took three ill-tempered men to get the job done. With horror, I watched as my dad lifted the branding iron alive, glowing with orange heat, his eyes aflame as he seared the cattle's flesh. Their moans of pain meant nothing to him. As it turns out, neither did the pain he caused us.

Worse yet was castration. It was done with rudimentary tools. You could not escape the pain bellowing from the bulls. I could not bear watching it; hearing it was bad enough. Something in my soul knotted when watching the defenseless cattle. In my mind, God must have been keeping score of these atrocities. I imagined the cows being able to turn the tables on the men. Horses were broken with whips, heavy boards, and discarded pipes. Usually, after many battles, they finally relented, surrendering to the blanket, saddle, and spurs dug deep in their flanks. Watching the will of animals leave their bodies felt like an upright death. Every creature was living in fear, including me. My soul cried out like a baby to the deaf around me; it seemed to bother no one. The ache of my silence took root; I was being broken, too. In my powerless state, I floated from scene to ugly scene, hushed by my insignificance. I could not turn my back on the cruelty; they deserved a witness, even if it was just a helpless girl.

My childhood was spent going to rodeos, tending horses, and bailing hay. Weekends meant heading to rodeos, carving out dusty desert back roads in my dad's white Ford pickup. Windows down, radio up, the twang of Johnny Cash, Glen Campbell, and Waylon Jennings pulsing through the speakers. The side view of my father was burned into my mind. He was as handsome as a movie star and dangerous as the devil.

I knew what he was capable of, and I needed to outsmart him to survive. The sun always seemed to be on his far side, making the perfect silhouette of a man, one I would never really know. A cigarette was often precariously balanced between his lips, and his mind was sunk deep in thought. He told his pain through violence instead of words.

In the glove box of that pickup, a loaded .32 caliber pistol was cocked and ready to go. Stray boxes of ammunition and his police badge lay within clear view. Two horses rode in a trailer behind us, staring with their dead, wet eyes.

The rodeo arena would come into focus, and we would find our place in the parking lot, with unimpressed horses tied up in every fashion imaginable and trucks of all sizes and colors. Cowboys and cowgirls dressed in skintight jeans, shimmering rhinestones, and etched silver buckles. I felt so small in this world, floating like an apparition trying to escape Hell.

The bullpens held a variety of enormous, pissed-off bulls—a beastly scene of twisted horns, gristly noses dripping strings of snot, and foam collecting at the corners of their mouths. Each with its reputation, each willing to kill anything that had breath—if only given a chance. My dad would walk by and size up his opponent in preparation for the ride. The chosen bull would be ushered to the holding shoot. I would follow my dad in a quiet hush, alone with my thoughts.

His hard grip would grab my upper arms and lift me onto the platform above the bull he was preparing to mount. I would feel the heat of the animal. I could feel its fear and anger, smell its sweat. A flank strap was tied and ready to pull around its boy parts. My dad would adjust his hat, gloves, and chaps. Then, in an instant of horror, he would drop down on 2,000 pounds of cantankerous power. The bull would slam back and forth, snorting as my dad yanked the strap, ensuring he knew who he was dealing with. With a quick nod (I hated the nod), the gate would open. With one hand flung high in the air, my dad would ride a living tornado into the arena, spinning and twisting. The eight seconds felt like a lifetime. An ambulance was always parked in the distance, the crowd whistling and cheering as he was thrust and bucked—a rodeo clown with a painted-on smile, rolling a barrel, weaving in and out of danger, all ending with my dad being cast off onto the floor of the arena.

The bull usually charged him. My father never backed down; instead, he would stand at full height, almost begging to be confronted, with hellfire in his eyes. The beast was his soul, angry and vengeful, the ride his reckoning, the crowd his validation.

My secret mission became animal helper at the rodeos. I would sneak underneath, in between, and above their enclosures. My tiny hands and tiny voice would tell them how sorry I was, running my palms and fingers over their smooth hides, telling them I would rescue them if I could. Bits of carrots and apples snuck into the big-lipped horses from my lunch sack. When I ran out of snacks, I would pick desert flowers and offer them to the livestock. I loved to see their small joys as their jaws chewed with pleasure. Their eyes amazed me, with their deep pools of unending dark brown, with paintbrush eyelashes sweeping their blinks. It was a communion; they never feared me, and I never feared them. We saw each other, and I imagined what it might be like if I unlocked the gates and all of us ran for it. Part of me wanted to see what revenge they might impart. I suspect that they would not have sought revenge; they would have basked in freedom.

RELENTLESS

My father's upbringing had been harsh and abusive, setting the stage for his rage. As a boy, moving from ranch to ranch where his stepfather cowboyed, they eked out a living. In the family, my dad was demoted to "the other man's son" after his half-sister, Carol, and half-brother, Butch, were born. Punishments were cruel and often. He didn't share much, but my mother told me some. After working for twelve hours, he would be tied to the kitchen chair for no justifiable reason and left there hungry, angry, and vengeful until morning light. Relentlessly beaten before he was big enough to compete, he was only fourteen when he left for good. Working ranches one after the other, he grew into a formidable man carrying a heart of stone. Finally, landing in Tucson, Arizona, at twenty, he enrolled in the Police Academy, offering the force two decades of undiluted grit, fury, and fearlessness.

He met my mother at the University of Arizona in the cafeteria. She remembers seeing this movie-star-handsome cowboy strutting in, and she fell hard. They married, and she knew she had made a mistake on their wedding night. That night gave her a first glance at his rage. By the time they had been married six months, he had choked her, pushed her, and had several affairs. In her young mind, she thought she could change him by starting a family.

Years passed without a pregnancy. At her insistence, they started the journey toward adoption. The marriage continued to deteriorate. After seven years, they divorced briefly and then remarried. The intended solution came when I was born in the middle of the 1965 race riots and passed to them. During the adoption finalization process, my dad told my mother, "I can sleep with a woman in our bed, and you can't do anything about it if you want to keep that baby."

He was cold, cruel, and wildly unpredictable. My mother's attention shifted from him to me, the fire that was his cheating, violence, and anger fueled.

My childhood was spent immersed in fear. My dad's volatile temper kept everyone on edge. He was not capable of being gentle; even his playing hurt. His hugs hurt. Everything he did hurt. Even his laughter was diabolical. You could feel the danger in his presence, the evil in his glare, the coldness in his clenched teeth. The danger was always there—fumes of violence ready to ignite with the smallest provocation.

We had a pool in the backyard of one of our homes, and I dreaded when he would ask me to swim with him. It would all start out okay, but soon, he would push me under the water and hold me down. I would come up for breath to hear his laughter, only to be held under again. I remember looking up at his blurry face above the water, the strength of his body bearing down on me. There were many times I thought I would die before he stopped. To my shock, he was unaware of how much he was frightening me. I cannot recall one time he ever touched me that it didn't hurt in some way.

I stayed close to danger by studying him; this was my tactic for survival. I became agile at sensing even small shifts in his mood. There were only a few ways that I enjoyed being in my father's company. Sunset rides were one of those exceptions. My dad would saddle up our black stallion and quarter horse several times a week. With him by my side, I was allowed to ride our quarter horse, Dollar. She was a beauty, with a satiny chestnut coat and a distinct white geographical island on her forehead. Her muscular build, glassy eyes, and thick blond mane enamored me. Her shiny black waterfall tail was always in motion, swaying from side to side. Dollar posed with one knee kicked in just to show off her beauty.

Dad would place me on her back, and I would hinge my feet in the stirrups and grab the reins. Trying to remember that horses are a conduit for our emotions, I would quiet my fear by petting her muscular neck and making tiny braids in her mane while I waited for my dad. He would stare down his ill-behaved black stallion in silent intimidation. No matter what my father did, the horse would rear up, buck, or refuse to move. My dad would finally get the best of the stallion, and we would be on our way.

My father was ruggedly handsome on horseback. There was an ease, a oneness with the horse. The trail dropped into a dry desert wash, a river of beige sand ribboned with streaks of colorful iron and mica. The sky blazed with rich pastel hues melting into the last light of day. Our horses were calm and rhythmic from head-to-head, their coats glossy and shining. We would liven up the pace to a trot, then a floating gallop against a warm mesquite breeze. For a moment, the world would slip into a place where fear had no existence. Then, the horses would run out. Their strides would shorten, their gate slowing under our bodies. The rich sound of the leather saddle rubbing against the sway of my stirrups would remain. With a half-dark sky against our backs, we would ride back to the corral in silence, each stride a step toward the reality I wanted to escape.

GIDDY UP

Just like Grandpa, he tried to make me a cowgirl, too—with minimal success. Since the bigger horses put the fear of God in me, he decided a pony would do. Teddy was a rich taupe-colored Shelton, with large freckles and an even larger attitude. He strutted like a purebred stallion, swishing his inadequate tail. He enjoyed biting the other horse's bellies and legs, sending them into the far corners of the corral.

When it was saddling time, I would tether Teddy to a hitching post by the water barrel, where he would slurp and snort. Fitting the bridle and bit was no easy task. He would fidget, neigh, and kick. He often lifted his upper lip like the hood of a car to show me his huge, flat teeth. Tightening the saddle properly was crucial. If the saddle wasn't fitted, it would slide sideways, and off you would go. Dad had demonstrated the belly kick, followed by the pull of the strap, while the horse exhaled in shock. I just didn't have the heart to power kick my horse, so whenever I saddled, you could predict that I would end up in the dirt while Teddy ran away, saddle under his belly.

My favorite way to ride was bareback on Dollar. She tolerated a lot and was easy with me, perhaps out of pity. I loved to sit on her curved, warm back and hold her amber mane. Her soft caramel hide, big deep breaths, and slow moves rocked me into ease. She would move at my whim, with the click of my cheek and the slightest pull on her reins. Our spirits flowed together as we enjoyed a break from the tyranny of my father's anger. I favored her, offering thick, crunchy carrots and stolen apples. Her sweet face would greet me through the fence, sharing breath and kisses. Dollar feared my dad. Her eyes would grow wide in his presence, and her chiseled muscles would tense. She knew his whip, his sawed-off boards, the bite of his mouth on her ear; the pain of his pointed cowboy boots took her soul.

JUSTICE?

We had big dogs, big guns, and locks on all the doors. My dad spent most evenings pacing the house, waiting for danger, for threats to become reality. Deep in the night, I would hear the friction of his cigarette lighter. My ears were keen, and I could hear him inhaling and exhaling the smoke. The fear he kept so well-placed during the day could not hide in the darkness.

My father had become a well-regarded police officer with vice, homicide, and undercover experience. He imprisoned many men who wanted to see him suffer.

Our family boldly moved to a small mountain town in Arizona after we learned there was a contract on his life—and possibly ours. In our neighborhood, a well-known mobster was in witness protection. He was an informant who disclosed to my dad regularly, making him aware there was a "hit" aimed right at us. It was a dangerous life filled with a cast of very frightening characters.

When he was home, there was a strong current of fear among us all—a riptide of irrationality that could sweep us away at any moment. His rage was not far below the surface, anchored by nothing. At his hand, I learned hate. I literally hated him and felt powerless against what I witnessed. It was clear that our survival wasn't guaranteed. His rage was one-hundred-percent pure—never induced by drugs or alcohol. There was nothing to quit, no bottle to hide.

More than a few memories marked my soul permanently. Wonderland Acres was where one of my childhood homes was located, a home that butted up against reservation land. No matter what time of year, I lived on the carpet of meadow grass, the sky my ceiling, a fallen tree my bed, pinecones my earrings. Outside was my safe place, a place of unending beauty and freedom.

After school, I would feed my rabbits, Chocolate and Vanilla, amongst other chores. One spring afternoon, when I was twelve, I didn't shut the rabbit cage properly, and Vanilla hopped into our yard and helped herself to Dad's garden. I heard my father yelling my name, and I returned to find him chasing the escaped rabbit, who had been nibbling his vegetables. He was enraged. I ran after him, begging him to let me catch her. With a carrot in my hand and my begging voice,

I began chasing her—to no avail.

Her keen skills far exceeded mine; I could smell the storm coming. Dad reappeared on the porch and snuffed out his cigarette under the toe of his boot. He told me to get inside in no uncertain terms. I ran frantically past him, crying my way into the house, the heavy sliding glass door shutting behind me. I watched as he took each step down the stairs; I had seen this look before. He was going to kill, or hurt, and there was nothing I could do. There was no one to call, no one to hear my screams, my begging. My hands pressing against our picture window, my rapid breath fogging the glass, and tears streaked across my face, burning my skin. I watched in horror as he pelleted my rabbit with rocks until she was stunned. Cornered by the chain-link fence and him, she cried and screamed as he violently stoned her to death. Blood covered her creamy coat, trickling from her still nose. He held her by her back legs as she hung lifeless; I ran to my room, crying into my pillow, hatred gripping every ounce of me. When he entered the house, his stride stopped at my door and drifted past. His violence was purged.

The next night, I was called to the table for dinner. I was told to serve up. I noticed the strange small bones in the meat. They looked flat and fragile, and the meat was unfamiliar to me. When I asked my mother what it was, she said it was rabbit. My fork dropped; it was my rabbit. My dad looked up from his bite to assess my reaction. He told me to pick up my fork and eat the dinner my mother had prepared. I took one bite, spat it in my napkin, and ran to my room. My dad had spun a story about what had happened to the rabbit and convinced my mother to put it in a Crock-Pot, knowing full well that we didn't waste good meat. At that point, I built a wall so high that he could never get over it.

The cruelty was relentless, so I did what I could to protect all of us. My efforts fell short because most of the violence was unprovoked. The worst fell on my beautiful Charlie Brown, a Great Dane-Shepherd mix my dad had "rescued" from the pound. Charlie quickly became my companion and my father's punching bag. He would hold Charlie in the threshold of the doors and slam him. He would kick him in the gut when he would walk by. He made him stay outside no matter the season, chaining him in the beating sun or numbing winter.

Charlie would walk for miles to reach my uncle's house for refuge. There, he would curl up in front of the wood stove, defeated. Soon, my dad would show up and beat him all the way home. Charlie's yelps and cries became part of an existence I didn't want to endure. Ten-year-old Charlie's last command was "sit" as my dad shot him point-blank in the head. Charlie was beautiful, and I still ache that I wasn't able to stop his abuse.

ONE OF THE RECKONINGS

Years passed. A medical retirement caused by sprue disease whittled my dad's 180-pound frame down to 126 lbs. Emphysema from smoking shortened his breaths and his patience. His days were spent in bed or on the couch in the flicker of a Zenith TV. During one of his naps, it all came to a head. My brother and I were fighting over the phone. Dad woke, yanked the phone from my brother's hand, and started to come for my brother. In one fell swoop, I tucked my brother behind me to shield him.

My father charged toward me as my anger usurped my fear. As his hands pushed into my chest, I felt my feet lift from the ground. I landed up against our huge console stereo. My breath knocked out of me. I was so angry that I bolted right back up, with every ounce of my thirteen-year-old skinny self, and met him halfway as he charged me again. I told my brother to go upstairs and shut his bedroom door. My brother scurried around me and disappeared. I could feel the heat of my dad's breathy rage sweating out of him. His fist cocked back as he gritted his teeth. He stared me down. His eyes were wide and bloodshot. But it was over; I was done, and even if it meant my end, I did not care. I begged him to hit me—I taunted him—telling him he was a coward, asking him what kind of man enjoys hurting things smaller than him. His fist was shaking and ready to strike.

I told him I wanted to show his police friends who he really was—a weak, evil man. I begged him repeatedly to hurt me, bruise me, bloody me. He grabbed my shirt and pulled me closer, but I was ready—*fearless*. I thought I would get my wish to exact my revenge. I was done, and he knew it. I was ready to fight back. Our eyes met in an epic glare until I felt his grip release. I melted to the floor in an exhausted heap and watched him storm off in his open robe. He never looked so small. I knew I had changed, and so had he. I had gotten my horns and my ability to charge. I was locked and loaded. I was dangerous in my own right—and it was because I could ruin his highly regarded reputation.

As soon as I could, I left home. I graduated high school at seventeen, and his gift was a pistol. I filled it with bullets, put it in the glove box of my Chevy Chevette, and drove off, leaving that life in a cloud of dust, once again fearless, as I felt his grip on my life loosen. I didn't consider what was next—only that I had managed to survive and escape.

EMOTIONAL CASTRATION

My father's illness forced him and my mom to move back to Tucson, where he would spend his final years. The cheating and marital strife continued, and my adopted brother remained in the crosshairs. I managed to thrive in college, and then I married the love of my life and moved to Hawaii. I saw my dad a few times during his final decline. It seemed that his illness didn't soothe his cruelty. Even with a terminal illness, he managed to have an affair with a younger woman. This time, my mother was done, and she moved in with my grandmother. My father spent his final months living with his girlfriend, who enjoyed my mother's towels, decorating, and the beauty of the home she had made.

He had taken my mother's soul so many times, but this time, my mother stood tall despite her enormous humiliation. She would not give him the divorce he wanted, determined to reap the financial benefits of being married to him. It was my turn to stand tall, this time as a twenty-six-year-old woman. I asked my dad if I could come to "their" house to speak with him without his girlfriend present. He agreed.

When I entered, I could smell and see evidence of the other woman. A Crock-Pot was full of stew, and there was the smell of cheap fruity candles. Her coat hung on the rack, and a few pictures of them together were displayed amongst his badges on the shelf. We settled across from each other on two matching blue tropical-patterned sofas, a glass coffee table between us. He had his shirt off, which wasn't uncommon. An oxygen tank next to him, he had a cannula coming out of his nose. His chest was enlarged from emphysema, and his arms were covered in lakes of deep purple bruises. His hair was perfect, still an impressive mop of salt and pepper gray, and his mustache curved around his gasping mouth. His muscles were small; the rivers of veins that used to run like roots under his skin lay flat.

I asked him if he would listen to a letter that I had written to him and not say a word until I was done. He agreed, and I read pages and pages of pain. I said it all just the way I wanted to, and I didn't look up until I was done. As I folded the letter into thirds, I looked over at him. His head was hanging, his silver cross hanging too. His face was wet as he lifted his chin to look at me, and he said, "I don't remember doing most of those things, but I believe you, and I am sorry." He did not defend himself. He did not push back as we sat there in the overwhelming pain. He wiped his face and fumbled with his oxygen hose, asking me if I wanted something to eat or drink. His weakness provided a safe barrier for me to exert my will. High stake's role reversal, I had become his mirror, and he had become mine. I had turned the tables and hurt something weaker than I was.

THE FINAL RECKONING

The call came that my father was in his final days. The man I thought could never succumb to death, who seemed invincible, had withered away into a wisp. I decided to come home for our final ride into the sunset. This time, it would be on my terms. I came home to see the death I had begged for so many times, knowing that if he were just gone, everything would be okay. I didn't know that he would never leave me; we would be forever bound by the trauma branded on my soul.

When I arrived, he was lying in a dimly lit hospital room that smelled of his sweat—his bruised hands tied to the bed, tubes down his throat, his skin thinly laid over his bones. His demonic girlfriend stood by his side, acting out her lies. The nurse came in and said, "Mrs. Hamilton," to her, and I lost it. She had lied and said that she was his wife. My nostrils flared, and my hooves started kicking the dirt. Apparently, she didn't see the horns hidden in my hair. All 5'7 ¾" of me escorted her to the hall and showed her to the door. As she reached for the handle, I noticed my dad's cross necklace twisted around her hands. With snort and spit, I said, "Hand it over." She looked shocked. I repeated with gritted teeth, "Hand it over!" She dropped the silver cross into my hands and huffed away.

The stampede of my anger relented, and my forehead hit the wall outside my dad's room. I could see him through the tiny window in the door. He was a cowardly yellow, covered in stiff white sheets. This death that I had waited so long for wasn't bringing me any relief. There was no satisfaction in this tragedy. I went in and sat on the bed, which was still warm from his girlfriend's sorry ass.

"Dad, can you hear me?"

His eyes strained open, and his mouth gave me what was left of his one-sided smile. The whites of his eyes, stained with red, filled with tears, beginning a journey through the deep hollows of his face until they rolled under his chin. I asked the nurse to untie one of his hands so I could hold it. She warned me he might try to pull his vent out. When his hand was free, he made a writing motion. I grabbed a pen and pad of paper from the nurse's station. He could barely clasp the pen as I held the pad of paper to steady his attempt to write. In craggy letters, he spelled out two phrases: "I love you," and "I am sorry."

I put my head on his heart and listened to its sporadic beats. His untied hand rested on the middle of my back. I wept for everything that was and everything that would never be. I wept for the pain—so much pain that never needed to happen. I wept for what he had done to me—and for me. As I said my final goodbye, the nurse tied his hand back down again, and I watched him resist death.

He continued to buck his vent until his last breath; I guess a cowboy is always a cowboy. In the night, the call came that he died. For whatever reason, I wanted to see him dead. I rushed back to the hospital, his cross in my purse. It's funny what we remember and what we forget. I entered the room, dim except for one light above his head, and noticed the vent tube in the trash. There he was, cold and alone, his mouth open, eyes bleached, arms clutched to his sides like useless wings. I grabbed his face and yelled, "You are not allowed to go. You weren't the father I needed. You need to come back. I need you to come back. We are not finished."

My tears ran through the deep crevices in his cheeks until they rolled off his chin. I put my ear to his chest, my fingers against his hollow mouth . . . nothing . . . just death . . . cold, hard death. I thought I would feel relief and justice in his suffering. Instead, I just felt empty. I kissed his right cheek, the one with the hole in the bone from a bull's horn. I took the silver cross out of my purse, the cross he had worn all his adult life, and walked out, holding all I had left of him.

CHAPTER 4
TRUE GRIT—THE COWBOY WAY
THEME 4: AGGRESSION, HOPE, AND MINDFULNESS
Alysa Zalma, MD

The chapter on Heidi's adoptive father is a difficult one due in part to the explicit content of physical and psychological abuse directed at Heidi, her brother, and her adoptive mother. This may resonate with many readers. Our hope is that within this experience of resonance, the reader may have the opportunity to heal some of their unique history that may be similar. We also offer other tools and information beyond identifying the chapter's traumatic content in the form of mindfulness work and other healing modalities that are particularly relevant to the healing of such traumas. The reader may use these offerings for their healings relating to aggressions and anger that they may have experienced as part of their adoption story.

Among other traumas, Heidi discusses the violence involved in cruelty to animals. She discusses her horror at how her adoptive father treated animals.

> Every creature was living in fear, including me. My soul cried out like a baby to the deaf around me; it seemed to bother no one. The ache of my own silence took root; I was being broken, too. In my powerless state, I floated from scene to ugly scene, hushed by my insignificance. I could not turn my back on the cruelty; they deserved a witness, even if it was just a helpless girl.

There are many ways to release oneself from the atrocities of these types of traumas. Mindfulness meditation, originating from Buddhist teachings, has been shown to have healing effects on traumas such as these (Hanh 1975, 61-62). Loving-kindness meditation attempts to utilize a three-tiered model of offering compassion at first to a loved one, then to a neutral person, and finally, to one whom feels is a hostile person, as noted in the Buddhist text, *Path of Purification* (Buddhagosa 1975, 293).

Loving-kindness meditation, which I use often in my psychiatric practice, instructs the patient to practice compassion and unconditional love in three stages, ranging from easier to difficult. The first stage is to practice and energetically send (in a nonverbal way or by speaking aloud to oneself) the compassion and unconditional love one has for a loved one, someone in the patient's immediate sphere of communication. The practice is easiest when the patient is feeling a sense of harmony with this loved one, but it is harder (and has more positive clinical implications) when the patient is upset with this loved one. The second stage of difficulty is with a neutral person in the patient's life, such as someone at the grocery store or bank. Again, the same rules apply. The third and most difficult—but the one that yields the highest results—is the practice of loving-kindness meditation toward someone who has hurt them—someone with whom they're angry or resentful. This third scenario is most relevant to the relationship between Heidi and her adoptive father.

Toward the end of his life, Heidi's adoptive father, Ellis, tries to make amends with her. He asks her to help him write something while she is with him in the hospital before his death.

In craggy letters, he spelled out two phrases: "I love you," and "I am sorry."

This calls to mind the Hawaiin *Ho'oponopono* healing prayer, comprised of four phrases: "I'm sorry. Please forgive me. Thank you. I love you." This prayer is meant, among many uses, to offer means of forgiveness to the one who has been wronged, especially if the abuser cannot say it.

Forgiveness does not mean absolution of wrongdoing but acknowledges that it has occurred and allows space for the wrongdoing. This allows for more of the conscious choice to move past the abuse (Grace and Lightness 2023). It also may be powerful for the one who has been wronged to say it to themselves, to forgive any guilt or blame they may be harboring for why the abuse happened.

For Heidi, her father's words did not offer relief.

I thought I would feel relief and justice in his suffering. Instead, I just felt empty. I kissed his right cheek, the one with the hole in the bone from a bull's horn. I took the silver cross out of my purse, the cross he had worn all his adult life, and walked out, holding all I had left of him.

What might the psychiatrist say about this scenario that might offer any healing? Perhaps an interpretation, perhaps a validation, but what may be most important is that the psychiatrist and patient, in the presence of each other, bear witness to the abuse as it is told by the patient to the doctor. This is a highly co-created process of vulnerability, and much healing may occur not only in this process but also after the story is told.

After listening to a traumatic one, providing a healing story may encourage neuroplasticity and help repair various limbic system processes. Reparation of the limbic system may occur through various psychotherapies, such as expressive therapies that use language, art, music, and dance in patients with PTSD (Ho, JMC, et al. 2021, 2). By melding core shamanic practices and expressive therapies, it may be extrapolated that the ritual and ceremony undertaken from soul retrieval work attempts to repair the limbic system from trauma.

The most successful Soul Retrievals occur when I find the most healing story for the client as their soul pieces return to them as part of the ceremony.

Like Heidi, I had a client for whom I did a Soul Retrieval, who suffered from severe abuse from her father. Her father had died of alcohol complications when the client came to me. She confessed that she had a bond with her father that her brother and mother did not have with him. They, unlike her, outwardly disliked him and would "taunt and disown him." Despite the abuse, she felt the relationship with her father was meaningful and did not want to disown him the way her mother and brother did.

During our second meeting, when the actual Soul Retrieval ceremony occurred, one of the soul pieces returned to her was a cloak with beautiful purples and golds. It had significant meaning to her; it reminded her of a tapestry her father purchased while working as an anthropologist. She felt a sense of profound healing.

Later that year, she invited me to her father's celebration of life ceremony and wore a purple and gold scarf. After the ceremony, I commented on it, to which the patient noted that she had not made the connection between the scarf and the piece of soul that had been returned during her Soul Retrieval. About a year later, in follow-up, she noted that she was able to stop taking her psychotropic medications, Lexapro and Zyprexa, medications that assist in the treatment of PTSD.

CHAPTER 5
BUGS AND WINDSHIELDS

IN MEMORY OF MY ADOPTED BROTHER, JUSTIN JON HAMILTON

"You were born a child of light's wonderful secret—you return to the beauty you have always been."
—*Visions of a Skylark Dressed in Black*, Aberjhani

NOT HERBERT

There were no telltale signs of pregnancy—my brother's conception—an adoption process I didn't understand. All I knew, as a seven-year-old girl, was that a baby was coming, and we didn't know when. The ring of our phone would launch my mother into a furniture-bumping, toe-stubbing race, hoping for good news. This baby she didn't carry in her belly was certainly being carried in her heart. The disappointment that would wash over her face when the phone call wasn't about the adoption would send her directly into sadness. I, however, wasn't in any hurry to dilute the attention I was getting by adding a sibling.

Furthermore, if we had to have another child, I had decided it would be a sister. I had envisioned countless hours of playing Barbies, braiding our hair, and trying on my mother's forbidden red lipstick in the slick black tube. It never occurred to me that a baby brother would be my fate. I could not stop his arrival or warn him about the danger he was facing. This baby boy would be another attempt to mend a broken marriage—his innocence placed to fill a void so deep and wide that he would never get out.

Justin was tucked inside a body that weighed him down. He was thick from the beginning—better than ten pounds at birth, with deliciously roly-poly legs and a chin so chubby, you couldn't see his neck until he was thirty. His eyes were pools of brown with gold flecks, his eyelashes lush, his hair thick as plush carpet. A perfectly cleaved dimple sunk deep in the middle of his square chin. His size would end up being his grace—and his demise. His spirit had no barrier; it was susceptible to pain and irrevocable damage. Justin did not deserve his fate, and I could not save him.

On March 23, 1972, Justin was born in Phoenix, Arizona. The call my mother had anticipated for so long finally came. Her face filled with light; her smile was as wide as her dreams. It would be another five days until we could bring Justin home.

Months before, a wash of blue came over the nursery, and I was thoroughly disgusted with my parents' lack of concern for my preference to have a sister. When I finally came to terms with what was happening, I asked if I could at least name him. My suggestion was Herbert. Both my parents' eyeballs bulged in cartoon style. I insisted that our names should both start with an "H" so we could match. As it turns out, nothing about us matched.

KEEP YOUR ROBE OPEN

My brother lived what I call an "open robe life." From the time he was an infant, he was always peeling off his diaper, clothing, or anything else that came between him and his skin. As he grew into his manliness, his orange terrycloth robe became his uniform. Without an ounce of modesty, he regularly walked around with his robe untied, revealing his Buddha belly, hairy chest, and tighty-whities. He had an ease and ownership of his body—all 300-plus pounds of it.

Although he could not move fast on his own, he put his body inside or on top of anything with wheels as often as he could. I could see this was his way of being free from the weight of all things.

His happiest days as a child were spent on his three-wheeler, flinging mud and popping wheelies. His desire for nudity even then was always a part of him—he was content just to wear shoes and a cowboy hat until he was three. It was quite the sight to see him riding his tricycle buck naked. He even had the audacity to show up at my bus stop when he was two, wearing only my father's cowboy boots. And the unmeasurable audacity to show up to my ninth birthday party naked—completely naked! That time, his life would have been even shorter if my mother hadn't come out to save him.

As he grew older, he slowly began to comply with society's rules regarding clothing. Nevertheless, the moment he was home, off would go the clothes, and on would go the robe. His presence had fluidity about it, a kind of knowing. Enfolded in so much physical and psychological weight, he found a way to be himself, with robe open and belly out.

NEVER ENOUGH

My father valued appearances, particularly physical attributes. My brother did not fit his idea of a son. He was not thin, athletic, or movie-star handsome. Nor did my brother show any interest in sports, horses, or rodeos. From the time I can remember, my father called him "Princess Poopy Pants," laughing diabolically. Something inside me would cringe as I saw my brother try to fit my dad's idea of what he should be.

I recall one time when my brother was about ten years old. He decided to ask my dad to play catch. I observed in the kitchen as my brother worked up the courage to approach. Justin's favorite tattered T-shirt showed his milky-white tummy rolls. His arms were filled with two baseball gloves, a bat, and a few baseballs. My father was sitting tensely in his dark green recliner, yelling at the TV, a teetering cigarette riding his words. A commercial came on, and Justin made his move.

"Dad, you wanna play ball with me?"

My father pulled the cigarette out of his mouth with his forefinger and thumb and flicked the ashes into the ashtray. His brow crumpled, and he pulled the wood side handle on the recliner to perch his feet up, simultaneously saying, "Not now, Princess, the game is on."

It felt like the air left the room. Everything dimmed and was framed in slow motion. My brother's back was facing me; the outline of his hanging head and curled shoulders astonished me. His pain radiated; it penetrated every part of me. I watched as Justin fumbled to open the door to the front yard, only a hand's reach from the back of my dad's chair. Inside that chamber of my brain, where I tortured my father regularly, I secretly stabbed him in the eyeballs with a dull, serrated knife. Glaring at him, I made my way to my bedroom, down a hallway that was not nearly long enough.

The sun was highlighting the dirty window. I folded my arms on the sill, watching my brother struggle—aimlessly throwing the ball in the air and trying to catch it while the other glove, bat, and ball sat at his feet. I had a front-row seat to his fresh injury of the soul. Tears ran down my face as I saw his little spirit trying to play alone. I was about to go out and join him when it happened. The ball. The bat. The unexpected home run hit right into the window next to my father. Glass shattering. Justin's horrified face. And then my father's words. "GODDAMMIT, JUSTIN." The rant started.

I had little time. I peeled out of my room, yelling, "RUN, JUSTIN, RUN!"

His fat little body moved faster than I had ever seen it go. He disappeared into the far reaches of the meadow, leaving behind all things baseball. My dad cursed him inside the door's threshold, calling him names too painful to repeat. I remember little more of that day, and that is probably best.

ARE WE EATING OR DRINKING OUR FEELINGS?

My brother frustrated me with his food choices. His weight was an issue for everyone but him. Among his culinary masterpieces was the infamous bean sandwich. After school, he would come home and grab a whole loaf of white Wonder Bread, a bag of brown sugar, a can of baked beans, and a squeeze bottle of yellow mustard. He would make the sandwich straight on the counter before I yelled, "Use a plate!" He would happily lay down twin slices of bread in neat rows. Start with brown sugar on the bottom slice, squeeze mustard strands on the top slice, and then slather on spoonfuls of cold baked beans. He would stand at the counter, devouring one sandwich after another, chasing each one with full-sugar Pepsi. Then he would down whatever was left of the stale Oreos, open the refrigerator door, and drink right out of the milk jug as I glared in disgust. His cheeky smile was framed by a thick, frothy milk mustache.

Grossing me out was one of his greatest pleasures. His way of dealing with food just seemed reckless to me. I didn't understand self-comforting and self-medicating; I just thought he was being a brat. Now I know food was his best friend, a simple pleasure in his hellish existence. My mother understood; in her pity of his plight, she would indulge him with treats.

Food became medicine to numb the pain of heartbreak and rejection. His weight became a garment of protection, a padding around a spirit too tender for the place it found itself in. His weight collapsed the very physical life out of him, too much to carry. He ate and drank his pain, happiness, unrequited love, wishes, and dreams. He spoke so little because no one was really listening. He cried for help in the darkness of our ignorance until his voice was silenced for good.

I MISSED MY CHANCE

As my brother's older, wiser, and big know-it-all sister, I felt quite proud of myself for earning a college degree, living in Hawaii, and marrying an amazing man all by twenty-five. As Justin landed on Oahu, I greeted him at the airport in my chest-puffed stance of wisdom. Hell-bent to set him on a path of health and happiness, I would cut him *zero* slack. He would need to take notes and carefully observe the ways of his superior sister.

Justin came to Hawaii broken, hurting, lost, and needing everything that I was *not* about to give him. We even went so far as to buy different colored eggs so he wouldn't eat ours—*WTF?* What he needed wasn't portion control but to be seen, heard, and valued just as he was. Instead, we took it upon ourselves to parent him during his four months with us.

No surprise—he left as soon as he could. His last morning, when I went to wake him up, he was lying on top of a horrible, flowered mauve and lavender comforter that I thought was beautiful. He was sleeping soundly in his tighty-whities, hair a mess, quietly snoring. He seemed so small, even though he was so big, childlike in his slumber.

Instead of saying I was sorry for being an uptight asshole, I woke him and instructed him on how I wanted him to leave his room. I have many regrets; how I didn't love my brother the right way is high on the list. The woman who types these words now would burn the comforter and hug him until her arms couldn't squeeze anymore. I would say I understand why you eat and drink your pain. I understand because I was your witness. I would say I love you just the way you are. I would tell you that the weight I carry will always be greater than yours.

DEALING WITH ME

My brother had a way of looking at me with his head cocked to one side as if I was speaking in shrieks. His curious "what the hell" face is easy to remember. He thought all my worry, curiosity, and fussing was a waste of time. When I talked to him about being adopted, he wasn't interested in knowing anything about his own history. My endeavor to know about my story seemed to annoy him.

It gives me pause to accept that each adopted person has their journey and that each journey is personal. I wish now that I hadn't applied so much pressure to his wounds. It wasn't my place, and I can see his cocked head confirming that.

GOODBYE STRANGER

Supertramp was one of our favorite eighties bands to sing to. My brother had an incredible singing voice. I can still see him driving through the Salt River Canyon with one hand on the steering wheel—

the hand with the distinct birthmark below his pinky. The other hand hung out of the window, the sun flooding the car, the wind tossing his hair while we sang "Goodbye Stranger" at the top of our lungs. The six-disc changer moved from disc to disc, my shoeless feet on the dash, the scenic snakeskin roads smooth and empty. It felt like the world was ours on that glorious summer day. In a cruel twist of fate, my brother would die a stranger to me.

Justin never left home. He lived with my mother and grandmother, tied by the chains of obligation. His life was never his—always someone else's—and he resigned himself to that fact. I sadly thought it was a lack of ambition and laziness. As his pain grew, so did his weight. His private life was just that: *private*. It took his death to reveal his life.

Troy and I were living in Northern California then, and my brother was back under Wongee's roof in Tucson. It was April 29, 2004. I had just poured a beer for a friend, and we were getting ready to play a board game when the phone rang. I decided not to get up—let the answering machine do its job. The annoying beep sounded, and I heard my mother's scream, a scream of such anguish that it leveled me.

I ran to the phone and picked up the receiver to hear my mother repeating over and over, "It's Justin, it's Justin, it's Justin."

I asked rapid-fire questions. "Mother, what happened? Was he in an accident? Is he okay?"

Her breathless words moaned as she said, "He's gone."

"Gone? Gone where? Where did he go, Mom?"

"He died, Heidi. Justin died."

My back hit the pantry door, my body melting onto the cold floor. I collapsed, the phone in my lap. The sounds of my mother's grief poured from the tiny holes in the speaker.

HALF OF ME

I don't remember packing; I don't remember anything until I touched down at the Tucson airport. I don't remember who picked me up or how I got to my wongee's house. I do remember the sound of the gravel under the tires as the car pulled up, the painfully loud, gritty sound. I did not know what I would find behind the door I was about to open.

It took a while, but my wongee came to the door, pushing her walker with the two silly tennis balls on the two front legs (can't someone invent another option?), her eyes glazed with the redness of spent tears, her body trembling as she said, "Heidi, your mama, go to your mama."

I made my way through the quiet kitchen into the family room. The house smelled stale, with the lingering scent of cheap, brewed coffee. The sliding glass door was smeared with handprints and dog nose art. A few feet beyond, in the yellow grass, was my mother, her head surrounded by a cloud of cigarette smoke. Everything was sepia. She was pacing, as she did when something was wrong. I ran to her, and she dropped her cigarette to the ground. I smashed it with my shoe and pulled her close. She uttered quietly in my ear in the hot breath of pain, "Half of me just died."

She held my face with her perfectly smooth hands and looked at me with her tiger gold eyes, eyes that would never have light in them again. I now had a mother who was only half alive and barely functioning. Nothing could prepare me for the horror of the days to come. To see a mother—my mother—experiencing one of the most painful heartbreaks a human can feel took a part of me, too.

EXTRA, EXTRA LARGE

Four days before, at home in my kitchen, I had talked to my brother on the phone, hearing his words through the same tiny speaker that would carry the news of his death. He was coming to visit me, and we had plans to see San Francisco and drink wine in Napa. Now I was faced with planning his funeral.

Wongee's house was pulsing with pain, confusion, and shock. Even though it was seventy degrees, the air seemed subzero—everything frozen. I made my way to Justin's bedroom, which faced busy Tucson Blvd. The traffic whizzed by with no concern for the heartbreak a few feet away. I just wanted this to be a bad dream. I wanted to fling open his door and find him hanging out in his robe, listening to his beloved CD player.

Even without him, Justin's bedroom brought comfort. I found him there inside my collapsing grief. I pushed the door shut to find his orange robe hanging on the back of the door. I ran my hands down the well-worn terrycloth fabric. I made my way to his dresser and picked up one of his colognes. I sprayed the smell of him into thin air.

With hesitation, I opened his creaky closet doors. His double extra-large clothes, mostly neon-colored T-shirts, were tightly packed, hangers going this way and that. His extra wide shoes, cowboy hats, and sweaty-brimmed baseball caps told stories. He was extra-large in all the ways a life should be. His heart was the biggest part of him; it held the greatest weight. As I contemplated, I stared into the open closet at his spacious clothes.

For a moment, I felt unsteady. I sat on his brass bed, holding the weight of my own heart, noticing how tarnished the brass on his bed was. I laughed, remembering how I had caught him peeing on one of the bedposts when he was two. He had left the bed unmade—because, in Justin's opinion, why make it if you're going to be sleeping in it again soon?

I leaned over on the breeze of memories of him and grabbed his bunched-up pillow, noticing a few strands of his dark brown hair. One by one, I pulled them off and let them drift to the floor. The pillow became a soft place until the distinct sound of gravel broke my trance. A tow truck hauling his denim-blue truck pulled up.

Reality's fist punched hard, an uppercut that rattled my very being. The driver came to the door and handed me Justin's truck keys. I walked outside, hearing each step on that damn crunchy gravel. I unlocked the door and climbed into the driver's seat. I grabbed the steering wheel and cried until my chest was wet. I turned the truck on to see what he was listening to, and it was Supertramp. In the cupholder sat an oversized Pepsi cup, its condensation in the heat visible, a can of

Scholl's tobacco, and a bag of shells from his beloved sunflower seeds.

On the passenger's side, papers were tossed and scrambled. I fumbled, looking for any clues, using his leftover napkins to wipe my nose and eyes. Then I found them—the pink discharge papers from the hospital.

IF HE HAD JUST STAYED

Justin had gone to the emergency room by himself; he had been diagnosed with double bacterial pneumonia and given IV antibiotics. No one knew. He didn't call anyone. No one knew he was sick. He was advised to stay in the hospital to receive treatment, but he opted to check himself out. The pink papers I held clearly stated that he should not go. From the emergency room, he went to a pharmacy to fill his prescriptions. He had driven two hours from Tucson to Phoenix, checked into his hotel, and taken his medication. He had kept his plan to have dinner with his best friend, Casey, without mentioning his visit to the emergency room. Eight hours later, he was dead.

He did not attend training the following morning, and his best friend couldn't get him to answer his door. My mother was promptly notified, and she called the hotel to do a "wellness" check. When their knocks went unanswered, they opted to open the door, but the chain stopped them. Through the tiny opening in the door, they could see my brother's feet. When the police came, they broke down the door and found my brother dead between two beds, inches from a phone. He died in his signature white BVD underwear, alone, in a Best Western Hotel.

Those days were a suspension in hell. Justin's death was unattended, so an investigation commenced. His body would be held for a few days while an autopsy would be performed to determine the cause of death. In the meantime, we needed to plan a funeral. I had never done that before. This was before Google, so phone books were my only option for information. I picked three funeral homes close to my grandmother's house. My mother insisted on going with me, so we headed out to inspect them.

Our first stop was horrifying, to say the least. The building was long and skinny, painted a terrible color of dark brown. I pushed open the double glass doors and was met with eerie smells. I immediately noticed the absence of anyone at the front desk—just a hallway of closed doors. Off in the distance, I could hear a voice, and I followed the sound. My search ended three doors down on the right, where I could hear a man talking to someone behind the door. I gently knocked, and a shocked man opened the door, wearing bright blue gloves, standing next to the body of a deceased man. It was clear no one else was in the room but the two of them. Befuddled, he asked if someone had passed away and said, "If so, I can help."

Oh no, you won't, I thought. *We don't need that kind of help.*

Our last stop felt like the right place to have our celebration of life. The building was Spanish-style architecture, the stucco on the outside painted crisp white. Mission tiles lay like thick fish scales on the arching roofs. The sanctuary was beautiful, with a huge entry and a small bell tower. Gorgeous heavy wood benches faced a large stained-glass window. Wrought iron chandeliers reached across the ceiling. A kind man, without blue gloves, whispered his sympathies.

I suppose it's part of funeral employees' training to speak in whispers so as not to provoke the grieving. With a hushed voice, we were escorted into the casket room. He hemmed and hawed and said, "The coroner has let me know your brother is on the larger side."

Startled, I said, "Yes, he sure is."

In an even quieter whisper, he said, "A standard coffin will be too small. For another $1,000, we can fit him in this casket."

There it was: cobalt blue. The lid was wide open, with a carefully directed spotlight shining from the ceiling. White doves of peace soared above perfectly sewn pleats of white satin lining. Or the other option: a pitch-black coffin resembling a limousine without wheels. We chose the blue one.

HE IS COMING HOME

The coroner released my brother's body, and we learned that he would arrive about seven o'clock in the evening. My mother insisted that the funeral director allow us to be present for his arrival. In his all too familiar whisper, he said that was not a good idea. His body had just been autopsied, and there would be no time to prepare him for a viewing. My mother wasn't having it. She had waited for days to see her son. I could see that this was going to happen, and I had to be by her side.

All I remember next was driving in the darkness back to the funeral home. Our car lights cast shadows behind the saguaros that flanked the chapel. A tiny strip of fiery-red sky faded to black. It's funny how the desert smells different at night. We pulled into the parking space closest to the door. My mother paced outside the car until she finished a cigarette stub and slung her overly large handbag over her shoulder. I could see our friendly funeral whisperer behind a desk, waiting for us. In his predictable whisper, he said, "He should be here any time."

We whispered back, "Thank you," and sat on two horrible burgundy chairs, a dusty fake plant and a box of Kleenex separating us. My mother nervously grabbed a few tissues and began wadding them and patting her eyes. I prayed with my eyes half shut because the full view was too much. I prayed for God to give me strength to see this through.

Then I saw shadows cast by the headlights of a long, white, unmarked van. I swallowed my prayers; they felt like broken glass moving down my throat. Our whisperer excused himself and said he would come back to get us. The muffled sounds of unloading and more whispering people agitated me. I told my mother she didn't have to do this. She was steadfast in her decision.

The door opened; the whispering director said, "Are you sure you want to see him this way?"

My mother said yes. Everything in me said no. But she led the way into a long sterile room with a lot of stainless steel and painfully bright lights. The speckled white tile floor accentuated the horror of what was to come. My dead brother lay in the far-left corner on a gurney. I saw the top of his head first, a messy mop of brown tussled hair. His right knee was bent and sticking out of the white sheet.

My mother ran to my brother, touching his hair and kissing his face. I followed, with a few reluctant steps, until Justin's face came into view. Then I felt it—the weight, the gravity of his death, stiffening, slicing, and yanking its way through my body. My lips trembled as I turned to face him, my mother now at his feet. His eyelashes were so beautiful and long, and I noticed small stitches, forcing them closed forever. The dimple on his square chin was so perfect amongst fresh whisker stubble. I bent to kiss him and was slammed by the smell of formaldehyde; I coiled back. His skin was ice-cold and hard; I placed my hand on his heart. Frankenstein stitching revealed a massive Y-cut from the autopsy, his ample chest hair parted by the formidable stitches.

The constricting grief wrapped around every part of my being. The tightness, the suffocation, and the snapshots of my mother were permanently written into memory. Her tears, her screams, her talking to him as if he could hear. His body lifeless. His body would never again laugh, cry, or hold us. It was crushing.

TO WHERE YOU ARE

I drove myself mad planning his funeral. His sendoff was going to be one to remember. I bought hundreds of candles and asked the guests to light them around his body. In the flicker of candlelight and the colors of stained glass, his profile was posed perfectly. His favorite button-down shirt with tiny blue stripes tucked around his sizeable belly. His friend, Casey, discreetly tucked a can of chew into his pocket. A young man dressed in a suit and sneakers from the University of Arizona sang "To Where You Are" by Josh Groban.

An open microphone brought up a dozen people sharing their fondest memories. His best friend, Chad, told of an afternoon when Justin brought over a plastic pool for his kids. My brother filled the pool with water and tried to talk the little ones into a dip. They declined. He took it upon himself to strip down to his tighty-whities, pop a beer, and sit in the pool alone.

I learned so much about how he loved to dance and how the girls all loved him. Story after story—my brother was described as kind, funny, and lovable. The life he had kept so private was being revealed in such a beautiful way. As the guests exited to meet us at the grave site, our whispering funeral guy opened a side door, and a hearse pulled up.

Death was not new to me, but this death felt so underhanded and cruel. As I watched my mother's body arched over his casket, I saw the ground zero of grief. My uncle lovingly peeled her away as the lid lowered forever. He held her weeping body as the casket was loaded. The funeral director discreetly handed me an evidence bag of my brother's personal belongings. The ride to the grave site was eternal. Pensive funeral staff ushered people about until we were all seated, the blue casket glistening in the sun. The spray of flowers on top seemed contradictory, too beautiful for death.

Then it was over. I gathered my mother. My uncle Jack asked me to take her home. He would stay for the lowering of the body. I did not know then that after we left, my uncle had them open the casket, and he cut a lock of my brother's hair that he later gave to my mother.

After we took care of my brother's affairs, I drove my mother from Tucson to California to allow her to lick her wounds. Once there, I watched as she relentlessly paced the backyard and smoked cigarettes with such strength that the embers lit for inches. Her eyes were swollen, wet, and vacant. I did not know what to do. No one did.

He has been gone fifteen years now as I write this. Until my mother couldn't write anymore, she wrote a letter to my brother every night. When I cleaned out her apartment, I found dozens of journals, which I still can't bear to read. Her grief was so profound that she wanted to be laid to rest next to him.

YOU SHOULD HAVE BEEN THE WINDSHIELD

His simple yet poignant way of looking at the world and life came down to two things—*bugs* and *windshields*. In my brother's infinite wisdom, he encapsulated all of life's answers into one quote: "Sometimes you're the bug, and sometimes you're the windshield."

Justin, you should have been the windshield!

"Goodbye stranger,

It's been nice.

Hope you found your paradise" (excerpt from Supertramp's hit song "Goodbye Stranger").

CHAPTER 5
BUGS AND WINDSHIELDS

THEME 5: GENDER EXPECTATIONS AND TRANSGENERATIONAL LOSSES

Alysa Zalma, MD

Children seem destined to unsuccessfully fulfill the unresolved needs of their parents. In their attempts, they find many ways to carry the intergenerational torch of these unresolved losses. There are many collective fantasies within the adoptive family about who the children will be and how they will fill the hunger and void of the adoptive parents. There are the fantasies of the adoptive children about how they will measure up and fulfill the fantasies that the parents explicitly and implicitly convey to their adoptive children. In some ways, the fantasies around how the children will "make right" the family are not specific to families who adopt children, but this is the story of how one adoptee has understood her own adoptive family of origin and how she now understands the highly personal journey of each adoptee. In Heidi's desire to find out more about herself, she has more understanding of the different ways each adoptee attempts to find their own identity.

Heidi learned more about this from the outwardly different way Justin struggled with fulfilling the unresolved needs of their family. That Justin seemed to "rebel" against their family seemed inexplicable and foreign to her experience for many years, but she eventually realized that there was much they shared, even though they shared no biology. She realized they shared the wish to have safety and freedom to explore one's identity while not feeling threatened by losing love and connections to parents and family.

Heidi's experience outlines that adoptive children carry the burden of specific losses and the expectation to fix them. In her family, this included the inability of their adoptive mother to have a biological child. They also were expected to provide stability to an otherwise troubled marriage. Heidi observes the expectations and the fate of her adopted brother.

This baby boy would be another attempt to mend a broken marriage—his innocence placed to fill a void so deep and wide that he would never get out.

Heidi realized that Justin felt the pressure to feed the metaphorical "hunger" and voids of the family, which was acted out in his relationship with weight and food, as well as the complexities surrounding his experience of gender.

Justin was called upon to fill the impossible void between their father's limited ambitions for a male heir and their mother's demands for love and loyalty. He was expected to be nothing less than the savior of the family, to bestow more "feminine" aspects of a savior child for their mother and more "masculine" aspects for their father. Christ has been depicted through the centuries as having both masculine and feminine aspects, highlighted in Middle Ages and Renaissance art, more notably through the art of Leonardo Da Vinci and Michelangelo (Adhikari 2017). These masculine, feminine, and, at times, androgynous traits depicted in the paintings of Christ (and other disciples and characters) are found in many of Da Vinci's and Michelangelo's most famous paintings, such as *The Last Supper* by Da Vinci and *The Last Judgement* by Michelangelo.

Heidi talks about her brother's "Buddha belly." As an adult who never left home, he would don his "uniform," a bathrobe with his belly protruding. Bellies have been revered and respected in pregnancy, a core aspect of the feminine. It is wondered if this presentation of Justin's was somehow related to his psychological burden to fulfill in some symbolic way Joy's desire to have a viable pregnancy. A review of the relevant literature discusses the juxtaposition of overeating and pregnancy and suggests that the symptom (overeating) may be symbolic of the repressed sexual impulse of "the desire to become pregnant" (Hamburger 1997, 162).

For Heidi, much of her brother was not known to her while he was alive; since his death, she continues to make sense of this. The fact that Justin was so internally private yet unabashedly naked is a paradox. Even though he did not seem interested in being adopted in the same way as Heidi, both had to make sense of adoption's challenges.

The Supertramp song "Goodbye Stranger" speaks to Heidi's grief and loss surrounding her brother's death. Her conflicts stem from her wish to know her brother more deeply. His untimely death did not afford her time to reconcile her experience of him as a "stranger." In part, she blames their father. She also blames herself because she felt that she was too keen on trying to solve his problems rather than accepting him.

Heidi describes her brother as a loving, gentle golden giant, a rebel against society. Part of his rebellion, which Heidi termed "the open robe life," referred to his orange terry bathrobe. Supertramp's "The Logical Song" discusses the individual's innocence until society bares down with its judgments about individuality and insistence on conformity. Heidi felt these two things killed his spirit and eventually took his life.

In the song "Breakfast in America," from the album of the same name, Supertramp comments on the hope of a better life. The coveted food and women ("tickets for breakfast" and "the girls in California") were markers of fantasized success despite the reality ("not much of a girlfriend, but she's the only one I got"). The hunger for autonomy, independence, and success was yearned for by both Heidi and Justin. While they shared their love of music through many venues, they especially connected through these particular lyrics and melodies.

The desire for autonomy and independence are germane to youth in general but may be harder for some adoptees to attain due to some of the impossible expectations that may be placed upon them to fulfill the unresolved needs of the adoptive family. The "Breakfast in America" CD in the CD player and the hospital paperwork that Heidi found in Justin's truck gave her some of the tragic clues surrounding his death. The song gave her some insights into how he may have felt regarding the expectations of their adoptive family. The burdens of solving these unfixable burdens were too high for him and made the transition into an independent adulthood tragically beyond his reach.

CHAPTER 6
MY QUEEN, MY WONGEE, MY GRANDMA

*"Some women fear the fire.
Some women simply become it."*
—RH.

MY KINGDOM COME

I am so excited to have the chance to describe the *queen of my heart*, my wongee. She lovingly accepted the name I created for her with pride. My attempts to say "Grandma" somehow became Wongee, and it stuck. Her self-appointed crown always stood tall in her waves of fiery-red hair. She smelled of White Shoulders perfume and thick drugstore hairspray. She used all colorations of pastel lipsticks to blush her cheeks and paint her smile. Wongee used hairpins to clean the wax out of her ears. She loved statement bracelets, necklaces, clip-on earrings with lots of sparkles, and turquoise rings. On her left hand, she proudly displayed two wedding rings from two marriages. She would never remove her first husband's glistening diamond ring. Her second husband would always be second. Wongee would wash her hair once a week—in the kitchen sink—because she hated showers. She also prided herself on coloring her own hair and eyebrows with a box of Clairol red hair dye.

She loved a clean house and used lemon Pledge to shine her sinks and counters. We would spend hours polishing her tea set, silverware, and platters. Having an unmade bed was a crime worse than capital murder. If anything was ever misplaced, she would say, "In God's Kingdom, nothing is ever lost. Just keep looking."

Per her description, she was a right-handed, farsighted, overweight Capricorn. Her heart, arms, cupboards, and mouth were always open.

Wongee was tough as nails and could bite a raw onion like an apple. She loved pickled pigs' feet and pickled bologna and could suck the meat off any bone in 2.5 seconds.

Food was a huge part of her world. She loved to cook and make messes so grand that it would take hours to clean up. She kept an overflowing fridge, and her cupboards were full of expired goods and stale crackers.

Wongee stood nearly six feet tall, with ample bosom and belly. Her shoulders pulled back as if they were tethered to the sky, her head held high, and her chest pushed into tomorrow. Her bright pale-blue eyes, wide nose, and pleasant lips made her look regal. When she was too hot, too cold, or too angry, her cheeks and the tip of her nose would turn hostile pink. She kept a massive number of formal gowns in a small closet at the end of her hall. We often had to force the door shut, the dresses packed so tight that removing one was considered exercise.

Wongee dressed up every Friday night for her weekly Eastern Star meetings. I would go and sit in the audience as she would parade around with a bunch of other fancy ladies. She loved the art of dressing up and made sure she always had a reason to. She ran her kingdom without mercy—loving and hating with equal enthusiasm. She loved family, God, and country.

Wongee loved holidays—or any reason to celebrate. She always sat at the head of the table. The German rose-patterned bone china was used for Easter and the ruby dishes for Christmas and Thanksgiving. She was convinced that she would live to be at least 100 years old; I was convinced she would never die. A survivor of the Great Depression, she knew how to stretch a dollar. Buicks were the only car she would drive because they were American made.

Raised Methodist, she decided to follow a more controversial path and became a Christian Scientist when she was twenty years old. She read the Bible and *Science and Health* daily. She sang hymns so out of tune and with such volume that I am certain God had to cover his ears. I remember her preaching that our minds are our medicine; our evil thoughts are our undoing.

The first boy who ever tried to kiss her got punched in the face. When that same boy asked her to marry him a few years later, she punched him again. She could breathe fire and angel dust in one breath. She fancied friends named after jewels—Garnet, Ruby, Opal, and Pearl. Her friendships were long and deep.

Wongee was more than foundational; she was a pillar sunk deep in my unsteady life. Her steadfast reign never wavered, no matter how many attempts were made to dethrone her. She stood her ground in her pull-on polyester elastic-waistband pants. Given her domineering presence, you felt her shadow as well as her blinding light. Her path was her own, and she walked it with red high-heeled shoes. She was a matriarch in every sense of the word; her German bones were thick, sturdy, and seemingly unbreakable. Her example shaped my soul; her influence still runs through all my days.

TWO LISTS

Wongee was a force to be reckoned with in both presence and demeanor. She kept two distinct lists: she either liked you, or she didn't. There was no middle ground. If you were on the "good" list, you could do no wrong, even if you were wrong. If you were on the "shit" list, you could do no right, even if you were right. No matter which list you were on, you stayed there forever. This was to my advantage because I was always on the "good" list. I can say without hesitation that I enjoyed a lifetime of immunity and favors, curiously watching as those on the "shit" list were dished out all varieties of punishment. Everyone needs to be someone's favorite, and I was my wongee's. It didn't hurt that I was the only girl in a mess of rambunctious boys, most of whom deserved the shit list they found themselves on.

SHE DID WALK IN THE SNOW

Her given name was Alta Maxine Coville, and she was the eldest girl of ten children. She was born on a sprawling Michigan farm in the coldest part of winter, January 3, 1914. Her life was condensed into what she could do for others. School was a break for her, a chance to dream, a chance to learn, a chance to think. She willingly walked three miles in the snow, her books carefully tied with twine, protected under her jacket. Every frozen step was a step toward her own ideas and eventual independence. Her mind was as fiery as her hair; her intelligence was electric. She made it all the way to ninth grade, when her parents abruptly pulled her out of school. The only evidence of her lack of education was her inability to spell some words.

At that point, as the oldest girl, she became her mother's full-time helper. I could see her face change into deep sadness when she recalled that period of her life and how her days plodded with the tasks of daily living on the farm, the relentless pulse of need. She woke with the sun each day to stoke the woodstove and put on her parents' coffee. Kids had to be dressed, fed, and readied for school. Baths had to be given every few days, butter had to be churned, cows had to be milked, eggs had to be gathered, meals had to be prepared, and clothes had to be mended and hand-laundered; she even had to clip her father's toenails. The needs of small children yanking on her sleeve, a cold mother, and a chauvinistic father took any remains of her childhood.

HERE COMES THE KING

At seventeen, her stature had reached 5 feet 10 inches, and her body had filled out in all the ways that give a woman power. Fiercely independent, she called the shots—her heart calloused from digging out of a life not meant for her, making her tough as nails. A handsome, mild-mannered gentleman, ten years her senior, named Ralph Kurzhals, began to court Wongee. He treated her like a queen. He held her heart tenderly and bowed to all her wishes. When they married, alone at a courthouse in Michigan, they exchanged two thin gold rings, and he promised one day to give her the diamond of her dreams. At just eighteen years old, she became pregnant with my mom, Joy, and gave birth to her at home on October 21, 1936. Five years later, my uncle Jack was born.

Wongee wanted to leave behind the heaviness of relational obligation and bleak memories. She wanted more for herself and her children. Her world was too big to be someone else's "get me this, get me that" girl. She cast her eyes to the west—where the dreamers were migrating.

WEST COAST GIRLS

It can be said that people on the West Coast may be a little more daring. It seems to be the place where all the rebels moved to congregate in the sun. Arizona called her, with its lavish warmth and freedom. They loaded up their little family and a smattering of belongings and headed to Tucson, Arizona, in 1942. My grandfather had saved all his earnings. They bought a small dirt lot and started constructing a modest 1,000-square-foot home on 2637 N. Tucson Blvd. With his own hands, he placed every brick.

Her dining room and kitchen were perfect for feasting—ample cabinetry, a pantry, and a large sink with two big picture windows kept her happy while she cooked. Her dining room was anchored by two open corner cabinets so she could display her wide array of dishes. A quality bathroom with a smooth pink bathtub for her soaks and a medicine cabinet to hold her makeup completed the setup.

Ralph built a suitable carport to cover her series of Buicks. The backyard was generous, with a concrete fishpond, clothesline, hedges, and a eucalyptus tree. He built a covered porch with a swing to help keep them cool on hot summer nights.

She loved her home and insisted the only way she would ever leave was feetfirst. Her determination to stay never ceased. This was her castle—a space for her dreams to live and breathe. Even when the roads were paved and traffic and crime infiltrated around her, she stayed.

UNTAMABLE

We came into each other's lives at the perfect time. I needed her, and she needed me. Nine months before my adoption, her dear, sweet Ralph died of a massive heart attack at fifty-four. They had just celebrated their twenty-fifth wedding anniversary, and he had presented her with her long-awaited diamond ring. It was a perfect solitaire, full of brilliance and color, that he had saved for years to buy. Once he gave it to her, that ring never left her finger—until I took it off in her final days. I remember so vividly how the ring always fell off to the side of her finger. I loved placing it upright and admiring the sparkling life inside the stone.

Wongee had loved him entirely but had rarely treated him as if she did. His job was to please her, and from what I understand, he didn't mind. He took pride in being married to this untamable woman.

His sudden death was a crash course in survival. In spite of her feminist ways, she had never written a check, paid a bill, or run the "man" side of things. He left her a home that was paid for and enough savings for a few months.

She applied to become a missile inspector at Hughes Aircraft and started working full time. Ralph's spirit was never far from her; she talked about him so much that I felt I knew him. I remember visiting his grave weekly after church. On the way, Wongee would take me to Dunkin' Donuts. In the back seat of the car, I would eat at least three of the dozen donuts we bought. The thin paper napkins were never enough to keep me from being covered in donut dust and sticky jelly by the time we arrived at the cemetery.

The distinct sound of her white Buick's turn signal blinker would wake me from my sugar coma. The car would rock up and down on the bumpy gravel road toward his grave. After parking, she would laugh with me as she attempted to clean my face with spit and a handkerchief. Once my face was acceptable, she, in her finely pressed church clothes, would kneel down and kiss the headstone.

As I got older, I asked her why one side of the headstone was blank, and she told me that she would rest with him one day, and her name would be next to his. I couldn't wrap my mind around that ever happening, so I avoided the thought. Even in my youth, I instinctively knew that these visits were sacred. I would meander off, picking dandelions and reading epitaphs to give her time. I would glance over occasionally and see her talking to him and praying. Watching her love and honor him every week showed me the depths of true love.

NO DUST ON THESE MEMORIES

My memories of Wongee are clear, precise, and uncluttered by dust or debris—our five shared decades, woven together like stars and sky. She was one of the greatest loves of my life. According to legend, I was a crabby baby and didn't see the point of sleeping. My exhausted mother would go to Wongee for rest. Wongee would rock me in her oak rocking chair and sing nursery rhymes as I adoringly looked into her eyes. Our bond was instant and unmatchable, each of us better with the other. I grew up in her arms, nourished by her words, food, and laughter. Her love shaped all I ever am or will be. We enjoyed all the simple things, fully immersed in the joy of each other's company.

We spent warm Tucson nights in matching, handsewn, floral nightgowns. Wongee was never modest in front of me or my mother, and that helped me accept my own body. Her dressing and undressing were done shamelessly and in full light.

I vividly recall how she would put on her bra. I was usually perched on her bed next to the clothes she had picked for the next day. Her nightgown would drop to the floor. She would grab one of her huge, stretched-out lace bras with pointy cups. She would put each arm through the straps until the bra was hunched up under her chin. Then, she would bend at the waist until her breasts were suspended in midair. Apparently, this bent-over action helped her capture them more efficiently. In an undergarment dance, she would swing the bra and trap her lady lumps. In one fell swoop, she would stand up and simultaneously secure the clasps behind her back. Then, she would finish the job by prodding, pushing, and pulling until everything was in place.

In the evening, her bra was the first thing to go. The removal procedure was done in reverse. I am happy to say I continue the tradition of nightly bra removal. At the end of our fun-filled days, I loved tumbling into her double bed. The well-worn lavender sheets always smelled like fresh grass and sun. Free of any confining lady wear, we would rub our cold feet together and pull up the buttery covers. I would lay my head on her chest until I could hear the muffled beat of her beautiful heart. The minty smell of her words washed over me as she took me into the world of books and spoken stories. It was the safest place I have ever known—her with me and me with her. When she would get tired, she would make a wide, noisy yawn, remove her glasses and hearing aids, and set aside our collection of books.

Then, she would tell stories born of her imagination. We would enter magical, mystical forests, with fairies, princesses, and dinosaurs. When it was time for lights out, she would tell my favorite story, "The Three Little Pigs." I loved how she would give my ill-behaved cousins flimsy houses and save the brick one for me. That wolf could huff and puff all he wanted; my house was never coming down.

FRIDAY NIGHTS

As a child, Fridays were my favorite days because Wongee would pick me up to spend the weekend with her. It was a welcome break from the turmoil of home life. Dealing with the complex issues of my parent's volatile marriage tore at my tiny soul.

Wongee was not perfect; she loved hard but hated even harder. Despite her religious stamina, she used many "choice" words, coloring her sentences with profanity and volume. Her disdain for my father and others on her "shit" list was shoved into my ears. I would sit on her velvety coral sofa while she ranted. Her words would be vicious, venomous even, and they would make my body recoil. I spent hours watching my legs swing as she released her venom.

Her grievances were justified, but they damaged me. I couldn't process the toxicity, so I distracted myself by thinking of donuts, bedtime stories, and what treats might be hidden in the pantry. At those times, I avoided eye contact because I didn't want to see my wongee filled with rage.

Once she had purged her emotions, though, we were free to play.

We would hang baskets of fresh laundry to dry in the sun, roll up our pant legs, and abandon our shoes for the warm grass. She would run the sprinkler so I could dance in the shimmering water. We would pluck the seeds from her arching sunflowers, swirl them in salt water, and bake them for an afternoon snack. We would feed her turtle, brush the dog, and make homemade noodles. I was allowed to make mud pies and display them on her china. There was no limit to how many Twinkies, Ding Dongs, or SpaghettiOs I could have. We would spend hours swinging on her back porch and drinking sun tea (tea steeped in a gallon jar in the sun) out of her cheap, dime-store, appliquéd glasses.

When darkness came, she would draw me a bath filled with Calgon crystals. The water would swirl with clouds of blue as the granules dissolved. She would dip a washcloth in the scented water and wring it out on my back. Her bathroom was tiny, but she would give me a good scrub while sitting on the toilet. Her talcum powder was kept in a hand-painted china container. After I was dry, she would pick up the abundant white puff and dip it in the powder. Generously, she would pat large circles all over my skin. I loved the way I smelled when she was done. Sometimes, she even let me use a few squirts of her perfume.

After I was squeaky clean, she would fill the tub with more warm water and hop in. Her large rolls of flesh and comfort with her nudity made me feel at ease. She understood her body was her consort. The holder of her spirit was her body; it was healthy, vibrant, and substantial. I always dipped the wash rag and scrubbed her back, taking notice of the galaxy of moles between her wide shoulders. We were a team in every sense of the word; there was a knowing that couldn't be explained.

The days would end in the living room, with me sitting on her prized oriental rug. I would wait as she double-checked all the doors and windows, carefully hanging pots and pans on the door handles to alert us if anyone tried to break in. The blinds would be shut, and the world put away. She would sit behind me as I sandwiched in between her two thick legs. She would gather my hair and start brushing, the two of us counting together until we reached one hundred strokes. Once all our grooming was out of the way, she would settle into quilting, and I would read. In the winter, the heat of the archaic gas stove would take the chill away as it hissed and glowed. In the summer, we would do late-night Dairy Queen runs and sit close to the swamp cooler vent to fight the heat. No matter the season, the weather, the storms, or the endless summer days, she was home, my place, my person.

RING NUMBER TWO

When I was nine, Wongee decided to marry again. Poor Norman was just not man enough to handle her. In fact, he was frail in body, mind, and spirit, which made him a pushover. She made it very clear that her Ralph was the love of her life. His ring would remain on her finger, and Norman would just have to deal with it. Wongee was a taskmaster.

They had twin beds from the get-go, and there was no doubt that she was in charge. I am quite sure they never consummated anything, and he never had the pleasure of seeing her put on her bra. As time went on, he was banished to his own private quarters for reasons unknown. My weekends were filled with the sounds of their muffled fighting instead of her muffled heartbeat.

She felt distant as she dealt with an unhappy marriage. I ached for the days we had spent in our nightgowns, holding the world in our hands. Now I was bookended between two conflicting worlds, with no escape. I never liked Norman very much, and more to the point, I didn't like sharing my wongee.

The troubles in their relationship escalated to a breaking point one blistering, hot summer morning. I was trying to sleep in, covering my head to avoid the details of their arguing. I was annoyed that the grandfather clock's Westminster Chimes kept dinging. In a flustered fit, I lay there, gritting my teeth, on the verge of hostility. Suddenly, I heard a scream of fear, a scream of pain—a scream I never want to hear again. My response was so primal that it pulled me upright, and I ran, my heart bursting in my chest. I arrived at the scene; there was my queen, lying on the kitchen floor, smeared with blood, tears running down her cheeks, her hair a tangled mess. Norman stood above her, his bifocals cockeyed and his cowardice on full display. Seeing me gave her strength, and she stood up, towering above him.

At the top of her lungs, she yelled, "*Get out*!" He fumbled, trying to defend his actions, claiming self-defense. I moved closer. He was sandwiched between us, which wasn't going to turn in his favor. I was ready to do whatever I had to do. I thought of the knives in the wood block, or the iron skillet filled with cooling fried potatoes. It wouldn't be hard to take this wimp down. Wongee's hands were now on her hips. She pulled out her vocal guns and started firing. "You miserable bastard! Get your stuff, and get out of my house *now*!"

Norman assessed the situation, tucked tail, and went back to his room to pack his things. We watched from the living room window as he drove his beige Chevy van away in a cloud of dust. When I asked what had happened, she reverted to a child, a side of her I had never seen. Shame changed her expression; she shrugged her shoulders and cast her chin down. "We were arguing, and he pushed me. My arm hit the corner of the counter, and when I fell, he kicked me a few times."

A strange silence blanketed us as I saw my queen fill out to her full stature. Her strength was never far away. Norman was moved to the top of the "shit" list, his name in *bold* letters. I helped Wongee clean up the cut on her arm, along with the blood on the floor. Seeing the red on the paper towels angered me deeply. She seemed distant as we removed all evidence of their ending. I knew she felt awful about me witnessing her in that position. I knew she needed to hear what I was thinking. I told her it was just *fine* with me that Norman had left. I never liked his white shoes, his bad breath, his crusty nose boogers, or the way he wore his pants too high. Soon, we were laughing, and I watched as she found her crown and placed it back where it belonged. It didn't take long before happiness came back, and we resumed our routine. She would never marry or date again.

BRA STUFFING

Wongee loved me fiercely and completely. In her eyes, I was perfect. As I came into my teenage years, when she visited, everything she did embarrassed me. In my immaturity, I would roll my eyes when she would wrap her restaurant leftovers in a napkin and put them in her purse. Her food handling was not for the faint of heart. She would grab raw meat and scatter blood and juices with no concern for the hard-to-pronounce illnesses she was distributing. Handwashing was optional, and I often prayed for a strong immune system. Her bra or "high pockets" were a place to stuff wads of cash and/or a tube of lipstick. I would die a thousand deaths when we would go shopping, and she would reach under her shirt to pull out warm twenty-dollar bills.

Wongee talked very loudly, and due to her hearing loss, she was unaware of her volume. Her vocabulary was rich, unique, and boisterous; she called cheating men *womanwizers* instead of *womanizers*, hamburgers were *hamburgs*, couches were *davenports*, and she always told me to get my tail out of a knot. She yelled, "WOO-HOO-HOO-HOO" whenever anyone came to her door. I avoided being with her in public at all costs, even pretending I didn't know her.

I regret my treatment of her during my teenage years. I should have been put on the "shit" list, but I wasn't. If I could pull her down from heaven right now, I would join her in bra stuffing and reckless food prep. We would wrap all the restaurant leftovers in thin napkins and throw them in our purses. Then, we would laugh too loudly and sing even louder, making everyone wish they were having as much fun as we were.

FEETFIRST

Her eighties came, and her hearing was almost nonexistent. The squeal of her hearing aids, along with her yelling "*What*," became the bulk of our conversations. If she did hear you, she often heard you wrong and would get madder than a hornet. The most horrible part was watching her go legally blind and lose her ability to read, sew, and drive. The job of caring for her fell on my mother, whose own health and attitude were declining.

Living thousands of miles away, I would return a few times a year. The progressive deterioration contrasted with her former self. There was no more "WOO-HOO-HOO-HOO" when I would ring her doorbell. Her kitchen smelled of old trash and rotting fruit; the counters were cluttered with used coffee cups. The pantry that once overflowed was reduced to a few expired canned goods. Her once-polished furniture was smothered in dust and cobwebs. In the yard, Wongee's previously lush grass was dead, brown, and abandoned. Her trees, plants, and prized hedges all begged for water. There were no more sunflowers, goldfish swimming in the pond, or laundry floating on the line. There weren't any more turtles named Henry or dogs named Happy.

On these visits, I would achingly try to persuade her to move next to me in Washington. She would always become agitated and indignant at the suggestion. Her mantra remained the same—*she was not leaving the house*—unless it was feetfirst on her way to the morgue.

The deciding point was during one of my visits. It was clear the situation was unhealthy and unsafe. I had to be the Big Bad Wolf and take her away from her white brick house and everything she loved so much.

IT'S NOT A BRICK HOUSE

We were living in Battle Ground, Washington, at the time, and we had just purchased a 2.5-acre property on a hill. It had a main house and one outbuilding. The view stretched all the way to Portland, with over 100 evergreens piercing the sky—a piece of earthly heaven if you ask me. After heavy negotiations with my mother, we decided to remodel part of the outbuilding to make an apartment for the two of them. The design/build began, and nine months later, it was ready to move in. It was a bold choice to take on two strong elderly women. That choice came with bold consequences. I was convinced that if they were nearby,

I could heal the relationship with my mother and help take care of my wongee. That didn't happen.

HIGHWAY TO HELL

One problem with being a dreamer is that the dream doesn't always pair with reality. My idea of "rescuing" my wongee and mother via a thirty-eight-foot RV seemed reasonable at the time. Since Wongee had horrible issues with her bowels and bladder, flying seemed out of the question. Why did I think a five-day RV trip was the solution? To make matters worse, this trip would happen in the hottest part of August. Destination: Tucson, Arizona. In a nutshell, it was the highway to hell—and back. I was determined to fill the trip with delightful memories, campfires, and sightseeing (despite Wongee being blind as a bat). Oh, and let's take my eleven-year-old son along and traumatize him enough to need extensive therapy one day.

It was brutal, long, and *nothing* like I had romanticized. Troy insisted on driving the entire time because no one else could be trusted with "the bus." When we arrived in Tucson, haggard and on the cusp of divorce, Wongee's house was in a shambles. The packing that was supposed to have occurred hadn't. My mother had just shut down. I found her smoking on the back porch while Wongee nervously rocked in her recliner. We spent the next three days getting things in order and shoving what we could into the RV.

To add further excitement to the journey to Washington, we added to the passenger manifest "Suiki," my mother's hyper, miniature schnauzer, who suffered some kind of dermatitis. My husband called her Scabby instead of Suiki. Her incessant scratching and foul smell did not help my deteriorating mood. Then, we decided to tow my mother's car, a silver Kia hatchback, a.k.a. *The Ashtray*. Now, instead of being thirty-eight feet long, we were forty-five feet long.

Wongee sensed something was not right and became scared. We just told her we were going on a family vacation. Perhaps we should have considered more heavily how to deal with an eighty-five-year-old suffering from advanced dementia, incontinence, and outbursts of anger. It is only by the grace of God that we made it home alive.

NORMAN!

A few hours into the trip, Wongee started yelling, "Norman!" She was under the impression that her ex-husband was driving when, in actuality, it was my husband, Troy. Troy patiently spent the first day correcting her until he realized it was futile. For the rest of the trip, after he caved to her insistence, Troy was renamed Norman. Although I'll admit that I thought it was funny, he wasn't amused.

I rode shotgun and took my role as copilot seriously, but whenever I blurted out a piece of driving advice, I was banished by "Norman" to the back of the RV. I would sprawl out on the bed and hold onto the sides of the unpleasant mattress as the RV wagged its tail. The toilet was constantly sloshing, the dog was scratching, Wongee was yelling, my mother was yelling, I was telling her not to yell, and my son was rolling his eyes and covering his ears. Troy, "Norman," would be swerving, and me . . . I'd be on the verge of vomiting. After five hellish days, we miraculously arrived in Battle Ground, Washington—exhausted, exasperated.

LIVING IN THE GARAGE

The apartment we designed was adorable, and I worked hard to create a home for them. I was so excited to show Wongee. When we got her through the door, she said firmly, "I will not live in this garage. I want to go home."

Garage? What? NO! My heart broke that she thought I had moved her into a garage. It didn't matter how much I showed her the fireplace, the beautiful bedrooms, and the way I made her bed with lavender sheets; to her, it was a garage. Eventually, she settled in and focused on other things, but it wasn't easy.

Over the next three years, I went over several times a day to love her and bring food for them. One day, when I was headed out, she yelled my name and patted her lap. Tears welled up in my eyes as I remembered the millions of times I had sat with her. As I approached, she smiled bigger and patted more enthusiastically, wanting me to sit on her frail legs. I told her I didn't want to hurt her, but she grabbed my arm with surprising strength and pulled me down.

The moment I rested on her chest, everything she meant to me pulsed through my entire being. The whole world fell away, and it was just us—me better with her, her better with me. She was starting the process of saying goodbye, reminding me that our love would always remain. My grief opened as wide as the sky, my tears as uncountable as the stars.

SOMEONE WITH A BRAIN

It wasn't long before things started to become unmanageable for me and my mother. Wongee was a hearty 180 pounds of stubborn, sassy woman. Her falls became frequent, and she required at least two struggling people to get her up. I begged God so many times to take her in a sweet dream, but that would not be her end. She was a fighter, a lover of life, and she was determined to finish her last breath with gusto. On a chilly January night, everything changed—as it sometimes does when we don't want it to.

It was 10:30 at night, and my mother called and said Wongee had fallen in the bathroom. I grabbed my robe, closing it as I ran up the stairs and out into the cold in my bare feet. I ran across the driveway and into their apartment. When I opened the door, the smells of urine, tomato soup, and cigarette smoke assaulted me. Wongee and my mother were cornered in the bathroom. My mother had dropped her while trying to lift her off the toilet. It was horrible to see Wongee's saturated diaper collected at her knees, her naked body void of its robust curves, now bruised and red.

A puddle of warm urine under her bottom made the whole scene a living nightmare. I grabbed a towel and tried to clean her and cover her privates while I assessed her for injuries. Soon, Troy entered to see what was going on. He burst in with a loud, "Hello!"

Wongee looked up and said, "Is that Troy?"

I answered, "Yes," to which she replied, "Finally, someone with a brain!"

Troy smiled wide as he walked over and effortlessly placed her on the toilet. Mom and I stood with folded arms and rolling eyes. Wongee's screams of pain worsened, and she started to moan. I knew something was very wrong, and the debate about what to do started. Against popular demand, I called 911—so what if it would be another false alarm? Soon, the ambulance, with its full siren, arrived, spinning its cherries and berries, and all the neighbors filtered over to see if they could help.

I watched in horror as the pain swallowed Wongee. Her screams reminded me of that horrible time I found her beaten on the kitchen floor. The gurney was lifted to waist height, and they tightened the straps to keep her from moving. A thick strip of tape pulled across her forehead, catching a large wisp of her gray hair. I asked to ride with her in the ambulance, and they agreed. How I wished the ambulance wasn't so well lit. I didn't want every detail visible at full strength.

I patted her clammy head as her agony escalated. Every bump, every turn made her wail. I could not believe this was our truth. Everything felt cold, heavy, and unfair. I wanted to ask the ambulance driver to transport us to another time. Maybe he could take a hard right and head to Arizona? He could drop us off at 2637 N. Tucson Blvd. Wongee would have a boiling pot of homemade noodles on the stove. We would have the backyard grass under our feet and donut dust around our mouths. There would be turtles, dogs, flowers, stories, and nightgowns. But that was not going to happen.

I saw the emergency room come into view as the slowing of the ambulance pulled me back into reality. Soon, she was rushed off for X-rays. Her hip and femur were fractured. There would be emergency surgery, steel rods, pain, and rehab. She would never come home again.

REHAB MY ASS

A week in the hospital led to a "rehabilitation" facility, which was, for all intents and purposes, Hell on Earth. The staff was overworked, underpaid, and void of compassion. The smells, sounds, and suffering overwhelmed me; every open door offered a view into someone's personal purgatory. Her time there ripped at my soul, and I know it ripped at hers. There weren't any other viable options, so we had to make it work.

I became the campus police and sneaker of treats. There were a lot of breaking points, but the worst was when I entered the building and heard her cries. As I made my way down the hall, I found her lying half on and half off her bed. There was my precious wongee, red-cheeked, red-nosed, hair disheveled, naked from the waist up, crying out into a world she could not see. She was scared and confused and had clearly been in that position for some time. There was no dignity for my queen, and I was pissed. I pushed every button and stomped down the hall, yelling things I shouldn't have been yelling. I was fully prepared to be arrested for my actions. Their excuses meant nothing to me, and I threatened to call 911.

I devised a strategy of layering my visits in unpredictable spurts so I could catch any problems. It was exhausting trying to take care of teenagers, my husband, my mother, and our home while still keeping her safe. I am surprised I was not arrested during that time or committed to an insane asylum. In a state of lethargy, I would sit by her side and touch her hands, memorizing the softness and warmth. Her skin was so thin but so beautiful. The wrinkles told stories. I would brush her tufts of thin gray hair, counting to 100, and put on her favorite gold lipstick. I would sneak in milkshakes, donuts, and candy. Gradually, Wongee became almost unrecognizable to me. Sliding from this world into the next, she was in the gap—in between them. During most of our visits, she would stare into a place far away, and I wondered what it was like. *What did she see?* Her slow leaving felt thick, heavy, and cruel.

ALWAYS FINISH STRONG

I should have known that Wongee wouldn't go down without a fight. I wanted so much for her to surrender and stop resisting, but that wasn't her way. When pneumonia came into her lungs, we found ourselves back in the same hospital where I had birthed my son. My precious Wongee was heaving with each breath, fighting and agitated. I was distraught that she no longer seemed to recognize me or respond to my voice—or to anyone's voice, for that matter. When my husband (the one with the brain) came for a visit, I burst into tears, asking him, "Why won't she let go? Why won't she say she loves me?" He asked me if anyone had bothered to see if her hearing aid batteries were dead—*Seriously?*

Before I knew it, Troy changed out Wongee's batteries, and she was with us once again. Her words were not really audible, but she mouthed "I love you" and began to nod when we asked her questions.

As the days faded into one other, her breathing became more sporadic. The hospital walls were folding in around us—I just wanted to run. At night, I would stare at the stars and sky, wishing I could put us on a cloud next to the moon. The nurse warned us her last breath was coming as she placed a syringe of morphine on the counter. I had never been present for anyone's death, but I was determined to escort my queen. My head rested quietly on Wongee's chest as I listened to the muffled sound of her final heartbeats. I wanted to feel the warmth of her minty breath as she laughed and told stories. I wanted her to wake up and tell me the wolf couldn't hurt us. I wanted the brick house. I wanted us to be beside the old furnace, her quilting and me reading.

The wolf of death has no regard for bricks. I watched for hours as she clung to life, with her warm hand in mine. Eventually, I fell into a scattered sleep. I was awakened by her hand losing its grip. I looked up as her head fell softly to the side. She took in a huge, noisy breath through her mouth, and the air sputtered back out. Stunned, I sat up and started crying, thinking it was her last breath. Then, she straightened her head, opened her mouth, and took her final breath. It was grand, loud, and exhaled into the first day of spring.

It is fitting that she died on a day that was bursting with new life. I asked for time alone with her. I shut the door and turned off the bright lights. I pulled down the sheets and the blood-stained bluebird quilt and crawled into bed beside her. I wrapped my arms around her back and pulled her to my core. The last bits of air moved out of her nose and mouth while I rocked her, thanked her, kissed her, and hugged her. Then, I heard her voice in my head say, "Get your high boots on, and let's get out of here." I gathered her hand-stitched quilt and stood at the foot of her bed.

I wanted to feel something, something holy. I wanted beams of light and singing angels with harps. *Nothing.* Just *silence.* This larger-than-life woman made it to ninety-four years old. She truly lived, but I wasn't ready to let her go. I crawled back into bed with her and rested my head on her quiet heart. I intertwined my fingers with hers and asked her if she wanted to hear a story about "The Three Little Pigs." I told her all of heaven is made of bricks, and there would be no more wolves at her door.

HOME AGAIN

It was time. Time to engrave her name next to Ralph's on the headstone that we had visited so many times. Time to lay her to rest in the Sonoran Desert she loved so much. It was time to get her from Battle Ground back to Tucson.

Her death crushed me in ways I did not anticipate. I had danced with death many times, but this death felt different. She was my skeletal structure, the person who strengthened me. I felt unattached, a blob of confusion melting into shapes I didn't understand. We were each other's heart. She flowed through me, and I flowed through her—a bond so intricate that I have never recovered from losing her. With her, I was truly seen, known, and loved.

I have no idea how I got through those first days after she passed.

But I did. It started by booking a room at Westward Look Resort for my mother and me. Nestled beneath the purple desert mountains that Wongee had adored, it was a place to rest during those torturous days of funeral planning.

There was the job of making her beautiful burgundy formal and matching shawl ready for her viewing. I remembered zipping up this dress for her. I could smell, feel, and embody those moments. The day of her viewing was difficult; when my mother and I arrived, it was offensively sunny. I just wanted dark gray clouds, thunderstorms, and pouring rain. We were escorted by a plastic-looking funeral director with overly gelled hair into the room where she lay in wait.

The room was huge. It had a horrendous green carpet and nineties mauve wallpaper. Her casket was flanked by two columns, with some strange fake flower arrangements. I could see Wongee's profile, her folded hands, and her shawl cascading around her. My mother approached first, kissed her on the forehead, and adjusted her hair. Her nose looked strangely pointed, and her makeup was awful. I reached into my purse and pulled out my Yves Saint Laurent lipstick, apricot, number 52. The gold tube glinting in the harsh light, and my hand shaking, I applied the golden-orange color to her hardened lips. I just wanted her to talk to me, to part her mouth the way she did when I would do her makeup. This would be the last time I would see her physical body. I focused on her hands, the hands that had done so much, touched so many, the hands that had shaped my life. I placed my palms over her still fingers and wept until nothing was left. The warm desert sun waited for me, and I needed something warm. I stopped at the doorway and whispered, "I love you," and blew her a final kiss.

THANK YOU

Wongee's burial was torture. I sat in the first row of uncomfortable folding chairs under a black canopy. Fresh dirt and a hollow hole, her coffin was cascading with spring flowers. It was hard to grasp that my wongee would be lowered into the ground. A gathering of about twenty-five people arrived, including her last jewel friend, Garnet. Their friendship had spanned six decades. She spoke first; then, it was my turn. I don't remember most of it, but I remember saying, "*Thank you*, Wongee." I could not stay after the service to see her eased into the earth. All my courage was spent.

The next day, I returned to the cemetery before our flight back to Washington. I was puzzled because I hadn't seen my own mother cry yet. But at that moment, it didn't matter. I had enough tears for both of us. I pressed my face against the cold granite of the stone and slumped over her grave.

I MISS YOU

I miss you, Wongee. I miss you like I have never missed anything or anyone. I know you hear me. I know you see me. I know you are never far from me. I set my table with your dishes and add mismatched chairs. I ring your rusty cowbell before dinner and say your prayer. "Let the rein of divine Truth, Life, and Love be established in me, and rule out of us all sin; and may Thy Word enrich the affections of all mankind, and govern them." I use your rolling pin and your well-worn recipe cards. You are alive in my hands, in my heart, in my words. I will always wear my high boots and keep my tail from being in a knot. I love kids, God, and family. You are the reason I am strong enough.

CHAPTER 6
MY QUEEN, MY WONGEE, MY GRANDMA

THEME 6: THE HOLDING ENVIRONMENT
Alysa Zalma, MD

The central theme in this chapter is what the British pediatrician and psychoanalyst Donald Woods Winnicott, MD, called the "holding environment." It was within this space, according to Winnicott, where, on the most primal level, the mother physically holds the infant; it was "understood," within the space of mother and infant, that the merge created everything that human experience needed (Winnicott 1960, 588-591).

This intimate space generates an infrastructure of supreme trust and safety, and thus, the ability of the mother-infant dyad to create a matrix that combines stability and spontaneity. The framework of this type of intimacy allows for the promise of individuation. As adults, this is the "space" we wish to return to, playing out these most primal desires in all our subsequent relationships.

This space has been called many things by many psychoanalysts, poets, and writers. Thomas Ogden, a contemporary psychoanalyst and author, in his partially Winnicottian treatise on this space, says, "This is a felt place . . . in a sense the creation of two people, and yet is the mind/body of an individual." He coined this space, in clinical treatment between doctor and patient, the "analytic third" (Ogden 1997, 142).

Winnicott, originally in 1953, wrote of this psychic space, the holding environment, on a broader level: "It is in the space between inner and outer world, which is also the space between people—the transitional space—where intimate relationships and creativity occur" (Winnicott 1953).

Heidi spends this most poignant, at times humorous, yet ultimately heart-wrenching chapter describing what it was like to have this holding environment with her grandmother. Heidi is able to say poetically, in a way that is easy to understand, what Winnicott meant when he originally described the mother-infant relationship (or dyad). She says of her relationship with her grandmother that they were

> **. . . woven together like stars and sky.**

She also explains the holding environment for us to understand with other descriptions of her relationship with her grandmother:

> **I loved tumbling into her double bed. The well-worn lavender sheets always smelled like fresh grass and sun. . . . The minty smell of her words washed over me as she took me into the world of books and spoken stories. It was the safest place I have ever known—her with me and me with her.**

Heidi puts more elegance to this most universally sought-after shared space:

> **We were a team in every sense of the word; there was a knowing that couldn't be explained. The days would end in the living room, with me sitting on her prized oriental rug. I would wait as she double-checked all the doors and windows, carefully hanging pots and pans on the door handles to alert us if anyone tried to break in. The blinds would be shut and the world put away.**

The lessons of adolescence and early adulthood, when individuation is more sought-after, are sometimes a place of confusion and complications, where individuals are taught societal norms, and the desire for the holding environment is shifted to more mature adult relationships. The price for these more "adult" relationships is at a cost.

Heidi looked back at her adolescence and noted her embarrassment. Her grandmother would refuse to acknowledge social graces by putting leftover food in restaurant napkins, defy good hygiene, and unabashedly reach through her shirt to find a $20 bill lodged in her bra.

As an adult, these were the memories Heidi understood as connections to perhaps the most healthy and sustaining relationship of her early development.

One of the most wonderfully comic yet deeply intimate passages is when Heidi's grandmother demonstrated her connection to and comfort with her body in the ceremony of putting on her bra at the beginning of the day and removing it at day's end. Heidi later saw this as a role-model moment of her adolescence, in her desire to be comfortable in her own body. The bra seemed to be a metaphor for the things that hold women "in" and the things they take "off" to be themselves.

> **Free of any confining lady wear, we would rub our cold feet together and pull up the buttery covers. I would lay my head on her chest until I could hear the muffled beat of her beautiful heart.**

To take the bra (as a symbol of public self and societal norm) off is to be enveloped in the experience of returning "home," to the holding environment, back to the experience of what it feels like to be truly loved.

CHAPTER 7
UNCLE SMACK

"Be virtuous and you will be eccentric."
—Mark Twain

"When everyone zigs, zag."
—Stephen Anderson

THE MAN. THE MYTH. THE LEGEND. DRUMROLL . . .

By now, after reading about the tragedy that has followed me so closely, you might be ready for a diversion. We need to spend some time with Wongee's only son, my uncle Jack, a.k.a., Uncle Smack.

There could only be one Uncle Jack. The world could not have handled more. He was tall and lanky, with a wide nose, big mouth, hooded blue eyes, and a mischievous upper-toothed grin. His know-it-all bravado was off-putting, and his flair for tall tales and boisterous exaggeration made him avoidable. Not to mention the offensiveness of the white spittle that would collect at the corners of his mouth during brag-offs. He was a red-white-and-blue swim trunks, farmer's tan, dirty white T-shirt wearing, beard growing, wealthy, eccentric human, and I loved him. Despite a few colorful qualities, his heart was wide, and his dreams were deep. In the breadth of his love, he gathered the lost, the weak, and the less fortunate—be they four-legged, two-legged, or otherwise. He will forever be the closest thing I had to a father—an embarrassing father, but a father, nonetheless. As Wongee would proclaim, Uncle Jack was born a "ripsnorter." His ever-curious spirit relentlessly tested her nerves until her last breath. Getting a reaction out of you was absolutely his highest calling, and he loved to tease Joy, my adoptive mother, until the day he died.

BUG ON A LEASH

A phenomenon happens in the desert every summer: bugs from Hell erupt out of the earth. Wongee's yard was full of locusts that left behind perfectly formed, transparent exoskeletons stuck by the hundreds to the bark of her trees, reflecting sunlight like tiny crystal chandeliers in the desert sun. Her back-porch light became a disco ball party for six-inch-long Scorcrockels beetles (the name I made up for them), moths that seemed to be the size of fighter jets, and the less offensive June bugs that enjoyed flaring their metallic blue-green wings.

This was the perfect scenario for my "rip-snorting" uncle, who used creatures both great and small to do his dirty deeds. Whether it was insect, mammal, fish, or amphibian, it did not matter; he would pick it up and give it a kiss without an ounce of fear. Never discouraged by whatever poison, fangs, or stingers they might have had, he captured them anyway. The small ones went into paper Dixie cups, the larger into Wongee's fancy bowls or pots and pans, and most of them escaped through an array of unsecured lids. Wongee kept an old straw broom next to the sliding glass door to usher out unwanted guests and to give Uncle Jack a smack.

Despite the trouble he found himself in, he continued to go above and beyond in his efforts to scare the squeamish. His favorite antic was to tie a long piece of thread around a captured June bug and fly it around the house, sending Wongee, my mother, and her friends up onto beds and behind doors. I can just picture his rooster tail hair and big toothy grin as their screams of disgust filled his ears. He loved bows and arrows, guns, slingshots, and fishing poles, and he often made his own lethal versions.

As he grew into an awkward misfit teenager in the fifties, my mother, in contrast to him, became a refined, popular cheerleader, the perfect ammunition for him to up his game. He loved to embarrass her in front of her "Elvis wannabe" suitors, who leaned up against their slick cars, with their greased-back hair and cigarette packs rolled up in their sleeves. Their macho stances evaporated the moment he brought a spider, horn toad, or snake into their view. My mother wasn't even safe when she was sleeping; he would find a way to pick the lock and put his hamster under her sheets at least three times a week.

WADS OF CASH

For as long as I can remember, Uncle Jack always had a wad of cash—not small bills but $100s. The roll was so big that he secured it with a rubber band. Any chance he got, he would slowly count the money, wetting his thumb with his tongue. Once he found the perfect bill, which was usually in the middle, he would slip it out to pay for something cheap, sending the cashier into a silent tantrum. As my mother often said, he was "a bragger and a world-class blowhard." I suppose I would brag if I had enough money to retire in my thirties, too.

He seemed oblivious to everyone's eye-rolling and admonition; his lack of self-awareness was his freedom. His earnings had come hard. He had spent two years right out of high school living in a camper shell, building the Trans-Alaska Pipeline System, and living on cheap canned food. He got his general contractor's license when he returned and started flipping houses before that was even a thing. His keen business sense made him a multi-millionaire within a decade.

EWW, THEY ARE KISSING

I was the only girl amongst the five spunky grandchildren. My uncle had two sons, Jarrett "Smilie" and Richard "Ricky" by marriage, and an adopted son, also named Richard, by his second marriage—this one to my aunt Pat. She had dander-soft, curled blond hair that was always piled in an updo. They had met at a trailer park that my uncle owned in Prescott, Arizona. Aunt Pat was a tall drink of water—almost six feet—and she had a ready smile. Seeing couples being affectionate was foreign to me. They did a lot of kissing, tickling, and rolling around on the living room floor; all the while, me and my cousins would be screaming "gross" and "stop it"—and then jumping in. I remember curling Aunt Pat's hair once a week with an old steam curling iron while she smoked cigarettes. She was a fiercely loving mother. She had suffered seven miscarriages before she adopted her son, and she was going to protect him—and that became very clear. Unfortunately, her attempts at talking us into being kinder never worked; the moment she wasn't around, we did what most kids do: test limits. But Richard never crumbled. He passed every test of endurance with flying colors. When we saw that he wasn't a tattletale, things got easier for him.

WE COULD JUST BE KIDS

My uncle Jack and aunt Pat didn't mind that we would raid their avocado-green fridge to make pizzas. Not just any pizzas, but the biggest pizzas we could make. Taking great pride in the wide variety of ingredients, from jam to lettuce, we had only one caveat, and that was that we had to eat what we prepared. Our continuing goal for each pizza was to beat the weight of the last one; to keep track, we used the bathroom scale religiously to weigh our masterpieces, which averaged ten pounds. She never yelled at us for those monsters or even for feeding watermelons to the raccoons or making forts outside with all the good blankets. The toilet lid didn't have to be down, and the beds didn't need to be made. Their home and their love were a refuge, a front-row seat to see how things should be, a place I could go and be free from the presence of violence and unpredictability.

COME HOME BEFORE DARK

Playing with my cousins when they would visit Wongee's house was one of my greatest joys before we moved to the mountains of Arizona. Wongee and I would go to the store beforehand and load up on everyone's favorites—cranberry juice, cheap powdered sugar donuts, bologna, Miracle Whip, Cheerios, and Wonder Bread. Wongee was rarely happier than when all her grandkids were under her roof.

If I wanted to be included, I had to do all the "boy" things they did, and those included firing BB guns, shooting rubber bands, playing tackle football, frogging, hunting, and playing army. One day, Uncle Jack took us to Kmart to buy the boys football jerseys. When it became clear that I didn't qualify, I went into silent but deadly mode. I watched with arms crossed, disgusted, as the boys searched for their sizes behind the numbered plastic rings. Their enthusiasm had me in a tither. The Barbies and dolls stared at me from across the aisle.

Halfway home, Uncle Jack noticed my upset, my dramatically heaving breath and tears. When he realized what was wrong, he pulled off the road, looked at all of us, and said, "I forgot to get our quarterback a jersey." He turned to me with that grin, waiting for my reaction, which was instant elation. We hauled back into Kmart, the boys helped, and I walked out with a thin plastic bag of happiness.

To be included, I had to learn to be tough, which meant not being a tattletale. My greatest weapons were silence, passive-aggressive plotting, and hairspray. There were a lot of things I should have ratted them out for—like the time they rolled me up in my Wongee's fancy Oriental rug or when they dared me to climb her giant eucalyptus tree and then ran away with the ladder. More disturbing was when they shot our prized extra-large goldfish in her fishpond with their homemade bows and arrows. I distinctly remember giving them a heavy dose of Wongee's Aqua Net hairspray directly on their faces after that massacre.

They taught me how to fight physically and verbally. I learned quickly that my legs were stronger than my arms and that a swift kick to the "boy" region would always buy me time to escape. I learned that a few well-placed "choice" words gave me street credit.

Where I drew the line was hunting. I did try, but it inevitably ended in disaster. They started me with low-grade frogging, which lasted all of 0.8 seconds as I accidentally sank the three-pronged frog poker into my thigh. Despite that, they graduated me to spotlighting jackrabbits—only, they had to console me when I shot the rabbit and cried with remorse when it didn't die right away. My last shot occurred when we were deer hunting. I pulled the trigger on the rifle without anchoring it into my shoulder. It knocked me off my feet and simultaneously scared all their hunting prospects into the far, deep edges of the forest.

Lucky for me, I learned how to spot animals, and that made me a valuable asset, or so they thought. I was skilled at finding fresh trails, spotting scat, and making animal calls. What they didn't know was how many animals I scared away from them, reducing their hunting down to the occasional basking lizard. All the while, Uncle Jack gave us all complete freedom as long as we would come home before dark.

ARCHAEOLOGY

Everything was about adventure with my uncle Jack. He was in love with life. He loved history, archeological digs, and hunting for Native American artifacts in the Arizona mountains. The whole landscape was a treasure trove. During our adventures together, I became adept at finding pieces of pottery and arrowheads. We would spend hours bent over in the unforgiving sun, digging, sifting, and gathering while he would monologue about Native American battles, and I would dream about ice cream.

There were no phones, and his truck was usually parked sideways at the end of some dusty road, windows rolled down so it would be a little bit cool when we returned. At the end of our dusty, well-spent days, we would walk back to his truck with the sunset, hands in pockets that bulged with finds. His old Ford pickup was always a welcome sight. He prided himself on the 160,000 miles it had traveled. The creak of the passenger-side door was enough to test the capacity of our eardrums. The cracked peacock-blue leather seats were always hot as a two-dollar pistol, the wide, deep cracks of stained padding filled with goodness-knows-what. The predictable hunt for his blue-handled wrench would commence. Once he found it, he would use it as a replacement for the missing gearshift lever. The ashtray forever overflowed with bent cigarettes, and old soda cans rolled around on the floor in harmony with the bumps, breaks, and turns as we sped down the road. The radio would broadcast a menagerie of static-filled voices and songs, all interrupting each other as I would turn the knob, searching for a station. Unlike my dad, Uncle Jack had no problem being seen in dirty clothes, wacky hair, and a beat-up truck. On those long rides, he would brag about how he could afford anything he wanted, and I would ask the obvious as he shifted with the wrench. "Then why don't you buy a new truck?"

"Because then we wouldn't be able to leave the windows down." He would grin and wait for my reaction.

During those no-one-else-in-sight rides, he would take time to reach into my heart and ask about my situation at home. He always kept his response simple. "Heidi, your dad is a very sick man."

In an odd way, his acknowledgment helped me feel vaguely understood and less responsible. He never dove deeper; he knew my time with him would give me a place to heal, a space for my soul to move. When I stayed over at his house, I usually took the back bedroom, down the hall to the left, across from the bathroom that I avoided—it had a metal spatula on a hook above the toilet so we could avoid clogs (don't ask).

Almost every room in their house had wood paneling, with dirt-filled grooves, cream and brown shag carpet, a large wood stove, moose horns hanging on the wall above the mantel, and some very disconcerting examples of taxidermy mounted throughout the living room—their eyes following you. On more than one occasion, I put some of Aunt Pat's dishtowels or hats over their faces. Uncle Jack's closets and cupboards were packed. There was no such thing as taking bullets out of the guns or hiding weapons. The "don't touch it without asking" rule was never enforced. We somehow managed to set our own limits—and stay alive.

LIMON LAKE

Uncle Jack knew how to have fun; the parts of his skin that saw the sun would become rich, espresso dark, which paired beautifully with his clear blue eyes. He had the whitest legs, chest, and upper arms that you have ever seen. The differentiation was stark. I don't even want to imagine what the birthday suit version looked like.

During the summer, he would take us to Limon Lake on the

Apache Sitgreaves National Forest reservation to waterski, fish, and frog hunt. The kids' jobs were to clean the boat, help pack up the coolers, and behave—none of which ever happened. Instead, we would joust each other with fishing poles, spray each other with the hose, and pinch, tease, yell, and laugh until he would give up.

After everything was loaded up and the boat was hitched, the five cousins would crawl into the bed of the pickup. We each had a coveted spot. I loved to lean up against the passenger side, where I could talk to Uncle Jack through the small sliding window while his gray Weimaraner, Spooky, sniffed the wind. Once he hit the open road and wrenched it into high gear, our voices would be silenced by the face-numbing wind. In the glory of it all, I would open my arms like giant wings and pretend to fly.

We might not have shared physical DNA, but we shared the spiritual DNA of gypsies and rebels. The wind would turn to a breeze as the turn for the lake would come into view, and once we reached the shore, we could not unpack quickly enough and begin begging Uncle Jack for a ride on his eight-seater white boat. Once the boat launched, the rough afternoon waves bucking like a bronco under us and the lake reflecting a million coins of light, the cooling spray on our faces cleaned all my wounds, and my soul always danced in this place.

When night fell, the repeated dinner of hot dogs, salty chips, and cheap candy would fill our bellies. After the flimsy paper plates were thrown away, all of us cousins would travel from the campsite back to the boat, where we slept, our flashlights darting back and forth as we navigated the rough terrain in our thin rubber flip-flops. In the darkness, the boat would be transformed into part of a magical floating world. The air would hold sounds differently. The sky and water would become one with us. I was always the last to fall asleep, entertained by my imagination. I felt like I could walk on a glittering path of light up against the round moon and open it like a door. My hair would be decorated with stars; silver dust lay across my eyelids. I would swirl in a gown of Milky Way particles, dancing on the other side of everything.

REPUTABLE

My uncle's reputation preceded him in all instances. He was hard to deal with socially because he had a flare for exaggeration and rarely smelled pleasant. I am sad to confess that I always used a disclaimer before introducing him to anyone. I made sure it was known that I was adopted, and this apple did not fall from that crazy tree. His eccentricities created unease when I saw how others reacted, and that worsened as I got older.

LIFE IS STICKY

After everyone moved away, Uncle Jack and Aunt Pat stayed on the mountain, continuing to enjoy life with each other. Then Aunt Pat started having health problems. Her thyroid began creating heart palpitations. Pinetop was remote and not known for its specialized medical care, so she headed to Phoenix for a follow-up cardiology appointment. Uncle Jack stayed home to work, and until his dying day, he regretted that choice. She passed out in the Salt River Canyon, halfway to Phoenix, and she never regained consciousness.

Aunt Pat was put on life support in a run-down hospital in a small town named Globe. Within hours, scattered family members arrived at the hospital, but she was already brain-dead. It was the first time I ever saw my uncle cry. There was no June bug dancing on a string that could help us now. Aunt Pat was only forty-seven years old. It all felt cruel and underhanded. But someone still had to decide whether and when to take her off life support.

We all went to a Denny's restaurant so everyone could sit and have coffee. The windows were unacceptably dirty. Our family smashed into a stiff leather booth, large purses getting in the way; everything felt sticky—the air, the mugs, the coffee, and the moment. My uncle sat down last, in a heap of despair, his elbows on the menu, his head in his hands, facing a decision that didn't take him long to make.

He looked up, raising his hooded eyelids. "She would not want to live like this. I will let her go and donate her organs. She would want that."

Uncle Jack stood up, leaning on the table as he calibrated his movements. A rush of images ran through my mind as we followed the shadow of his pain. In full spectrum color, I could see him and Pat rolling on the floor kissing, hugging, teasing, joking—recalling the fun they had, her blue eyes, her soft hair, and the way she loved us. I realized that she would never get to see her son marry. She would never see her grandchildren. But most of all, I felt despair; I did not know what would become of Uncle Jack without her.

Aunt Pat's funeral was open casket. She looked peaceful, with a slight smile on her face, her soft blond hair styled in wide curls piled high on her head, and the fabric of her favorite pastel-green dress falling over her body just right. I stood close to her casket, feeling the smooth, cold edge of death.

BUM HEEL RANCH

For a while, my uncle tried to live in the home they had shared, but the memories were too heart-ripping. He would tell me that he always thought she would come through the door at any moment, and that sensation never let up. He could still smell her perfume and feel her presence in everything. So, he moved out of the house, making it a museum, taking only his clothes and an old RV.

He spent two years driving that RV as far left and as far right as he could until he drove his grief into the pavement—the dirt rounds, the sharp turns, the storms, the sunrises and sunsets—until he was ready to come home. Most of us predicted, by the length of his beard, that he would live out his days counting money in his swim shorts and a white T-shirt while eating food straight out of the can.

GLORIA, GLORIA

After being a widower for way too long, Uncle Jack decided to quit his lifelong smoking habit. He joined an archeological club, and there, he met wife number three, Gloria. They were perfectly paired in their eccentricities and free-spirited ways. Their love of Kachina dolls, old books, artifacts, animals, and canning gave them plenty to work with.

The whole family was up in arms when they announced that they were buying a remote chunk of land outside of Heber, Arizona—WAY outside of Heber, Arizona—beyond any paved roads, electricity, or plumbing. For them, it was a canvas for their dreams; for us, it felt like insanity.

Regardless of the harsh family judgments, they turned their ranch into a sanctuary that antelope, hummingbirds, and people flocked to, with orchards of thick apricot, peach, and cherry trees, a pond with fish and a canoe, and a pig named Lily.

They built it on their own, and they took pride in each step of its evolution. They allowed the downtrodden to live and work and find safety in that place. They had epic Halloween parties and two decades of nights under the stars. I visited the ranch more than a dozen times over the years, and I was always inspired by the bounty of their dreams.

As Uncle Jack got older, the ranch became more dangerous for men who were still trying to rip and snort. Eventually, he fell from an old, rickety ladder and broke his heel, and for all his remaining days, he wore a special boot and walked with a limp. He always said the pain was worth it because, based on that, they named their ranch "Bum Heel."

OUTSIDE OF HEBER

It was my fifty-third birthday, September 30, 2018. I made it just in time. I was outside of Heber, way outside, pulling up to an old ranch-style building with a gravel parking lot. The sky was just the way I like it—crisp blue, with a few scattered, lovely, plump white clouds. My cousin Richard was waiting outside to greet us in his red ball cap, cowboy belt, and dark sunglasses.

Inside, my uncle lay, dying of lung cancer from the cigarettes he had put out long ago. I was so glad that Wongee wasn't there to see her son die this way. These are memories no one wants to share. Her two children would die five months apart, in two different states. I could barely inhale the grief.

Inside the lobby of a ranch-style hospice facility, my senses were assaulted with ads, newspapers, quotes, calendars, and bright artwork stuck to a corkboard the size of Texas. The breeze was quick, rushing behind us, fluttering the pinups. I squinted.

The smell confronted me—a mix of mashed potatoes, Pine-Sol, and the sweet, fruity smell of those weird plastic air fresheners. I reminded myself that I could do this. Gloria appeared, leading us—me, my son, his girlfriend, and my husband Troy— into my uncle's room.

I was taken aback by how small the room was. Uncle Jack was lying on a low, cot-like bed, covered by a thin white sheet so transparent that you could see the pattern of his hospital gown through it. When I saw his hollowed face, my heart shattered. His messy hair was white as the clouds, his skin still a rich brown. He smiled a toothless grin and waited for my reaction. Any attempt to contain myself slipped away. I was startled by his appearance. How quickly cancer had taken its toll.

He asked me for his dirty, large-frame glasses so he could see "his favorite girl" better. As I placed them crookedly on his face, his thick goodbye tears dropped in soft succession. I sat beside him; we drove back in time to his old truck and all those dusty, dreamy days. As we recalled memories, he nodded and whispered, "I've had a good life."

I collapsed into him as deep as I could, my head right on his heart. His calloused hand patted me, and he said, "It's okay, Heidi, it's okay. Everything is okay."

I told him he was ornery, and we laughed again. I stood above his bed and held his hand until our fingers slipped away. The lobby was no less offensive as I walked out crying. Then Richard came out and said, "Heidi, don't go. He wants to see you again."

When I walked back into the tiny room, the breeze had picked up and was lifting the curtains in waves. The light seemed ambient. Voices of a church choir next door entered the room. I fell into him once again, and while he patted me on the back, he repeated, "It's okay, Heidi. I just wanted to see you one more time."

We looked at each other. I saw the man who had saved me, the man who taught me that we should all live a windows-down life. He was the person who allowed my soul to move on the dance floor of imagination. If I could do it all again, I would have announced his presence with a red carpet, been proud to be an apple falling anywhere close to his crazy tree, and, without a doubt, tied my heart around him like a June bug on a string.

CHAPTER 7
UNCLE SMACK

THEME 7: UNCENSORED
Alysa Zalma, MD

This chapter offers some comic relief to the previously heavy chapters that precede it. Heidi had a positive male role model to teach her not to take herself too seriously. Her humor is one of the many healing qualities she provides to the reader. In humorous and poignant references to adapting to a more "male-dominated" household of sibling peers, she also comes to understand how she saw the value of the generous, kindhearted rebel that was her Uncle Jack.

> **Despite a few colorful qualities, his heart was wide, and his dreams were deep. In the breadth of his love, he gathered the lost, the weak, and the less fortunate—be they four-legged, two-legged, or otherwise. He will forever be the closest thing I had to a father—an embarrassing father, but a father, nonetheless.**

In his rebellion and seeming disregard for the mores of society, he taught Heidi to care less about what other people think.

> **He seemed oblivious to everyone's eye-rolling and admonition; his lack of self-awareness was his freedom. We might not have shared physical DNA, but we shared the spiritual DNA of gypsies and rebels.**

She found healing from her adoptive family at her uncle Jack's house, where the lack of rules was an oasis, and the environment of love and affection between her uncle and aunt was new to her. Having adults who loved each other and displayed affection was healing; it provided a framework for healthy adult relationships.

One of the most healing aspects of Uncle Jack was his ability to be present in Heidi's life as a more stable, empathic, and psychologically healthier man than her father. He did not ask her too many questions about her home life but provided his home for healthier child development. He nonthreateningly let her know that he felt that her father had psychiatric challenges that were not her fault. She felt, in some ways, healed. She did not feel that her father's abuse was due to her shortcomings or something she did to anger him. She felt absolved of the responsibility. In this way, Uncle Jack helped Heidi dispel some of the guilt she felt about her adoption. Her abuse was unrelated to her inability to be a more perfect child.

In an odd way, his acknowledgment helped me feel vaguely understood and less responsible.

When my patients tell me their stories of abuse, it is sometimes healing to acknowledge their parents' psychiatric challenges in a nonthreatening way that does not prompt them to run to the aid of the abusive parent to protect them. Many patient responses are similar to Heidi's. They feel tremendous relief from guilt and feelings of fault.

Heidi also learned about adventure, fearlessness, and freedom from her Uncle Jack. Sailing with him proved to be some of her most profound healings.

Once he hit the open road and wrenched it into high gear, our voices would be silenced by the face-numbing wind. In the glory of it all, I would open my arms like giant wings and pretend to fly . . .

. . . the cooling spray on our faces cleaned all my wounds, and my soul always danced in this place.

He took Heidi through nature; sailing and camping became some of the most sacred refuges of her life that she could build upon and return to later in her life. These experiences also inspired her to have imagination and deepened her spirituality to connect with herself through nature in a powerful and healing way.

I felt like I could walk on a glittering path of light up against the round moon and open it like a door.

When she became older and more in tune with the social mores of her environment, she felt conflicted between what Uncle Jack offered her and what society might think of him; she started to make excuses for his eccentricities.

I made sure it was known that I was adopted, and this apple did not fall from that crazy tree.

As she grew to adulthood, she realized how vital he was to her survival. At his death, she could tell him how much he had been one of her saviors.

We looked at each other. I saw the man who had saved me. . . . I would have announced his presence with a red carpet, been proud to be an apple falling anywhere close to his crazy tree . . .

To be a psychiatrist is to have the honor and challenge of being offered an attempt to be an Uncle Jack. Some of the tools we are afforded in psychiatry allow us to come close. This chapter speaks to the resilience of the human experience and offers hope that through a character such as Uncle Jack, a corrective emotional experience is possible. Even if adoptees such as Heidi have varying levels of abusive households that they relate to their adoptive experience, the presence of a positive parental figure or mental health professional at any time in their lives may stimulate neuroplasticity and allow the adoptee to traverse these traumas.

CHAPTER 8
WEEZY

"Sister, the day I found you is the day I came home. You decorated the walls around my heart and opened a door that I never knew existed."

—H. Marble

WEEZY

Jennifer Louise, my biological sister, is, beyond doubt, the "aggressive" to my "passive." She takes less-than-zero bullshit while I allow myself to be buried in it. She is the woman that I, in the safety of my conservative constructs, can only imagine being—bold and beautiful.

Her eyes are denim-blue, with glints of deep green, and her nose is rounder than mine, which makes me jealous. She is also a lot more photogenic and seems to have a much better sense of fashion. I lean toward all black (okay, that's all I wear). If someone sasses me about it, I just tell them I am dressing for their funeral. Her closet is a bounty of colorful prints, thick sweaters, sexy shoes, a lot of expensive perfumes, and Louis Vuitton bags that I occasionally get to hold (grab).

My daily grooming ritual is to put my hair up in the same clip, in the same style that I have been wearing since the 1980s. Also, I apply the same pale lipstick from the same era, which my sister insists is what the dead wear. She's not afraid of plums, pinks, and corals. She takes her time getting ready while I stand by and watch in my plastic clipped-up hair. She sleeps naked but is forbidden to do it when we share a bed. I wear pajama sets with long sleeves and extra-large bottoms. We both love food, but I love it more. She introduced me to the glory of homemade chicken soup poured over mashed potatoes, baked pineapple, spinach balls, Blue Moon beer, flavored vodka, and chocolate cupcakes with peanut butter frosting.

Everything she touches becomes more wondrous. To think that she lived in this world and that I didn't even know about her until I was thirty-three sends shivers down my untattooed spine. Considering how close I came to never knowing my sister gives me breath-into-a-paper-bag anxiety. What happened after we discovered each other is as complicated and beautiful as all love stories.

TOO MENY

Let's just get this straight before I rant. I love men, especially the blond, beachy ones. I can't resist golden hair in the sun. But growing up with all boys eventually became exhausting, especially after I veered into puberty. Their adolescent ways did nothing but annoy me.

I *always* wanted a sister. I even made up an imaginary one. I named her Rachel; she helped me plot revenge against boys with smelly armpits. I would envy the bond I witnessed between my friends and their sisters, even though it was fraught with drama. I was captivated by what it must be like to have someone so like/unlike you, and I wanted that. I had no idea that I had a sister 3,000 miles away, in another world. We were living parallel lives, both immersed in boys—one brother and two stepbrothers, to be exact. She knew about Marty's "extra" baby, but because it was assumed that I was a boy, Jen didn't have a burning desire to chase me down.

HALF HAS NEVER BEEN SO FULL

The ricochet of emotion that befuddled me when I heard my birth mother say, "You have a sister thirteen months younger than you," is hard to describe in words; it is not often that a dream like this walks into reality. Marty told me that when she flew back from Pennsylvania after giving birth to me in Arizona, John Schuster, who would become my sister's father, was waiting for her with a bouquet of flowers. Marty and John had an on-and-off relationship that had been further complicated by my birth father; the two men had collided in a robust physical altercation to win her affection. Now, with my father and his baby out of the picture, John saw his chance to win her back. You don't need to do the math; it wasn't long until my sissy was on her way. Marty married John, and three years later, they had my brother, Jeffie "Pangy." But Marty wasn't meant for staying.

YOUR NEW BROTHER IS A GIRL (OH MY GOD, THERE ARE TWO OF THEM!)

This baby "boy," or so they thought, who had been relinquished in Arizona, was never a secret. Every member of this big, welcoming Pennsylvania Dutch family supported Marty Jo's decision to give me up for adoption, understanding the harsh circumstances of her youth and my father's untimely death. My biological mother's eagerness to meet me in broad daylight and invite everyone to join her gave me a luscious feeling of acceptance. Her shock that I was a girl started this permanent saying: "Oh God, there are two of them."

The afternoon when Marty and I were reunified slipped away quickly into freckled gray twilight. She was absolutely giddy to unite her daughters for the first time. I repeatedly wiped my sweaty hands on my high-waisted jeans as we waited for Jen's arrival. When her rhythmic knock sounded on the door, Marty Jo bounced up like a baby deer, holding my sweaty hand. The thick brown laminated door opened, and just like that, my sister appeared, reflecting my own features.

I screamed—cried—screamed. I had never seen anyone who looked like me. There she stood, a taller version of me, with better hair and an espresso-colored suit. Her reaction was much the same. As we giggled and hugged our way through those first moments, Marty was aglow beside us. That night, I would also meet my brother, Jeffie, for the first time. A tall, handsome, manly man, he put me at ease with his humor and wit. Members of my extremely tall biological dad's family joined us, helping to unfold the mystery of my beginning. It felt as if some parts of me that had collapsed were filling out, opening, and expanding.

HEREDITY VERSUS ENVIRONMENT

The next day, the snow from the winter storm that had tried to kill me a few days earlier started to melt. The sun found its full glory in a periwinkle sky, highlighting the streaked dirt on our windshield. The car smelled of perfume and clean diapers. My sister invited us for an early dinner so I could meet my eleven-year-old niece, Ronni, and my five-year-old nephew, Tyler. I was in a dreamlike state as we settled into a parking space right in front of Jen's apartment. I noticed that her door wreath, made of twisted vines, was almost identical to mine. Through the small kitchen window, I could see Marty busy at the sink, a luminescence around her. Jen's hair was pulled back, so we looked like identical twins. A wave of delicious smells and adorable children with thick hair and peachy skin welcomed us.

Jen and I had the same cookbooks, the same style of decorating, and the same mannerisms—so many sames. There was a feeling of home that I had never experienced before. As I watched Jen and Marty Jo side-by-side in the kitchen, teasing, laughing, and cooking, I felt my chest tighten as a sense of confusion and curiosity set in. How could this relationship be so strong after Marty had walked out on them? How could she have left behind all three of us? Marty left the family when they were just children.

SHE WATCHED HER GO

When Jen told me about the leaving, I shattered inside; breathing felt difficult as she described the cold winter night when Marty walked out. Jen was three years old, and Jeffie was just six months. Jen stood on the stair landing of their two-story house on Curtain Street. Dusk rushed winter's cold breath through the open door. Jen was holding her fear, Marty was holding her suitcases, and John was holding Jeffie in a wooden rocking chair. There had been a fight about Marty's infidelity, and when John told her to leave, she took him up on it. My sister begged her not to go, but Marty said to her, "I have to leave. You and your brother are going to stay with your dad."

Marty took her suitcases, loaded them into a white wood-paneled station wagon, and drove away from a life not meant for her. My sister did not recall which of her mother's lovers had caused the breakup. It was either "Pooch," a brown-haired, whiskey-drinking state police officer, or the sexy, tall, blond flared-pant photographer. For dramatic purposes here, let's just go with the sexy, blond photographer. The only evidence left of him now is a picture he took of my birth mother, staring intensely into the camera, her hair parted down the middle, her marijuana roach clip, with a burning joint sending up a ribbon of smoke.

That evening, as I watched Marty, with her short bob cut, and Jen bantering in the kitchen, it was hard to imagine that scene—her walking out on her children. I could not fathom how they could have such a great relationship after such a devastating blow. Had it been me, it would not have gone that way. I hold onto my grudges as if they were naughty children—they ain't getting away from me. It's hard for me to confess this, but I even held on to resentment of Marty on behalf of my sister and brother. I could never stop asking, "How could Marty have left all three of us?"

But my sister didn't ask probing questions or hold onto the pain. She accepted Marty with love and understanding. Jen's hurt was never fueled by resentment, revenge, or judgment. Her eyes saw deeper, and her heart remained open while my vision and heart shut like a vault.

RED RABBIT

Marty's sexy photographer lived in Harrisburg, 1.5 hours from Bellefonte, and that's where Marty unpacked her suitcases for a few years. John figured out a way to be okay with Marty spending time with Jen and Jeffie. He agreed to occasionally meet her at the Red Rabbit Ice Cream Shop, the halfway point, so Jen and Jeffie could spend a weekend with Marty Jo. Jen remembers picnics at Spring Creek, with buckets of Kentucky fried chicken, where they could run barefoot in the sun while Marty parented from the only platform she could—*freedom*. And, each time, Jen fell more in love with the woman who couldn't stay. Those greasy-fingered, barefooted days always ended too quickly. My sister recalls their dirty-footed, tear-filled goodbyes as Marty drove away. No amount of Red Rabbit Ice Cream could remedy that pain.

PARADE

When my sister was five years old, John fell in love with Nina, a beautiful, spunky woman with a hearty giggle, round curves, and two little boys. Jen was beyond excited because she had been looking for a mommy since Marty left. On multiple occasions, she had even tried to convince their housekeeper, Bessie, to marry her dad. Bessie had to refuse Jen's proposals because of her advanced age. That hardly felt like an excuse to Jen.

On a breezy spring afternoon, shortly after John and Nina married, Jen set up a chair under a sprawling cottonwood tree. She went into the house, grabbed a surprised Nina, sat her down under the tree, and asked her to wait. Nina did what she was told, enjoying the lacy shade. With tears in her eyes, she saw Jen grab as many neighbors as she could organize into a parade to introduce everyone to her new mother. Nina became and still is a steady force in Jen's life, a strong female who could dilute the constant barrage of testosterone in Jen's life. Nina gave Jen shelter and a secure place to attach her heart, and she never stood in the way of Jen's need to love both of her mothers.

AGAIN AND AGAIN

All grown up, Jen still loved Marty fully; she embraced the ebb and flow of Marty's presence and built a relationship that was rare and, despite it all, nourishing. For her part, Marty poured her free-spirited ways over Jen's children, lavishing them with time, adventure, stability, and Unimart hot dogs. None of that would have happened if Jen had allowed her resentment to destroy the beauty of her love.

Then there's me. I lost respect for Marty quickly after I learned about her abandonment of my sister and brother. It seemed shocking that she would give me up, then turn around and get pregnant again with my sister—and then *again* with my brother—and then leave *again*. My understanding was surface level, I admit. But I had no desire to go deeper. I just saw it as a slurry of selfish decisions. I was in no mood to entertain Marty Jo's reasons why; leaving one child was bad enough, but leaving all your children is something I couldn't reconcile. I wanted Marty to feel bad at some level. I kept her at arm's length. For her part, Marty accepted my feelings without judgment—even with understanding and compassion. She never played the guilt card. She was just happy that her children had a relationship.

BICOASTAL

Within a year of meeting my sister, I was diagnosed with breast cancer. We both got caught up in the frenzy of young children, new marriages, and health issues. Despite having our problems to contend with, we found a way to see each other and celebrate our newfound sisterhood. In the beginning, I would tell my adoptive mother about my plans, with full transparency. I would even try to include her. But with every effort I made, she exerted her power over me. My guilt became so unbearable that I made a decision I still regret.

The wrath of my adoptive mother's disapproval was relentless, and when we moved to Northern California, I emotionally collapsed under the pressure. In Mother's view, any kind of relationship with my biological family was a slap in the face to the family that raised me. My heart became a mud puddle of sloppy pain. I came to feel like an ungrateful shit for wanting them in my life. The spiritual debt was flaming red with grief, anger, shame, and guilt.

Under that pressure, I literally had to focus on surviving for my son and giving myself a chance to heal from the cancer that ravaged me. I decided, reluctantly, to pull away from my sister—a vain attempt to keep the peace. That turned out to be the wrong choice because, no matter what I did, peace was beyond our grasp. Now Jen and I were back where we started, living parallel lives, 3,000 miles apart, while I stayed chained to my obligations, trying to pick the lock and escape so I could find my way back to my sissy.

REBELLION ROAD

Apparently, the women in my family of origin do not take kindly to being controlled. After nearly five years of sparse communication, my sister called out of the blue. My first thought was that maybe she had news about Marty, who had been battling cancer on and off. Her voice felt so good in my ears; then my heart split open when she said, "I thought you would want to know that I have breast cancer."

As I took in what she was saying, I felt the lock break and the chains fall away. I was done giving her up. Never again. With the delicate nature of an enraged bull, I called my adoptive mother and told her that I was going to have a relationship with my sister, period. Exclamation point! I told her about Jen's cancer diagnosis, hoping that would "be the change" that made it all right. Nope. My mother's response was unrelenting. "Do what you have to do. I don't want to know about it, talk about it, or hear about it."

It seemed unimaginable that not only my very real brush with death but now my sister's wasn't enough to bring her around. This time, though, I didn't feel shame. I felt rage.

WHIMPY

I started off all big, scary, puffed up, and spiky. I was ready to blaze a trail straight to my sister, no matter the ramifications. Instead, I deflated back in the face of my mother's blaring disapproval, quickly sending me slithering my way into evasion—either lying by omission or just flat-out lying. Basically, I started to have an "affair" with my sister.

My career in speaking provided the perfect cover for my traveling lies. All my keynote speeches focused on breast cancer survivorship. My career took me all over the United States and provided opportunities for secret adventures that my sister and I could want. During our times together, my sister tolerated my daily calls to my mother while she had to remain silent in the background. I am not sure if my sister was flattered, annoyed, or both. I justified my lying by convincing myself that my mother expected me to do that because she didn't want to hear, talk, or know about it. So, it was okay.

I can't imagine what a priest would think of that confession. I would probably be dipped in holy water and thrown out like a wet cat. Lucky for me, my sister loved, accepted, and understood that I was doing what I had to do, and she didn't judge me. We just enjoyed every second we had together. Thankfully, she survived her cancer, which was caught at an early stage, and although she endured a lumpectomy and radiation, she suffered no chemotherapy. She worked and lived fully during all of it. I, on the other hand, rolled over like a dead beetle, my legs sticking up in the air, dazed and confused by what cancer did to all the parts of me.

TIGHT MUSCLES

Whenever I would return from a rendezvous with Jen, the guilt would grow more intense, strengthening my bulging muscles of remorse. The belief that I was a bad person, with no hope for redemption, allowed me easy access to the dark alleys of the forbidden. After all, I had already done enough to get a one-way ticket straight to the fiery pits of hell. My "it's too late now, might as well have some fun" approach fueled the continuation of lies. I know now that I should have lived the truth, that all of us deserved that. But not then, and so the weight of regret, shame, and other "icky" stuff bulked up like a bodybuilder on steroids. I was, at heart, angry that my adopted mother didn't see that I wanted to be loved for all of me, and that included the adopted part. I wanted to stand in front of her and say, "My name is Heidi! I am adopted! I have two mothers! I have a sister, an adoptive brother whom I miss, and a biological brother whom I wish I knew more. Two mothers, a wongee, and two dead fathers. Why can't that be okay? Why can't I love all of you?"

It never—*never*—was okay. I could never make it right, so I chose wrong.

PRCLESS PCOFWRK

We both have vanity plates on our vehicles. Mine is *PRCLESS* because my husband called me priceless during an argument once, and so I went to the DMV to act out my revenge. My sister's plate is *PCOFWRK* for obvious reasons. Our vehicles, shopping carts with European engines, are important accomplices in our black-belt retail therapy sprees. We are both known for throwing a really good party. If you want to celebrate right, we are your girls. Together, we can spend our husbands' combined incomes in less than an hour and not even break a sweat. There have been countless times when we have driven down the road with a rug or other wide-load item sticking out of the windows. I even rode with my legs dangling out of her open trunk, holding a mess of branches to make a DIY arbor, her PCOFWRK license plate in between my legs.

We arranged weddings, funerals, showers, graduations, birthdays, holidays, move-ins, and move-outs, all of which tested our tolerance of each other. My sister's attention to detail and incredible physical stamina have contrasted with my "that's good enough; let's watch Netflix" attitude on more than one occasion. But when we are grooving, magic happens. In the end, we always step back in amazement at what we can accomplish together. When the guests arrive, we start clinking glasses. Watching people move in our world of too much food and twinkle lights brings both of us rich satisfaction. After my one drink and her ten, the faucet sprayer might become a microphone. We may even spread the edible glitter that we used on the raspberries onto our lips and dance until the floor is scuffed.

GLITTER IN THE AIR

I am far more morose, worried, and dramatic (okay, negative) than my sister. She sees absolutely no point in worrying about imagined outcomes. She prefers the world of denial, and the older I get, the more appealing denial sounds. Her "it is what it is" attitude is upsetting. When I want sympathy and attention from her, no matter my health concerns, relationship woes, or anxiety issues, the solution is the same:

deal with it when it happens. There is no time on her clock for wasting life on what could be instead of what really is. Jen gives great advice, and she is a great listener, even tolerating my personal funeral ideas, which have varied greatly over the years.

On a ride through Amish country, on the way to one of our shopping adventures, I told her to make sure that upon my demise, I would be dressed in my sparkly, pink cocktail dress with a matching pink coffin covered in jewelry. She could add a darker pink lipstick if she wanted. I told her to make sure to put a fire extinguisher in the casket in case I was going down instead of up. As soon as I started listing desserts for my heartbroken guests to enjoy at my memorial, she stopped me and said, "I *don't* want any of that. I am going to be cremated and mixed with glitter." Slightly miffed, I looked out of the window at the sprawling farms, with aprons hanging from clotheslines, and I made a decision—I want to be mixed with glitter, too.

GROUNDHOG DAY

My sister may come across as fearless—until you put her on an elevated roadway, in front of a snake, or around a dead groundhog. It has become my job to drive over, remove, and dispose of the aforementioned. The last time I visited her, I was in the kitchen, and my sister was in the yard, when I heard what I thought was a murder in progress. In the middle of her yard was a groundhog the size of a small horse, spread out like an ottoman, clearly no longer with us. She insisted I "take" it away, to which I replied, "I am not touching that thing."

I went into the garage and found a wide shovel while my sister screamed at her dogs to get away from the deceased. I approached in my calm "*I got this*" walk and placed the shovel under the groundhog. It turned out to be heavier than I expected. I held the shovel as far away from myself as I could, my arms shaking, and my sister yelled, "Fling it, fling it!"

What? Fling it? By then, I was laughing so hard that I could barely balance the hog. I swung the shovel, and the groundhog sailed through the air, into the stream, with a plop and a splash.

Secretly, I love it when Jen is scared of things that I am not afraid of. I can be Big Sissy. I will always be happy to be her hog-flinging, snake-removing, high-road-driving big sister.

FORGIVENESS

When I called Jen to ask her to help me with this chapter, what I really wanted to know was how she managed to not hold resentment toward her abandonment. I needed to hear her heart. Jen told me that shortly before Marty died, they sat at her kitchen table while Marty tried to coax anger out of Jen, telling her that she might be in denial. Marty wanted to give Jen a chance to be angry, to let Marty Jo "have it" before she died. Marty wanted Jen to deal with the pain and give her an opportunity to apologize for the pain she had caused her daughter.

That's when Jen looked her straight in the eye and said, "There is nothing to forgive. You did what you had to do. I don't judge you; I've treasured every moment we've had. You are my mother, and I loved you then, and I love you now."

As she spoke, I imagined them sitting together. I can see Marty's face soften. I can picture it all so clearly, one healing the other. That triggered me. I started crying and apologizing for not being a better big sissy, explaining that there are not enough hogs to throw to make up for hiding our relationship. I apologized for not having the courage to live my truth, for any distance I ever put between us. Not surprisingly, Jen said, "There is nothing to forgive. You did what you had to do. I don't judge you. I love you then, and I love you now."

I sat, stunned, realizing that the love she gave Marty is also the love she has given me. Her acceptance has allowed space for us to have a rare, nourishing relationship; she has given me the chance to love her amazing children, to share her life, as she embraced the ebb and flow of my presence. Thank you for the beauty, Jen. Thank you for being the "hell yeah!" to my "hell no!" Until we turn into glitter, I will always be a pain in your sparkly-jeaned ass.

CHAPTER 8
WEEZY

THEME 8: UNCONDITIONAL LOVE, SELF-LOVE, AND COMING HOME

Alysa Zalma, MD

Where is love?
Does it fall from skies above?
Is it underneath the willow tree
That I've been dreaming of?
Where is she
Who I close my eyes to see?
Will I ever know the sweet hello
That's meant for only me?

Who can say where she may hide?
Must I travel far and wide?
Til I am beside the someone who
I can mean something to
Where, where is love?
—Lyrics, *Oliver Twist* original soundtrack,
Oliver! Broadway production, Lionel Bart, 1968

The orphan Oliver, from Charles Dickens's second novel *Oliver Twist*, in the original 1968 Broadway musical production, sings of his yearning for unconditional love. Heidi, always searching for unconditional love from her adoptive and biological mothers, finds it in her biological sister. From Jen/Weezy, she learns some of her most valuable life lessons.

As an adoptee, Heidi learned that much of the experience of love is conditional. Heidi felt that one of Joy's conditions for love was complete allegiance. This may be a common experience for many adoptees, who fear this condition will arise if they become more curious about their biological families.

Many adopted children feel they must "earn" love and be grateful for their adoption, experiencing fear that they are not good enough. Heidi felt her adoptive mother's love became more conditional when she continued a relationship with her biological sister, especially after Jen suffered from the same breast cancer diagnosis as she did.

Heidi could not fathom how her sister was seemingly able to give and receive unconditional love. Heidi could not understand how Jen could love their mother the way she did after the abandonment. She felt the same way after their (Jen and Heidi's) five-year hiatus and subsequent reunification. How could Jen not harbor resentment?

The concept of unconditional love is elusive for many. The resultant traumas of not receiving it (or being unable to receive it) are, unfortunately, more accessible. Much of the psychiatric and psychotherapy literature since the 1950s concerning the "cure" focuses on the reparation of this trauma. American psychologist Dr. Carl Rogers became famous and revered due to his therapeutic interventions that approximated unconditional love in the therapeutic relationship. He pioneered the term "unconditional positive regard" to designate the technique and allow people to experience something akin to unconditional love in the therapeutic relationship (Rogers 1957). This concept worked its way into popular culture and eventually became part of the parenting norms. Parents were advised to love their children for who they are and not for what they do or don't do.

Mr. Roger's Neighborhood, which originally aired in 1967, amplified this theme. The program was one of the most watched television shows for children and their parents in television history and aired for thirty-one seasons (https://www.misterrogers.org). Mr. Fred Rogers (not unlike Dr. Carl Rogers) spoke to his audiences about the importance of unconditional love and how to offer unconditional positive regard. He would end each episode with a variation of "It's you I like. You always make each day a special day. You know how, by just your being you" (https://www.misterrogers.org/watch). One may wonder if things may have been different if Heidi's family had said this to her at the end of every day.

Because Jen was able to offer Heidi this "unconditional positive regard" and unconditional love, Heidi began to heal from some of the traumas related to her adoption, specifically concerning the "betrayal" of her adoptive mother. If Jen could forgive their biological mother for leaving them and Heidi for "abandoning" her for five years, then perhaps Heidi could start forgiving herself and others for all that happened as a result of her adoption.

Heidi loves and admires Jen. She feels that Jen is like their biological mother, bold and beautiful, and she does not seem to care about what other people think.

In contrast to Heidi's black wardrobe, Jen wears colorful clothes, has tattooed her body, and wears glittered jeans. Heidi loves that she has someone to look up to and admire. The clichéd Freudian symbolism of the handbag (the Louis Vuitton purse she gets to grab) is that it represents female genitalia (Freud 1965, 408). This interpretation had much to do with the social mores of Freud's day and the historical context of the Victorian era.

In a more recent and modern description of the handbag, *The New York Times* author Daphne Markin said, "Bags also serve as the portable manifestation of a woman's sense of self, a detailed and remarkably revealing map of her interior, an omnium-gatherum of myriad aspects of her life" (Markin 2006). Part of what Heidi admires in Jen is that she has a solid and beautiful sense of self. Thus, it would make sense that Jen's purses are valuable and beautiful and that Heidi "covets" them.

The initial meeting of the sisters was a fairy tale that came true. Discovering similar physical attributes and mannerisms was gratifying to Heidi. This is what many adoptees seek. They may wonder if their genetics can contribute to their feelings of love and acceptance within their shared biology.

Heidi describes the experience of meeting her sister for the first time:

Sister, the day I found you is the day I came home. You decorated the walls around my heart and opened a door I never knew existed.

The experience of "coming home" is one that the ancient shamanic Soul Retrieval ceremony hopes to accomplish. The ceremony is still practiced today by more contemporary shamanic practitioners (Ingerman 1991, 43). The ceremony energetically and symbolically returns the client's soul pieces to them. The client is "reunited" with themselves, the way that Heidi was reunited with Jen. Heidi describes this feeling of being reunited and "coming home."

The thick brown laminated door opened, and just like that, my sister appeared, reflecting my own features.
I screamed—cried—screamed. I had never seen anyone who looked like me.
There was a feeling of home that I had never experienced before.

The experience of unconditional love is an integral part of the experience of coming home.

Heidi felt "at home" with Jen from their first meeting when she saw the biological similarities she had with her sister. Heidi eventually "left" her sister for five years because her adoptive mother was jealous of their relationship. She experienced unconditional love when she returned to Jen after she learned of her illness, and Jen forgave her for leaving the relationship. The ability to receive love—even if one feels they do not deserve it, especially so—and forgive is what Jen was able to offer Heidi.

Heidi also saw Jen's ability for unconditional love toward their biological mother in that Jen was able to forgive Marty Jo for her abandonment.

> **. . . with buckets of Kentucky fried chicken, where they could run barefoot in the sun. . . . Those greasy-fingered, barefooted days always ended too quickly.**

Despite her ethereal experiences of the innocence of her childhood, Jen offered unconditional love to Marty Jo. Jen was "at home" in the world and within herself. She was able to be her own unconditional parent/sister/self. Being able to find unconditional love toward oneself is one of the definitions of true love.

One of my patients, a twenty-one-year-old adopted non-binary person, asked me how to find true love. I asked them for a list of traits they would want in their ideal partner. They were surprised but happy to provide the list. They had been compiling it since middle school. The partner had to be tall, good with kids, take a special interest in family, have a good job, know how to cook, and put them first and make them feel special. We looked deeply into why this was the list. The "tall" was really about safety and protection. The "good with kids" was about trusting that their partner would care for a younger version of themselves because they felt this piece of themself had never been taken care of. They understood that the list they derived was aimed at a potential partner who could be (at least in fantasy) their biological family. They had fantasized about their birth family and the unconditional love they longed for. At the end of this exercise, they also realized that the list was the attributes they wanted in themselves. They wanted to find a partner who symbolized their biological family and also wanted to find true love in their relationship with themselves.

The concepts of coming home, unconditional love, and self-love as "true love" are what Heidi learns from her biological sister, Jen. These are the experiences that every adoptee must find.

CHAPTER 9
LOVE CAN BUILD A BRIDGE

Regarding the love of my life, Troy Alan Marble,
a literal and figurative bridge builder
"Our love a bridge, two sides connected
over the otherwise impassible."
—H. Marble

"Burning a bridge takes too long. I prefer explosives."
—Rusafu

"A bridge has no allegiance to either side."
—Les Coleman

"To embark on the journey towards your own goals and dreams requires bravery. To remain on that path requires courage. The bridge that merges the two is commitment."
—Steve Maraboli

LIFE SPAN

This chapter has the greatest span to cross: our forty-year relationship. I am married to a bridge builder, and as it turns out, marriage has a lot in common with bridges. My husband has built some of the country's most beautiful structures. When I considered how to tell our love story, bridges, their purpose, and their structures came to the forefront. Bridges connect two sides, rising above whatever obstacle is preventing passage from one to the other. I wanted to understand how bridges are built and what fundamental qualities are required to create the ultimate structure. I asked my husband to sum it up. These are his words:

A bridge is strong if it has a good foundation. A bridge takes the weight placed upon it and transfers the load back into the foundation. If the foundation is not sturdy or it's placed in weak soil, it will be compromised, unable to sustain the weight. Bridges that stand the test of time and the ravages of nature are well designed to carry more than their capacity so they can withstand daily wear and extremes. If those stressors aren't considered, the bridge will eventually collapse and take down anything on, in, or around it.

THE WATER BELOW

The metaphorical bridge on which we find ourselves standing is a stunning work, a well-worn masterpiece. Constructed from fate, decision, and indecision, it is a relationship built on the deep foundation of relentless, unapologetic hope, tethered by cables that have held our bond, even in the throes of unimaginable storms. It is a bridge that has felt the weight of all that has crossed over, under, above, and through it—a connection between two sides that have been exposed to all kinds of weather, including our own destruction. Our greatest weakness as a couple has been allowing everything else to be a priority and forgetting that our relationship deserved attention, continued renovation, and retrofitting. In spite of some collateral damage, our bridge still stands after forty years because we have never given up at the same time. At this moment, we stand on two different ends, staring blankly across the gap, wondering what happened. Look at what we've built! Look at what we've destroyed! Our adult son, Blake, is freshly married, and that has cleared an empty roadway, a wide-open space to ask, *Now what?* We find ourselves trying to reach the side where we both started together: the same side.

I CAN SEE CLEARLY NOW

The blinding glare of denial has given way, and I miss it. There is almost too much pain to bear when I think about how my relinquishment through adoption has impacted my marriage. Decades have piled on, and my efforts to protect my heart have broken my heart and his. Being vulnerable left me open to more abandonment, or so I thought. We can leave without leaving, and both of us are really good at that. The deep love we crave is ours, but damn, it is a hell of a battle to change patterns. Both of us are black belts in passive-aggressive behavior. Nonetheless, there is so much beauty, so much left to fight for. I can see that my side of the bridge requires the most work. If I can build a roadway instead of more walls, we can meet once again and finish what we started.

SCOOB

He calls me Heidi-Heib, and I call him Scoob. (Sometimes we call each other things I won't mention.) Troy comes from a family of four boys—two older brothers and one younger. His parents divorced after the first two were born, and when they got back together, they had Roger and Troy. Troy's mom, Betty Lou, was known for her beauty, red hair, and fiery temper. His father, John, was a social alcoholic and a highly regarded builder. Neither of us hailed from exemplary examples of marriage, which makes our lasting union even more impressive.

Troy prefers jeans that are too long, blue shirts, and baseball caps. In high school, he was popular, a good football and baseball player. He was, and is, especially fond of baseball. His big dreams of becoming a pro baseball player were quickly dashed during his first year at Scottsdale Community College, the home of the Artichokes (what a horrible choice for a mascot!). Troy then turned his attention back to construction and joined the carpenters' union. He bought a tool belt and a high-quality hammer and began to build his way to success. Troy grew up covered in sawdust, surrounded by measuring tapes, saws, scaffolding, and his father's constant criticism. Building and fixing are in his blood.

Aside from his building skills, Troy can eat a bag of sunflower seeds faster than a chipmunk, knows how to chill beer in a creek, and generously applies Tabasco to everything he eats. He insists on being buried with a hammer in case he needs to escape. He continually reminds me and others that Jesus was a carpenter. Troy is obsessed with Apple products, Virtual Intelligence—and anything related to technology. His ability to troubleshoot a tech problem merely requires him to show up. His hair, eyelashes, and eyebrows are so blond that they almost disappear. He says the only mistake he has ever made is buying a pencil with an eraser. His love of the Red Socks and team swag leave little room for fashion exploration. Troy is a world-class flirt, is fond of blonds, and has absolutely no discretion when looking at a beautiful woman. He is beyond obsessed with his 401(k), the stock market, and how much I spend on groceries. He's a horrible swimmer and acts delicately in the rain. He can drive another person absolutely crazy channel surfing. Troy's intelligence mirrors that of *Rain Man*; he can recall just about anything. Above all else, Troy loves his family, and he is an incredible father not only to our son but to the many young people in our lives. He has given so much to so many, but he is rarely celebrated for it.

HEART TAKER

I first laid my green fifteen-year-old eyes on Troy Marble in October 1980. I am fairly certain that I was wearing something neon, and without a doubt, I had on Jordache jeans with parrots embossed on the pockets. I was with his brother, Roger, one of my best friends at the time. In spite of our friendship, I had never had an encounter with Troy. I was a long-limbed, unskilled cheerleader, and Roger was a permed-hair football player. Roger was the designated DJ for all our school dances. His blue Ford Bronco was tricked out with all the woofers and tweeters you could want, along with a fancy 8-track tape player and a portable boombox for football and cheerleading practice.

The day I met Troy, we headed to Roger's house right behind the football field to grab a few more 8-track tapes. Their modest brown house was inviting. Rex, their black lab, wagged his whole body as we opened the screen door. When I saw Troy sleeping on the rust and brown plaid couch—his curly mop of blond hair rimming a dark blue baseball cap, a thick reddish mustache, his flannel shirt, with chest hair peeking out—I stopped in my shag-carpeted tracks. I whispered to Roger, "Who is that?"

Snarling in disgust, he said, "My older brother, Troy."

Roger thumped Troy awake with a poke, making some smart-ass remark. Troy gave me a quick, uninterested glance, shoved Roger, grabbed his keys, jumped into his white Toyota pickup, and drove away, taking my heart with him. I pummeled Roger with questions, and I learned that Troy was a senior at our high school, and he had a beautiful girlfriend named Michelle. (Cue buzzkill.)

EWWW!

The next day, it didn't take long to find my way to senior hall to begin my seek-and-discover mission. I decided to risk life and limb to find out more about the man/boy who had taken my heart without so much as asking. I looked at the dreadful scene. I saw Troy in the sun-drenched parking lot, pressing up against Michelle, her back leaning on his white truck. A spotlight of sun followed them as they smiled, kissed, and hugged. It made me want to vomit the Twinkie I had just devoured.

Michelle was pretty, the way movie stars are pretty. She had crystal-blue eyes and woman boobs. My head hung as I was standing there in my training bra and retainer, with a face full of overly concealed pimples. In complete despair, I wanted to fling myself dramatically on the horribly patterned senior hall carpet and exclaim dramatically, "Go ahead, seniors, stampede on my freshman body until it is no more."

Passing on that impulse, I made my way back to the freshman zone, where everyone looked more like me; their arms were too long, and their rubber-band-brace smiles were goofy. That pimple-filled year continued, with all the tortures of puberty, and my heartbreak was further exacerbated by Troy and Michelle's displays of public affection, especially offensive during the Friday night dances. Just to twist the knife, they would find their way to the center of the dance floor. You couldn't see an ounce of light between their bodies. Discouraged, I would focus instead on the diluted Hawaiian punch and the stale Keebler striped chocolate cookies. I would make frequent trips to the bathroom to apply my cherry-flavored lip gloss and spackle more concealer on my zits. When a great song came on, I would dance with my brace-faced freshman co-sufferers.

LAST DANCE, LAST CHANCE

Semesters achingly passed through the seasons until summer began, teasing us with longer days, greener grass, and warm, sun-soaked afternoons. Our final high school dance was only a few days away, and the mirror was showing me a different reflection. I was filling my zero-cup bra—was, in fact, up to a B cup—my hips curving, braces off, and tight pants on.

It was the last Friday night dance before summer break. I opted for a purple button-up shirt with thin silver threads running through it—the dream of every eighty's girl. I lined my inner and outer eyelids with pitch-black liner, applied blue COVERGIRL mascara, swooped my feathered hair into attractive wings, and spritzed myself from head to toe in Jovan Musk perfume. The duck honk of my friend Carrie's cream-colored VW called me from my primping; away we went, sputtering our way down our small-town highway.

We fought over the rearview mirror in the Blue Ridge High School parking lot, peeling the foil off Double Mint gum sticks. Feeling very *Charlie's Angels*, we walked into the dance in all our over-sprayed, overlined, too-tight, minty-breathed glory. Our friends collected a few of the stacked beige plastic chairs, and we made a strategic semicircle so we could gossip and still allow ample access for any males who might be interested.

There I was, sitting amongst my glittery, shiny-lipped friends, sharing Starbursts, when I noticed Troy come in without Michelle. *Humm,* I thought, *that's odd. Maybe she is in the bathroom? Maybe she became dizzy from dancing in circles for a year?* I ran up the stairs onto the cafeteria stage, where Roger was setting up his DJ equipment. His back was turned to me as he wrestled a speaker the size of a small rhino. I tapped him liberally on the shoulder. He turned around with a snappy "What?"

I asked him why Troy was alone.

"His girlfriend cheated on him," he said, "and they broke up."

The world as I knew it stopped.

My heart put its hands on its hips and said, WELL, MY GOODNESS, *we didn't see that coming.*

I ran back to my chair and began to track Troy's movements. My eyes may have been overly made-up, but they squinted with the intensity of a lioness on the Serengeti. My prey wasn't dancing at all. He was completely focused on his football player friends. The microphone shrieked out, the rhino speaker amplified Roger's voice, and the music started blasting. I danced with my friends and a few irritating boys while keeping my eye on the prize. Roger announced the last song of the night, a slow song called "Babe" by Styx. I lost sight of Troy when the dance floor filled with people. Color rushing in from the disco lights created a living rainbow of purples, reds, blues, and yellows. Then I saw Troy looking directly at me, the colors washing over his face. He started moving toward me until we were toe to toe. He lifted his open hand, smiled his high-wattage chicklet-toothed smile, and said, "Would you like to dance?"

I quietly said, "Yes."

His hand touched mine, and the world fell away. How was I supposed to breathe under these conditions, let alone successfully dance in a circle? There was no gravity as the tips of our fingers connected in a tender grip. He led me to the center of the dance floor, where he stopped and pulled me in by the small of my back. His other hand wove into mine. His cheek against mine, I felt his fresh stubble. He smelled of spicy cologne and fruity gum. The colors, the feeling, the song, the dance—I never wanted it to end. Then, in a harsh moment, Roger's voice came through the rhino speaker, announcing the dance was over, and merciless white florescent lights aggressively filled out their long bulbs until the magical colors were gone. Troy's hands fell away. He smiled at me and then walked back to his friends. I tried to keep track of his movements as my friends giggled around me. I watched as he exited through the thick paint-chipped doors. After stacking the chairs, I made my way to the parking lot just in time to see his taillights drawing ribbons of red across the darkness, as bright as the fire he had started.

HERE I GO AGAIN ON MY OWN

The following Monday, summer came, and I started bugging Roger about Troy and his whereabouts. He was starting to get the idea that I fancied his brother. "You know, Heidi, he is going to college in a few months. Plus, he just started seeing this girl named Barbara."

What, Barbara? That Barbara? She's my friend! Barbara was my tanning partner, a bleach-blond, kind-smiled girl two years older than me, a "can't compete with her" kind of friend. *How could he?* We just danced, and now he's with her. How about giving yourself a minute there, mister?

Now I was mad. Because neither of them was aware of my feelings—I was falling in love with him—I didn't say anything to Barbara as we lay tanning on tin foil beds, spreading iodine and baby oil on our skin. To add coarse salt and lemon juice to the wound, Roger asked me if I wanted to go on a double date with him, Troy, and Barbara. My first reaction was *Hell, no!* But then something in me said, *Do it!* Barbara was seeing another guy named Scott, so I figured I had an opening. I spent the rest of the week practicing makeup, hair, wardrobe, compelling conversation, and how to act like I didn't care that he was with her and not me.

Finally, date night arrived. The first insult came when Roger and I were told to ride in the bed of Troy's Toyota pickup. Did these men not realize the time and effort I had spent on my hair? At forty-five mph, in the cold mountain wind, my big flaps of coiffed, feathered perfection were flapping like giant goose wings. Strands that managed to get loose stuck firmly to my glossed lips. Streaks of black mascara ran down my cheeks, and both legs were completely numb from my skintight jeans. All of this greatly amused Roger. Finally, Pizza Hut was in sight. Troy and Barbara jumped out of the truck, with their perfectly combed hair, ignoring us as we scampered behind them, wind-whipped. Inside the Hut, we were greeted by a teenage hostess and the smell of oregano and cheap red glass candles. Holding four thick plastic plates and some rolled silverware, she escorted us to a red faux leather booth. *Why is there so much red?*

Now I was sitting across from Barbara and Troy. All I could see was Troy looking at Barbara and Barbara looking at Troy. Roger blew a straw wrapper at them, and once he had briefly captured their attention, he went back to slurping his Coke and chewing ice as loudly as he could. I punched him in the leg. I wanted to barf. How could Troy have been holding me just a few weeks ago? A tantrum and storm-out were brewing, but I knew it would not be appropriate given that the relationship Troy and I had was only in my imagination.

Dinner ended—not soon enough. I found myself back in the bed of his truck, with numb legs and flapping hair. Then I heard the blinker click. Troy turned off the highway and onto a dusty road on his way to Make Out Mountain. Could this night get any worse? My lips were now gritty from road dust.

Troy parked the truck. Wasting no time, he started kissing Barbara. Roger started banging on the window. The truck door flung open. Troy got out and yelled, "Both of you out!"

Roger yelled back, "Where are we supposed to go?"

Troy said, "I don't care!"

The door slammed. Roger and I walked in the dark until we found ourselves sitting up against the garage of an abandoned house while bats dive-bombed us. In our boredom, Roger tried to kiss me. The second attempt no more successful than the first, we decided to look at the stars and talk about UFOs.

A few hours later, I was dropped off, looking like a witch who had been riding a broom through a hurricane. I watched from inside my bedroom window as the red taillights faded into black. I sat on my slushing waterbed (the gift I received for my sixteenth birthday), defeated, without my own heart, which I had given to a man who didn't even know I loved him.

IS ROGER A BIRD?

The next day, I confessed to Roger how much I felt for Troy. Predictably, he made fun of me and then wasted no time relaying the message to Troy. I began to contemplate all the ways I could kill Roger. Maybe he would be found squished under his rhino speaker, with his permed hair shaved?

The day somehow made its way to evening. At home, we had just finished eating some Hamburger Helper when our phone rang. My mother answered and said, "She sure is. Hold on a moment."

Cupping her hand over the speaker, she whispered, "It's Troy Marble."

"What? Who?" I grabbed the phone, ran down the hall until the cord spirals were stretched, slipped behind my bedroom door, and pressed myself against the paneled wall. I mumbled something inaudible. I had a moment of prayer (more like a moment of begging). "Dear God above, let this really be Troy and not some cruel joke."

What could he possibly want? Maybe some lip gloss for Barbara? I gathered what I could of myself and said a cool, slick "Hello?"

"This is Troy, Roger's brother. He said it would be okay to call and ask you on a date."

My heart was clearly back in my body because it was trying to beat me to death. I managed to say "yes" without adding a "please."

MY PRINCE DROVE UP IN A WHITE TRUCK

On a balmy Friday night in 1981, Troy picked me up for our first date, his button-down shirt with rolled-up sleeves as white as his truck, his hair perfectly combed, framing his "I'm about to get myself a mouse" grin. He opened the passenger door, and I hopped inside, my sweaty hands sticking to the seat. A Pink Floyd tape was playing; a pack of Wrigley's Juicy Fruit gum was in the ashtray. Troy jumped into the driver's seat and invited me to sit closer. I didn't hesitate. His leg touched mine while he shifted gears. The sun faded in the sky until the first star appeared. I made a wish to marry this man one day.

By the time we got to the drive-in movie, the world was deep black, the full moon casting opalescent light, low stars creating a ceiling of dancing shimmers. We grabbed a large, greasy bag of popcorn, two Dr. Peppers with extra crushed ice, and a Nestle Crunch candy bar. Troy hooked the speaker onto the truck as the smell of hotdogs and french fries filled the night.

In the bed of his little white truck, we watched *Tarzan* on a nest of sleeping bags. It was quite a contrast to the last time I was in the back of this truck, wind-beaten and heartbroken. I smiled, thinking about the irony of it all. Now I was looking at his profile in the moonlight. I was consumed by the idea of him. I knew that this man was meant for me.

The rest of the summer was bliss. There were lots of trips to Make Out Mountain and a lot of "submarine races" at Rainbow Lake (code for making out). I had never been happier. And then, as summers do, it slipped by too fast, and as with any good movie, there is always an end.

On the night Troy left for college, he gave me a small jewelry box with a split-heart mizpah necklace. The idea was that each person wears one side of the heart, and when the halves of the heart are connected, it says, "The Lord watch between me and thee while we are absent, one from the other." He said he would wear his side, and I could wear mine as a reminder of our love. He promised me all the things I wanted to hear as he hooked the necklace around my neck. I watched as the white

Toyota taillights streaked through the darkness into black.

In the beginning, his calls from his rowdy freshman dorm were reassuring. I just knew my prince was at college to become more refined and educated. I was unaware that his curriculum of girls, beer, and marijuana brownies made that outcome impossible.

HE IS SPIDERMAN, NOT A PRINCE

It was only a matter of time until I learned the truth: that my prince wasn't merely sitting around with his half-heart necklace, going to church, and studying. My hope of eternal love was dashed when my friend Pam, also a freshman at Northern Arizona University, called me out of the blue.

> Pam: Heidi, I thought you would like to know that I saw your boyfriend last night.
> Heidi: That's nice?
> Pam: I saw him climbing up a four-story building with a hamburger in one hand.
> Heidi: That's my guy—the ultimate athlete. So coordinated, too! What was he doing?
> Pam: He was climbing into the girl's dorm through an open window.
> Heidi: That mother $%#@&.

I have enough of my adoptive dad in me to be off the chain when I am pushed too far. My fangs were out, ribbons of drool dripping from my snarling lips. It was to his advantage that he was 200 miles away. I was savagely angry when I placed the call to "Spiderman."

> Heidi: *Dials phone while foaming at the mouth*
> Troy: How are you, sweetheart?
> Heidi: Great, never better! What did you do last night?
> Troy: I did homework and studied for a test.

Heidi: Really? Are you sure that's all you did?
Troy: Yup.
Heidi: Bullshit!
Troy: What? Why would you say that?
Heidi: Pam saw you scaling a wall and then going into a girl's dorm room. Was that your homework assignment?
Troy: *silence*
Heidi: Was the test to see what you could get away with?
Troy: *silence*
Heidi: WE ARE DONE!
Troy: That's fine because you are so immature. I don't need a girlfriend who draws smiley faces on her letters and seals them with lipstick kisses.
Heidi: Mother #$@&%! Don't worry. There definitely won't be any more smiley faces, kiss prints, or letters coming your way.

I hung up the phone, burst into tears, gathered a framed photo of him and the Aldo Nova and Lover Boy records he gave me, and placed them on the gravel driveway, where I drove over them again and again and again.

HE LOVES ME NOT

Like most young girls, I would pick daisy petals while reciting, "He loves me, he loves me not." More often than not, it ended with "He loves me not." I didn't need a daisy to tell me that. It was clear that Troy loved me not.

I repaid him by getting together with Mr. Close Call: a twenty-seven-year-old, six foot two, Robert Redford-gorgeous, guitar-playing, songwriting, ski instructor, bartender kind of mistake. What could possibly go wrong? I thought I was hot stuff—an older, handsome guy who could have anyone (and, as it turns out, did—and often) was looking my way. It was my summer before college. He was the blond version of my dad—basically a narcissistic asshole. He asked me to run away with him to Denver, and I almost did. He used me. I let him. He made me feel less than. I let him. He cheated on me, I found out, I left, and it changed me.

MY LIFE IS A WRECK

After almost destroying my life in a predictable way, I headed for the Arizona desert to attend college. I was seventeen, broke, and unafraid, thinking I was escaping it all as I peeled out of the driveway in my tiny matte-gold Mustang that sputtered every time I turned it off. Despite feeling as if I were finally free from the grip of my father and my close call with his double, no matter how fast or slow I drove, I carried it all with me in a deep place. The road I had traveled was written into my marrow. But in my naivete, I thought the world was now mine; I could do anything or be anyone, even though I couldn't afford toilet paper and the gas tank was empty.

Troy's brother Roger headed to the same college with a similar plan, leasing a smelly first-floor apartment with a popcorn-textured ceiling next to the pool so his roommate Chad could practice scuba diving and Roger could watch girls sunbathe. The life of small-town freshman college kids was underway, with plenty of boxed macaroni and SpaghettiOs to keep us alive.

I moved into a neighborhood that four young girls should never have called home. We had one bathroom, one phone, and no patience for each other. The Band-Aid-colored phone was busy ringing night and day, the cord permanently uncurled from stretching for privacy.

It was a school night; I had just drifted off to sleep under my knitted bright pink and purple quilt when the phone started ringing. Each of us was yelling, "It's your turn to answer!" In an oversized T-shirt that barely covered my backside, I ran to the phone, zipping past a sink full of dirty dishes, prepared to tell whoever was on the line that they shouldn't be calling this late. I had barely answered with an out-of-breath "Hello" when I heard Roger's voice. His usually smart-ass greeting was replaced with shaking fear. He delivered the news that he had been in a horrible car wreck, accidentally turning in front of a truck. Our friend Danny, who had been asleep in the back seat, was in critical condition, a medical halo drilled into his skull. Roger was at the hospital, unable to pee from the shock of it all but otherwise unharmed.

I ran back to my room, put on some pants and a cheap bra, grabbed my keys, and made my way to Borrows Neurological Center. It was pitch-dark. Only the desert could offer the perfect stage setting for this tragedy. After hitting every red light in Phoenix, I finally saw the emergency room sign glowing brightly. I pulled in too fast and parked in a well-lit spot, pressing my purse to my side as I walked-ran to the colossal double doors. They opened into a corridor lined with empty wheelchairs and IV poles standing at attention.

I found my way into the elevator, and after a jolted ride, the doors split open, squeaking loudly. Then I saw him, not Roger, Troy. It had been almost two years. My anger showed up instantaneously. He smiled that smile, but I wasn't having it, and with a huff, I flipped my waist-long blond hair over my shoulder, corrected my posture, and swooshed right past him.

I found Roger standing by a water fountain, mumbling and grumbling that they were fixing to put a catheter in him if he didn't urinate. I took over water fountain duty so he could hold both hands under an arch of cold water. Troy hovered close by. The icy water worked its magic; Roger ran to the bathroom. We took our places on closely packed navy-blue chairs. I sat on the other side of Roger, pretending to be interested in an old magazine. Time seemed to stand still as we waited for our injured friend's parents to arrive. After consoling them, it was clearly time to go. The three of us piled into the elevator. I pushed myself as hard as I could into the corner. I held the round bar as tight as I wanted to hold Troy's throat.

A CAN OF BEANS

Danny survived, and Roger slowly went back to being a comedian. It was late evening at our icky, wrong-side-of-town house. I was grumpy, tired, and hungry. Our food shelf had been pillaged by my roommates. Only a stale box of Cheerios and an old can of baked beans remained. Three of us were having our periods; it was a hellish scene for sure. Well, beans it is. I dusted off the lid and cranked the rusty can opener until a ragged metal circle sunk into the brown goo. I ate one cold spoonful after another, my forearms sticking to the Formica table.

In the middle of this collegiate gourmet experience, the phone started its predictable ring-a-thon. I answered with a bean breathed, "Hello."

It sounded like Roger, who also sounded exactly like Troy. Roger derived great pleasure from telling me he was Troy and tricking me into saying things I shouldn't. But tonight, I was in no mood; then I realized Roger actually was Troy . . .

> Troy: Hello, are you still there?
> Me: What do you want?
> Troy: It was nice to see you at the hospital a few weeks ago. Would you go out with me so we can talk?
> Me: Absolutely not!
> Troy: I am sorry about what happened in college. I just want a chance to explain.
> Me: I need to go. I have big dinner plans.

I hung up on him. Insert sound of me throwing the can of beans away.

NINE MONTHS DOESN'T ALWAYS MEAN A BABY

After two weeks of dealing with Troy's relentless calls, I agreed to go out with him *one* time if he promised *never* to contact me again. I was sick of beans, and at the very least, he owed me a nice steak. Utterly convinced that I had no feelings for this dorm-climbing, smiley-face-hating man, his white Toyota truck pulled into the driveway, and my colorful, Troy-adoring stomach butterflies flapped their love wings and tickled my insides. The feelings rushed back in, and I sat pinned against the passenger side door in forced resistance. Immediately noticing his half of the mizpah necklace in the ashtray, I rolled my eyes and whispered, "Asshole."

Troy smiled at me and tried to make small talk as I gave one-word answers, keeping my eyes diverted. But his gravity was drawing me in. The voices of logic in my head were screaming, *Don't you dare let this cutie pie take off with your heart again.*

The standoff lasted only thirty-six minutes at The Black Angus Steak House as we sat in a black leather booth with dim lights and candles. In a storm of butterflies, I cut a big piece of my steak. My heart was dry fuel, and he was fire.

A STATEMENT, NOT A QUESTION

He had my heart. He had it from the first moment I saw him. He had my heart when I fell in love with two other men. They had never been Troy. There was no escaping this love. It could never be done. After we established some serious boundaries—like no ex-lovers can be friends, never leave angry, no overuse of alcohol or lying by omission, etc.—our bond deepened. We became a unit. Troy's respect and romantic endeavors deepened when he realized I was not a pushover, that I had ideas, opinions, and spunk. He gave me a ruby promise ring with a circle of diamonds. We talked about marriage and could find no reason to wait to start our lives together.

Privately, he planned his proposal. Originally, he wanted to hire a pilot to fly a small biplane, pulling the "ask" sign, but that idea was quickly snuffed out by a limited budget. It was time to devise a plan B and put it into action.

It took an entire summer for Troy and his sister-in-law, Linda, who was married to his eldest brother, John, to create a thirty-six-foot-long "HEIDI, WILL YOU MARRY ME" sign out of bedsheets and peacock-blue paint. The only thing that statement lacked was punctuation. There was no question mark. In the final days of August

1984, Troy placed his "statement" on a mountaintop in the middle of nowhere in antelope country.

When he hiked back down and looked up, he could see only a white speck in the distance; it was his sign. In a tizzy, he tore back up the hill and drove recklessly over terrain so rough that he broke the tie-rod on his truck. He found a small canyon that looked like a better choice, and he climbed the wall and secured the sign to the side with rocks.

It was a Saturday; he was supposed to pick me up by noon. He arrived at our clothing store late. Troy was hot, tired, and flustered, and both of us were irritated. I was ready to get this picnic over and started pointing out picnic spots. "What about that nice tree?" "How about that pretty creek?" "Come on, that meadow is perfect!"

He rejected every suggestion. Exasperated, I folded my arms and stared out the window as his truck clanked down the road. After an afternoon that seemed an eternity, he parked on the side of a dirt washboard road. We grabbed the picnic basket and started to hike. I wasn't having it. My suggestions were turning more insistent. "How about that shady spot?" "How about that tree?"

Nope. He was on a mission, charging ahead of me. Thirty minutes later, we arrived at the base of a small ridge. Troy fluttered a large, red, plaid blanket to the ground. I was so happy to come in for a landing, the warmth of the earth underneath my body, that the high mountain sun melted my grumpy mood away as we shared cold fried chicken, store-bought potato salad, and thin, salty chips. Just as I was easing into a nap, Troy stood up and pulled me to my feet with his thick, beautiful hand. He said he had something to show me. Our fingertips interlocked just as they had the first night we danced. The ground was flecked with filtered light. Pine and aspen trees whispered as we passed under their canopies, a blue sky amongst tall wind-swept grass moving in smooth patterns. Then, we reached the edge of the small rock canyon. Troy was full of nerves; he got down on one knee. At that moment, I saw the thirty-six-foot-long statement pinned to the canyon wall. I said, "Yes." It has always been yes.

LOVE IS PATIENT

We were married on December 21, 1984, on a perfect winter night in Pinetop, Arizona. The church was flickering with candles. Two hundred and fifty people were dressed in their finest 1980s formal wear amidst fresh Christmas trees adorned in shiny bulbs. A full moon hung low—the kind of moon so clear that you can see the geography of its surface. Fresh snow decorated every branch of the pine trees. Forests of giant powdered-sugared arrows pointed to the stars. Inside the church bathroom, a flurry of bridesmaids in electric-blue dresses and fur hand muffs struggled to put on pantyhose. Troy's "HEIDI, WILL YOU MARRY ME" sign hung from the rafters. A roaring fire blazed in the four-sided fireplace. I was barely nineteen. My groom was twenty-two. Our love was sealed in a winter wonderland under a thick wood cross. We promised to love each other in sickness and in health, for richer or poorer, until death do us part. I even accidentally agreed to obey.

UPHILL BATTLE

My nineteen-year-old married self was arrogant. I was certain that I was unscathed by my past, that it wasn't going to matter that I was adopted. I wasn't about to be the poor, pitiful person who leans on her parents' faults to excuse her own. But I was holding a torch of self-righteousness, packed full of toxic fumes waiting to combust.

We took our vinyl records and our waterbed and rented a small apartment in Mesa, Arizona. We bought a Lhasa apso puppy named Bandit. Little did Troy Marble know, he was about to choose a girl who would put him through every variation of hell. He was in for a lifelong uphill battle.

DON'T BELIEVE ME, JUST WATCH

I was determined to have a healthy marriage because I had seen up close and personal what unhealthy looked like, felt like, and smelled like. I knew from experience how unhealthy relationships damage children, take precious time, and devour the very essence of life, leaving a stench.

Never ever, ever would that be Troy and Heidi Marble! And so, we decided that our marriage would work. And it did.

The first seven years were filled with happiness, accomplishment, and adventure. Yes, there were challenges, but we met them together. Our bridge was shiny, strong, and well maintained. We had a plan—we were going to have four children, starting with a boy so he could protect his sister, then another boy to protect another sister. Then, we would teach the girls that they didn't need protection. Then, we would teach the boys that they should be protective without letting the girls know. They would all have Troy's blond curly hair, my family's height, Troy's intelligence, my eyebrows, and Troy's smile. We would live happily ever after in the same neighborhood, and our children would become doctors or famous intellectuals, providing us with loads of grandchildren. Troy and I would grow "cool" old, with a yacht and tanned skin, planning dinner for friends with our private chef every night. *Ready, set, go!*

HUMUHUMUNUKUNUKUAPUA'A

Our plan was working. I graduated with a degree in elementary education. I was working as a sixth-grade teacher in Arizona when Troy received a job offer from Kiewit Construction Company after impressing them on a joint venture job to build the Phoenix airport. Troy's work ethic and intelligence made him stand out. Kiewit hired him to help build the Hawaii Interstate Roadway through the Koolau Mountains on Oahu. Our dream of yachts and private chefs actually began to seem viable. That was until we realized that a gallon of milk would cost as much as our car payment in Oahu.

Hawaii was good to us. We immersed ourselves in the culture. I learned the hula. Troy went deep-sea fishing. We lived in a condo overlooking the Kaneohe Bay. We island-hopped and made friends whom we still have. I taught school. We drove a white jeep, ate pineapple with salt, and learned to windsurf and eat raw fish. Troy built really big things and worked his way up through the company.

But it required working six days a week. Our time in paradise was also our time in hell; we faced storms that we were ill prepared to handle.

GRIDLOCK

It was time to start trying to have a baby. I was convinced that we would get pregnant right away because my body was healthy. Yet my womb remained empty month after month, and that turned into year after year—until each false pregnancy test became a dirge of broken hope. It was excruciating to have our dreams bleed out every month. It seemed as if the universe was punishing me for some obscure reason. Doctors could not find an explanation for our inability to conceive. Were my crimes of drinking a few too many margaritas in college or hopping on a motorcycle without a helmet enough to deserve this fate? I wanted to call 1-800-what-the-hell to file a complaint. But much to my dismay, the universe doesn't have a customer service department.

HI, DADDY

After more than three years of struggle, I could not believe that I was finally pregnant. I gathered what I could of myself and called Troy at work, asking him to come home immediately. I had to assure him that no one was dead but that it was that level of importance. Back in the bathroom, Wongee helped me write, "Hi, Daddy," on my tummy with black eyeliner. Her wrinkled hand patted my belly as we anxiously awaited Troy's arrival. About thirty minutes later, Troy entered the house. "I am here as requested," he said. "What's going on?"

"There is something on my stomach."

"You made me come all the way home from work to look at your stomach?"

I slowly exposed the words on my belly.

He buckled. His knees on the large square tile, he grabbed me around my knees as his kisses and tears covered my belly, his smile as wide as Texas.

RIDE OR DIE

We were so thrilled! I had just turned thirty-two. My pregnancy was going great; I was nauseous but managed to drink chocolate milkshakes and eat cream cheese toast regularly. We found out that we were having a boy. Troy was already planning baseball practices and Red Sox games. We decided that we would name our son Blake, a name that felt solid and masculine. We had just crossed over the fourteen-week mark, eager to feel his first movements, when our lives spun off the road into a medical head-on. During a minor car accident, I learned I had blisters, or blebs, on my lungs. The impact caused one to rupture, which was followed by a succession of chest tubes and three lung surgeries, one of which took place during my pregnancy, causing near-death for both of us. After surviving, I gave us everything I could: sun, ocean, fresh air, fresh water, fresh food, and deep rest. I took nothing for granted; I enjoyed every strange, miraculous change in my body. I felt Blake's busy kicking, his punching, and all his movements down to his hiccups; it was incredible to have an entire human being growing inside of me. His strength was undeniable. My health problems took a seat in my soul. It was as if my body had abandoned me, too.

ALOHA!

Oh, I have an idea! Let's go ahead and move back to the mainland a few days before my eighth month of pregnancy! Destination—Vancouver, Washington. Troy's job in Hawaii had come to an end, and it was time to build another bridge. This one would be in Boston. But before we headed east, Troy was assigned to the district office in Vancouver for a few months of planning. All our furniture had started its float on a barge headed for the Pacific Northwest. Blake's blue teddy bear nursery items, crib, and baby clothes were packed away safely. We would have only one month to set up a home before our boy made his appearance.

We arrived safely and rented a small house next to a hospital. We went from paradise to Rent-A-Center furniture, a stiff cream-colored sofa. A multi-armed light from the seventies, which arched like an alien spaceship, had me questioning my sanity. Our household belongings were still out at sea, where, for some reason, our moving company was unable to locate them. My days were spent waddling around a strange house in my black sunflower maternity dress, grumbling that our baby couldn't come into this world without a proper nursery! What if his first memories included this hideous furniture? I missed our trade winds and our view of the ocean. I started a pity party, but there was no one to invite. I just kept reminding myself that our ancient ancestors had their babies in the woods, tied them on their backs with a sling, and carried on. Certainly, I could manage some rental furniture and a rented house for a few months.

JUST IN TIME

Finally, for the love of all things sacred, our household belongings arrived—just two weeks shy of Blake's birth. During those precious days before Blake's arrival, we sat in his nursery. I would crank his teddy bear mobile, sit in his rocking chair, stack his tiny diapers, pop the tags off his precious clothes, and rub baby lotion on my hands. My hospital bag, ready to go, included a baby quilt made by Wongee and a CD of George Winston's piano music.

When the ache of labor started, Wongee monitored my contractions on a pad of paper until it was time to go to the hospital. My new OBGYN, Dr. Bishop, was well-versed in my case and the surgical trauma we had been through. He was prepared to give me a C-section if any complications occurred with my lungs. As long as everything was going well, I would give birth the old-fashioned way. My adoptive mother Joy, Wongee, Troy, and my best friend Mary Pat were there to get me through. Each took turns helping me labor for thirty-six (well, thirty-four) hours.

I pushed for three hours until our healthy nine-pound, three-ounce baby boy came into this world. Troy cut the umbilical cord and cleaned Blake. As I watched my boys meeting for the first time, I felt the strength in my weakness, the conviction that I would fight to the death for both of them. Being able to hold Blake outside my body, knowing that each breath he took was his own, gave my soul reach.

RED SOX NATION

When Blake was only two months old, our brief stay in Vancouver came to a close. We got a call to move to Grafton, Massachusetts, forty miles west of Boston. Troy was going to build the Leonard P. Zakim Bridge and finally go to Fenway Park, the home of his lifelong favorite baseball team, the Red Sox. On Halloween night, we dressed Blake like a pumpkin for our red-eye flight, his plethora of pacifiers ready to go—one in mouth, two in hand—and we flew through the night into the morning. As the sun rose, the hills below us were on fire with fall colors. Boston grew larger as we descended. Blake woke up. Wheels touched down in a screech of rubber and pavement, Troy's beloved Red Sox and Fenway Park just a few turns away. For four years, we would live in this amazing place, where I would meet death again, find my birth family, love new friends that would save me, watch our son grow into a toddler, and end up crossing over bridges both large and small to get to the other side.

COLONIAL STYLE

The first day we walked into our front door and the last time we walked out of it would mark a span that would include both the most joyful and the most devastating days of our lives. Our colonial-style home on the hill would hold many firsts. I am certain that our pain and joy still cling to the walls of that house like the metallic wallpaper we left behind. It took all our resources to purchase the home. Our sparse furniture filled only a few rooms. Wongee treated us to a formal dining room table with tapestry-cushioned chairs. Mother put up taupe and gold wallpaper so we would have a special dining place. Our neighbors' homes were filled with young families and stay-at-home mothers. No fences to separate us, our yards un-bordered, it all felt safe and idyllic. Blake was thriving, growing, and ahead of schedule on everything (I am not ashamed to brag). I could not wait to fill the house with more babies, memories, and furniture.

TWO FOR TWO

Sweet Blake was almost two years old. The house was filling with furniture and memories. We decided it was time for baby number two. I was tired and losing weight, and I did not seem to have the vigor of the other mothers. I accepted the fatigue and my thinning frame as a side effect of new motherhood. Then, one afternoon, while picking something up in my closet, I noticed pain in the upper right quadrant of my left breast. My brow immediately gathered with concern. I was done breastfeeding and could not think of a reason why I would be sore. I stood up and moved quickly away from my intuition, brushing off the warning as if it were a buzzing fly.

THIEF

The pain became worse. Swelling and redness showed up. It was time to see the doctor. I started with my family physician, who sent me to a breast surgeon. At first, he treated me for mastitis, but the pain and swelling would subside only to return. The light in my eyes had lost its shine. Fatigue, weight loss, and a sense of impending doom set in. I was told it was too much caffeine or fibrocystic breast disease. No one seemed impressed by my problem until April 12, 2000, when the truth at last appeared, scattered in cancerous specks across my mammography films. Not only did I have breast cancer, but I had inflammatory breast cancer, the most aggressive and deadly of them all. Cancer would be the ultimate thief, the knife at my throat, unzipping my soul while huffing the hot breath of death on my neck. I was inoperable, given eighteen months to live, and I was forever changed. *We* were forever changed—our little family took a trip straight to hell. *Why? Why us? Why our son? Why would he lose his mother?* I was so angry, hurt, and utterly suffocated by it all. But as I held him, the objective became clear. I wasn't going down without a hell of a fight.

I would start high-dose chemotherapy within four days, lose my hair within thirteen, and lose all hope for the future when my adopted mother, who was then at the peak of her anger toward me, came from Tucson to help, as she put it. She moved in and began her revenge. There would be no turning back for either of us. I had no choice; I needed help, and my son needed care. My adopted mom's resentment would hurt worse than the poison that would run in my veins and would feel more insidious than cancer. I found myself duct-taped to guilt. A small part of me thought that maybe my captor would forgive me, that maybe a terminal diagnosis would extract some compassion, perhaps make the rift between us less important. But there was nowhere to run, nowhere to hide.

LIFE SENTENCE

I came home from my double mastectomy, and finally, we had something to celebrate. They could not find cancer in my lymph nodes or anywhere else in my body. For all intents and purposes, I had a real chance of surviving beyond my original prognosis of eighteen months. There were heaps of grief as I adjusted to my breastless, infertile, and weak body. It was Blake who kept me alive; I would look at his picture during infusions. I would watch him sleep. I would drag myself in unimaginable fatigue and nausea to sit with him at dinner. I would listen to the creak of the swing outside, hearing his muffled laughter and wishing I had the strength to push him. It was devastating; all of it was just devastating.

All the many unknowns beset me. If I did survive, how long would it take for the cancer to come back? It felt like a death sentence went to a life sentence of dealing with the fear. I resented that my lungs and now cancer had terrorized our marriage and my mothering. Would Blake be old enough to remember? What was this doing to his tiny soul? He had to feel something, even though he didn't understand. I sometimes thought, *Maybe it would be better if I just died.* I felt powerless, unable to hide the fear I was transmitting. It was heartbreaking that I couldn't give him a sibling. Soon, the aftermath of it became secondary, and I found enough courage. I needed to keep my promise not to let go until the strength of Blake's hand could rest in mine.

MUST BE MOVING ON

The call came to go west to Northern California. This would be a fresh start, a chance to heal our little family. The sun and spacious dreamer attitudes gave us a newfound strength. California was good to us, a stopping point to take notice that we were not only surviving but living. Troy built another bridge, Blake was thriving, and after five years, it was time to move on.

DON'T MOVE IN DECEMBER

Another call came to move to the Pacific Northwest. We chose a town called Battle Ground, Washington; the irony is that we moved from Fairfield, California. Can you see the writing on the wall? We found a house on 2.5 acres, on a hill overlooking unimaginable beauty. Blake was midway through fifth grade and not happy about leaving the sun and his friends. It was December when we made our way north, straight into the onslaught of gray, dark, and rainy. Blake's sun-kissed hair, tanned skin, and baggy clothes were not well received by the small-town kids at school. It wasn't long before the sun came out and Blake made friends. Moving, up until that point, had been an adventure. I made up my mind—I wouldn't disrupt Blake's life again unless there was no other choice.

I'M NOT MOVING

The call came to move, and we decided that Troy would commute so Blake would not have to move during junior high and high school. As it turns out, Troy commuted from Hawaii for eighteen months, New York for six months, Montreal for eighteen months, and Maryland for six months. Although we made the decision together, I felt abandoned—our bridge started to crack. Resentment grew as I dealt with daily life on my own. The space between us grew so large, we could no longer see the other person.

THIS HOUSE IS OUR HOME

Change comes as it will. Troy quit his job and now works from home; luckily, we haven't become a *Dateline* episode. Our home that has held so much for fifteen years—doors opening, doors slamming, meals, holidays, pets, countless people—is evidence of love everywhere. The shelves that have everyone's name on a coffee cup, the bumps and bruises on the cabinets from years of cooking, old college textbooks from the kiddos in our lives, a chalkboard wall in our pantry with hundreds of messages, and the upstairs closet full of forty years of photographs—it's everywhere. Soon, our son will be off to medical school, far away, taking his wife and their newborn baby. The nest will be empty and full at the same time. We have made it this far; our bridge is still standing. We can see the other person now—the years between us, the history, the relentless will to keep going.

YOU KNOW IT'S YOU, BABE

No one has ever made me as mad or passionate as Troy. He has never wavered in his love for me. He held on to hope in spite of unbearable odds. A brave man who signed up to deal with a very complex woman. Troy has helped me chase all my dreams; he is there to console me when those dreams die—or to celebrate when they work. He has dried my tears of grief, telling me my breastless body is beautiful. He has made me miss him to the point of desperation. He has picked me up off the floor and put my bald and sick body in a bathtub while whispering strength into my ears. He loves our son and all the kids in our lives, sharing all of himself. There would be no bridge that connects us without Troy. He has kept us upright, allowing the weight to distribute evenly on his shoulders, each segment of our lives paved with his heart. I hold the memory of the first time we danced to "Babe" by Styx, the tender innocence that laid the foundation for all that we have built. I love you, Troy Marble. Thank you for being my home.

> *"'Cause you know it's you, babe*
> *Whenever I get weary, and I've had enough*
> *Feel like giving up*
> *Giving me the courage and the strength I need . . ."*
> —"Babe" by Styx

CHAPTER 9
LOVE CAN BUILD A BRIDGE

THEME 9: ABANDONER OR ABANDONEE?
Alysa Zalma, MD

The experience of many adoptees is that they fear continued abandonment unless they do something magical, noteworthy, or extraordinary to prevent this loss. If they had been so worthy and extraordinary, the fantasy is that the adoptee would not have been adopted from their biological family. Disrupted and disordered attachments are some of the many issues in their development and adulthood. Heidi still grapples with abandonment issues in her adult life despite her ability to enter into secure, mature adult relationships.

Heidi also addresses the central issue of love and hope. Love can do "magical" and "illogical" things to heal previous traumas. The staying power of love may be deepened by one's awareness of their patterns of dysfunction, such as how one feels about not being worthy enough, magical enough, or extraordinary enough, and how this pattern unwittingly seems to repeat itself throughout one's relationships. Heidi felt unworthy to sustain love in her parent-child relationship. Despite how much love Troy has for her during the best and worst times, she has lived with much doubt about her extraordinariness, lovability, and worthiness to sustain his love. Despite his "building bridges" with her, she realizes that she has put up some walls, too—in her traumatic illnesses, when raising their only child, Blake, in their "adoption" of other children, and in their decision to sometimes live in separate cities to accommodate Troy's career and Blake's high school.

Nevertheless, Heidi illuminates hope that this dysfunctional pattern does not need to keep repeating during one's lifetime and into the next generation. Despite many adoptees' fear of abandonment, there is hope if they can recognize these patterns in their lives; they may be able to find and sustain meaningful, loving relationships, including the relationship with themselves. How we understand and experience love is how we "remember" our inherent and original strength, confidence, beauty, and lovability.

Heidi's husband Troy seems to understand how to traverse trauma and love through his profound gifts of engineering. He says:

Bridges that stand the test of time and the ravages of nature are well designed to carry more than their capacity so they can withstand daily wear and extremes. If those stressors aren't considered, the bridge will eventually collapse and take down anything on, in, or around it.

If one understands their essence of lovability as truly "well designed," then "the test of time and the ravages of nature" will not destroy it.

However, many adoptees feel that they are not "well designed" in the first place.

From an energy medicine perspective, adoptees may not feel "well designed" because their essences of self/soul have been lost through the traumas experienced through adoption. Heidi's "soul loss" may resonate with other adoptees. She felt unworthy of her mother's love. Her biological mother left/relinquished her, and her adoptive mother emotionally disowned her because of her "betrayal." She wanted to ask her biological mother "why"—why was she so unlovable that her mother would leave her?—or find out if there was another explanation. Heidi wanted to know where she came from and if others like her could love her.

Through Troy, she learns that she is intrinsically "well designed" i.e., worthy and loved.

The famous Harry Harlow monkey experiments of the 1950s and '60s, despite their controversies, looked more deeply into the variables of "love" (as defined as comfort and companionship) in terms of what type of love monkeys could receive from a "surrogate" mother in monkeys who were taken from their biological mothers. Harlow looked at how these variables were pivotal to "the nature of love" and if the mother-infant bond conferred other factors besides feeding behaviors (Harlow 1958, 673).

Research concerning maternal "warmth" and the adopted childhood experience of love continues to find itself in the current literature. Adoptees, on average, continue to score a higher percentage of ACEs (adverse childhood experiences) than the general population (Adverse Childhood Experiences of Children Adopted from Care 2019, 2212).

The awareness of persistent patterns of fear of abandonment may be a vehicle toward healing from adoption traumas. The adolescent portion of Heidi and Troy's love story is beautiful in its sweetness and the description of young love, before much of the traumas of their later lives. As they move into more mature and difficult experiences, Heidi describes the events that offer more "opportunities" to deepen their love instead of running from it due to prior experiences of abandonment.

When much of their lives get shattered during Heidi's health crises, is it harder for Troy to continue to love Heidi or for Heidi to continue to love Troy? She may have originally thought that it was the former. However, it becomes more apparent that in her fears of being abandoned earlier in life, she must gain some semblance of control amid the current traumas. She finds another "choice," which is, depending on how one sees it, a protective or dangerous one. This is the "choice" of becoming the abandoner instead of the abandonee.

She says later in the chapter,

> **. . . the blood on my fists from beating up everyone including myself upper cut passive aggressiveness and knockouts of silence that left our marriage bent over in pain. The facts started**

> **revealing I am motivated by fear of being abandoned. That fear of being left has caused so much leaving of self, blocking the very love that could heal me.**

Despite the previous delicious narrative of young love, the themes of abandonment are already too prevalent to ignore. Heidi's fascination and obsession with the irresistible and unattainable Troy becomes her challenge and her undoing. Heidi describes ways that Troy abandons her repeatedly. He dances with her and then carries on with her tanning girlfriend, Barbara. He "returns" to her right before he goes to college and promises her his love, giving her a necklace before he leaves for college. He abandons her again as she naively states,

> **. . . my prince was at college to become more refined and educated. I was unaware that his curriculum of girls, beer, and marijuana brownies made that outcome impossible.**

In the beginning, Heidi cannot trust Troy (but maybe that makes her want him all the more), fueling the abandonment fire, where she will try to prove her worthiness before he can leave. Attractiveness/allure pair with the danger of abandonment, which is part of what powers her early obsession with him. Heidi's adoptive father and biological father abandoned her through abuse and untimely death, respectively. By late adolescence, it became better and safer for Heidi to abandon first. She abandons Troy while he's trying to get her back. After their eventual dating and subsequent marriage proposal, the abandonment blissfully resolves until Heidi's illnesses.

Abandonment issues tragically heightened as Heidi started to have acute and life-threatening circumstances. She discusses her terror and despair with her lack of control over her illnesses. She describes her second collapsed lung experience that threatened her pregnancy and life. She subsequently describes her diagnosis of inflammatory breast cancer that she was not expected to survive. During this time, she felt that she "chose" her newborn son Blake over Troy for many reasons. In the irrationality and severity of facing a terminal illness she may have denied that her imminent death would be destructive for Troy. She concentrated more on her mission to spare Blake from the tragedy of her death.

To abandon her infant at this time seemed unthinkable. Blake would be put in a similar situation of abandonment that she had felt when her biological father died before she was born, setting off the cascade of events that led to her adoption.

Heidi notes that focusing on Blake's abandonment due to her imminent death may have distracted her from the thoughts of leaving Troy as well through her death. To this end, with each year she lived, Blake would remember more about her and have more to mourn.

Again, thinking in this way may have protected her from deepening her love with Troy during an uncertain time that would have only been destroyed by her death. Even after the threat of her imminent death passed some years later, she continued to hold the presumed more powerful role of abandoner instead of abandonee to protect both of them from further trauma due to her illness.

In the years after her health crisis, she continued to "protect" herself and "build walls" with Troy. When a new job opportunity came for Troy, she decided to have him live in another city instead of relocating Blake during high school. Despite the agreement, she felt abandoned by him.

Mythology discusses universal themes of human experience to reveal how they may be explained and resolved. The concept of hell may be one where people experience a lack of control over what is happening to them. This is how Heidi describes her multiple health crises and how they relate to themes of abandonment as a type of "hell."

In the mythological story of the River Styx, the boundary between earth and the underworld, during the boat ride to the underworld, there exists a chance that one could potentially "bargain" with the boatman and have some control over one's outcome for a price.

One interpretation is that Heidi's "bargain" with the boatman was that she would not die (and Blake would not be abandoned) but that the price would be the loss of the depth of her love relationship with Troy.

This famous Greek myth later became Gluck's renowned opera Orpheus and Euridice. In this story, Orpheus almost saves his love Euridice from death when he goes down the River Styx in an attempt to retrieve her from Hades. He is told that Euridice will be saved from death if he does not look back to see her as he goes down the river to cross into the underworld. He fails. The cautionary tale for Heidi is the metaphorical "not looking back" and thus not being doomed to repeat one's patterns of the past. If she keeps "looking back," she will repeat the patterns and thus the traumas of her abandonment.

The story of the River Styx is dark but hopeful. During this "ride," the adoptee may consider "what it will take" to not repeat the patterns of the past and repeat the transgenerational traumas associated with abandonment.

The enduring strength of Heidi and Troy's remarkable attachment and love was foreshadowed by the power of her experience of their first dance to the 1979 song *Babe* from the soft rock band Styx (a different allusion to this name). The song may be incorrectly interpreted as the composer's abandonment of his romantic love interest.

The truer interpretation of the song "Babe" is substantiated by the singer/songwriter Dennis DeYoung, who noted that he and his wife had recently married, and the commercialization and success of the band had necessitated him to tour various cities around the country to perform. He composed the song for her as a birthday present to assure her that he is not abandoning her.

> Babe, I'm leaving, I must be on my way
> The time is drawing near
> My train is going, I see it in your eyes
> The love beneath your tears

But I'll be lonely without you
And I'll need your love to see me through
So please believe me, my heart is in your hands
And I'll be missing you

Of her love story with her husband, Heidi says,

**. . . is a stunning work, a well-worn masterpiece.
In spite of some collateral damage, our bridge still stands after forty years . . .**

Heidi offers that despite the traumas of adoption abandonment and subsequent traumas that may trigger them, it is possible to move out of the cycle of dysfunctional attachments of the past by becoming aware of how previous abandonment traumas inform the more "here and now" experiences of one's life.

Newer, more mature adult relationships are possible through the awareness of these patterns. Creating the experience of one's worthiness of love through more mature adult relationships becomes more available. This is a highly individual journey. Heidi offers adoptees guidance through her life-threatening illnesses that reawakened her adoption traumas and threatened her adult relationships. She used these experiences to break the cycle of intergenerational abandonment traumas.

Her psychological defense mechanisms of choosing the abandoner stance, which may have formed earlier in her life due to her adoption abandonment trauma, helped her survive her illness. She understands that she must be conscious of this to move forward in her marriage. She must also forgive the stark imperfections of her life's events. To have been able to achieve all of this is to be fully able to celebrate her life's most important joys and accomplishments. This is her gift to her husband of over forty years and to the adoption community.

CHAPTER 10
SIMPLE KIND OF MAN

FOR MY SON, BLAKE

"No one will ever know the strength of my love for you. After all, you're the only one who knows what my heart sounds like from the inside."
—Kristen Proby

"May our sons walk beside the Lord, on a straight path in which they shall not stumble."
—Jeremiah: 31:96

HARD-FOUGHT

This chapter was hard-fought. It has been nearly impossible to explain a relationship so intertwined with my being. To consolidate twenty-five years of being a mother into a truthful, meaningful, and raw portrayal has been a process. I know that my truth and the way I tell it will be one of the greatest gifts I can give my son. He needs to know the human side of his mother, with all its complications. One of my truths is that Blake has been my "reason," which is something I honor and regret. To be someone's "reason" invokes a lot of pressure and obligation, none of which I ever wanted him to feel. I have been a parent's "reason," and I know from experience that it simply isn't fair. Now I must accept the mistakes I have made; I also accept that I played a role in raising an incredible man despite those mistakes. There is a softness in considering that my flaws may have strengthened his character. I hope he will read and reread my words and discover more about his heart.

With a sobering truth, I admit that I did not do the best I could. I could have done better. I did the majority of my mothering from a platform of fear, and that is hard to grapple with. It is even harder to swallow all the unhealed pain I handed him. He deserved to come into this world free of those burdens, but I neither had the wisdom nor the strength to understand the wounds of my heart or how to heal them.

The psychological reach of my relinquishment at infancy, coupled with the abandonment of my soul, defined how I mothered. Abandonment has been at the heart of all my decisions, both good and bad. What my son needed more than the over-the-top birthday parties, matching clothes, and the latest-and-greatest was for me to heal my heart and love myself. This book, this chapter, is part of my healing—and I hope a start to his. My knees are on the ground, and I'm praying that by cutting open my soul and confronting my issues, I can give to the man the mother the boy never had. I let a resounding cry out that these hard-fought words will turn into power in his hands—and long after my body is gone, he can come to these pages and find my heart. I pray that through this effort, he will know himself and his mother more fully.

ROAD TRIP

This is going to be tricky. I don't have a map, enough gas, or a clear destination, and I have *never* had a good sense of direction. I am just going to stop at places that feel important to unpack and explore. The journey between my son's birth and his wedding day has been full of unimaginable threats and triumphs. It seems intuitive to introduce you to my son on the eve of his wedding because I was able to keep a lifelong promise.

When he was born, I promised that I would not let go until I could feel the strength of my son's hand in mine. I have begged, prayed, and yelled that promise for two decades, and I would not take "no" for an answer. I was determined to live, to see him grow, even if all my body parts were gone—with the exception of my mouth. I was hell-bent on being there for every milestone, and those milestones became the pull that kept me going. Before I can talk about my only child as a squishy, adorable baby, you need to know he survived, that we survived, and that sometimes we have to backtrack to find our way home.

ALL CLASSICAL

It is the depth of winter, January 3, 2020. We are in the far reaches of the Oregon high desert at a gorgeous resort called Brasada Ranch, preparing for my son's wedding. A black Steinway concert grand piano has made its way over the snowy mountain passes from Portland. The movers carefully place the piano in the center of the barn, where the reception will be. The instrument's finish is as shiny as a raven's wing, the keys dressed in crisp white and black, a thick sheepskin rug placed under the tufted piano bench, and ambient light softly glowing. Classical piano has been the center of Blake's life for a long time, and on his wedding night, he, his teacher, and his talented friends will play this grand instrument. Blake has decided to share a piece by Schubert, the Impromptu, Opus 90 No. 3, with his bride. All around the piano, the barn hums with activity, people scattered, handling last-minute details.

As always, I am hungry and suggest Mexican food in the next town over. Blake declines the invitation. Afterward, back at the cabin, I am full of chips, salsa, and top-shelf margaritas, when Blake messages and asks if we want to hear him practice his piece for Sontia. We could not get there fast enough. The barn is fully adorned in wedding regalia as six of us gather around the piano, the space dim and subdued. Blake organizes his music sheets, adjusts the bench, and takes a few deep breaths. At that moment, I traveled back to the first time I heard Blake play the piano when he was fifteen years old. I wrote about that experience years ago; it is the next stop, a detour that needs to be traveled.

MAY 30, 2013

Narrative of Musical Miracle

Proverb to live by: "When the student is ready, the teacher appears."

It is important to connect Blake's musical journey with my own. I vividly recall being a three-year-old girl, in a dress with tiny yellow flowers, sitting on the bench of my wongee's old pine spinet piano, swinging my legs back and forth like pendulums, my tiny fingers working the keys as the creaky bench complained. I grew up playing the piano impromptu, eventually trying lessons that quickly failed. I was too busy to sit very long, and I always had better things to do–like playing Barbies and chasing boys. Nonetheless, I always loved the piano and visited on occasion.

When I became an adult, playing the piano felt like a conversation with my younger self; the silly songs I had learned to play never left my memory, and playing them always gave me great joy. When I was twenty-two, Wongee gave the piano to Troy and me for our first home. In time, the piano became just another piece of furniture, only getting my attention when it was time for some lemon Pledge. She didn't care; she had a purpose greater than I could have ever fathomed.

A year after the piano came to live with us, when we moved to Hawaii, we could not afford to transport her. I contemplated selling her to buy a few cute bikinis, flip-flops, and high-end sunscreen until my brother-in-law offered to keep her. She would stay with him in Arizona for seven years, waiting patiently, untouched, unmoved. Over that time, thoughts of her kept tapping me on the shoulder; she never allowed me to forget.

When I was eight months pregnant, we moved from Hawaii to Washington, and I was obsessed with getting her back. A few days before Blake's birth, she arrived, and I welcomed her by polishing her wood with lemon Pledge. I pulled out the creaky bench. I sat, adjusting my sunflower-patterned dress, my giant belly pressed into her keys, and I played my three songs. Blake heard that piano's voice for the first time and danced inside me.

After Blake's arrival, I had little time to polish, play, or even acknowledge her presence—or anyone else's, for that matter. Even her time with lemon Pledge had come to an end. Another move to Boston further de-prioritized her until Blake grew into a toddler. He became curious about her, and his little fingers and dangling feet brought the piano back to life. She endured pounding so harshly that some of her keys became stuck. She never seemed to mind the sticky fingerprints covering her bruised wood. It wasn't long before those tiny fingers moved on to toy trucks, sandboxes, and baseballs.

Once again, the piano waited, this time for the greater part of ten years. She had become a shelf with a seat, an accessory for elaborate candlesticks and picture frames, her bench now a holding place for her parts and pieces. She endured two more moves, one to California and one back to Washington, where she turned seventy-five years old.

The transformation she was waiting for finally arrived when Blake turned fifteen; one day, he noticed her and asked if I could play for him. I was startled since the piano had been ignored for so long. I sputtered at the thought of showing him my sad little repertoire, but he was unrelenting; so, I pulled out the old creaky bench, noticing the places I had missed the last time I polished it, and instantly, I became that little girl again. I closed my eyes to find the notes, and soon, the songs found their way back into my fingers. As I played for my son, he observed carefully and then asked if he could try. With no warning, he played back exactly what I had played for him. I was flabbergasted.

From that day forward, nothing could stop Blake from playing the piano five to six hours a day. He practiced with perpetual force, consistency, and commitment. Even in the infancy of his talent, he had become a conduit for something divine—his soul connected with classical music. The piano became Blake's voice, and I could tell what he was feeling when he was playing. The piano always knew how to translate his heart, and together, they were one cohesive unit. She kept him from the trappings of teenage life; she kept him safe for me.

It has been an incredible eight-year journey watching Blake take on the challenge of mastering classical piano. He has introduced us to Ravel, Chopin, Schubert, Mozart, Liszt, Debussy, Rachmaninoff, Beethoven, and other men with exotic names whose music still stirs the world. Blake has an expansive collection of biographies of men with stunning hair and serious faces. With his array of music books stacked as tall as the ceiling, he has built a fortress of beauty. My son's hands and mind have brought their soul-stirring music into the present. His tour de force playing provoked a need for a succession of pianos. The old pine spinet stepped aside for the Yamaha baby grand, with a clean sound, which moved out of the way for a 1966 Mason and Hamlin, with booming dimension. The old spinet didn't seem to mind; she was good at waiting.

There would be a journey to Europe to stand at the graves of the great composers and explore museums and institutes to see their instruments, original works, and artifacts. We touched the column inside a church where Chopin's heart is interred because he wanted his body in France and his heart in Poland! It seems these composers had a flare for living—and dying.

The dream of being a concert pianist is a harsh one. A life of performance can alternate between extreme adoration and extreme loneliness; often, there can be no other love. Furthermore, most performers start as soon as they are dry from the womb. Starting at the age of fifteen most certainly does not put one at an advantage. Blake trained under many possessive teachers who tried to tame him. His relentless focus and passion helped him quickly outgrow the basics.

The piano has many suitors who are technically perfect, but few feel the piano the way Blake does. He evokes shapes, layers, and textures—a galaxy of musicality that cannot be taught. He fell in love with the piano without provocation and hated her with equal vigor. Love and hate are closely related, providing the perfect tension for musical growth.

Blake knows the piano; he understands her. He knows that she must be in tune to speak and that the slightest shift in weather or treatment affects her sound. Sometimes, her notes can be dulled or stretched with the slightest push. She comes in all shapes, sizes, colors, and dimensions. She can stand proud in the corner of a dusty bar or in the center of a glamorous stage. And like most women, she is full of infinite possibilities if she is cared for. Her complexity has caused him to walk away many times, but he always comes back with his truth.

Although, in the end, Blake decided not to pursue a performance career, the piano nevertheless still lives through him. And, on occasion, he still visits our old spinet piano with the creaky bench.

BACK TO THE NIGHT BEFORE THE WEDDING

Blake is music, and tonight, we are invited to listen to this mastery. I thank all that is holy that the old spinet waited, listened, and spoke his heart. If she could see Blake now, readying himself to speak his ultimate truth, she would smile.

I come back to now. I hear Blake exhale. He corrects his posture and boldly takes command of the piano. His strong hands pull every emotion from the instrument. His fingers race up and down the keyboard. My heart races with the same intensity. The sound was moving in, around, and through us; now I know what true love sounds like, and it is magnificent.

NOTHING STAYS THE SAME

After hearing Blake play, we head back to the cabin to get a good sleep before the big day. I get into my favorite pajamas, a striped jersey two sizes too big. A plethora of emotions are nagging at me. I can't sleep; the clock reads midnight (ish). I fidget—at this time tomorrow, my only child, my son, will be married to his stunning bride, Sontia, in a ceremony meant for the ages. The darkness has never been a place for me to hide; sometimes, it reveals more than any light. I stare through the window of our spacious cabin as opaque winter moonlight casts shadows under the sage and juniper bushes. The Cascade Mountains pierce a velvet sky, their peaks surrounded by night clouds, while well-fed horses and cows rest in sepia tones of swaying grass.

Troy rests soundly beside me as I try to get comfortable, gripping, yanking, and adjusting the stiff, itchy bedding. After a lot of fussing, I clasp my hands over my heart and begin flicking my toes together. My eyes dart back and forth. I notice a fierce blue pilot light and then my deep blue dress, both equally vivid in the dark. The fabric of the dress is luscious and shiny, designed by a handsome Italian. The dress feels expensive, and I like feeling expensive.

The darkness coils around me; I remain belly-up, resisting the urge to curl into a fetal position. So caught up in the pomp and circumstance of wedding bliss, I failed to consider the full gravity of this transition. I now become one-hundred-percent aware that my relationship with my son will never be the same. Although this is a natural and necessary step for his proper growth and development, I buck the idea of not being needed anymore. This realization constricts my chest. I gasp at the intensity with shuddered breaths. I start to drift and swirl in the memories of the road we've traveled.

Remembering . . . him. As a baby, a young boy, a teenager, a man—it's all so consuming. I see his toothless smile, feel his tiny chubby arms around my neck, and see him dancing while I sang my made-up songs. I see him ride a bike for the first time; I see it all. I feel a sensation of being hollowed out as I consider the should haves, would haves, and could haves. The disparity of how tightly I have held onto him—how painful yet affirming that grip must have been. That harsh reality is done now. I can't go back. He is an adult who deserves to live his life without his mother Velcroed to him. Grief overtakes me as I roll onto my side and wrap my hands around my stomach to feel the tiny ridges of stretch marks from my pregnancy.

HOLY WORDS

Morning breaks. The uncomfortable comforter is now pushed into accordion folds at the base of the bed. My blue dress is showing off its deep hues in the fresh sunlight. The night that just swallowed me whole is over. I feel light, airy, and untethered. It is time to celebrate my son's marriage. I pull the dress off the hanger and let it float over my head until it covers me in softness. A few rounds with my favorite apricot lipstick, some spritzes of Versace perfume, a heavy dose of hairspray, and I am ready.

The wedding day is God-given; it is almost sixty degrees and sunny, with just the right amount of breeze. The ceremony is to be held outside, at three in the afternoon, on an elevated grassy knoll overlooking miles of unobstructed beauty. The officiant, with his thick English accent, enjoying his own humor, tries to assemble the bridal party inside the lodge. He messes with his bangs as he directs me to stand at the front of the line. I stand at the closed door. Blake and I will be the first to walk out. I squeeze my innocent Kleenex into a wad. My blue, suede, pointed-toe pumps torture me. I vow that after the wedding, I will insist the CEO of Birkenstock start making dress shoes. Despite my foot pain, I notice Blake enter the room. A spotlight of energy follows him as he moves with towering confidence. He floats by the bridesmaids, in their pale-blue dresses, and they giggle, clutching their wildflower bouquets.

I am overwhelmed at how handsome he looks—his thick, curly, golden hair perfectly combed, his bright green eyes washed with love, his black-on-black suit perfectly fitted over his broad shoulders, and a winter flower boutonniere pinned above his heart. Time accelerates as he makes his way to stand beside me. I feel the rush of his warmth as his arm links with mine. Thick crescents of tears fill the bottom of my heavily lined eyes.

He looks at me, a wide smile spread across his face. I mop up tears with that handy ball of Kleenex. We wait as I try to keep it together, doing my best not to make eye contact. I stare outside. I want everything to slow down, and I want to live the rest of my life in this moment. Time does not wait; it takes what it wants. As our English officiate opens the door, a ripple of cold air billows the hem of my blue dress.

We step over the threshold. Blake pulls me in tighter. The crisp breeze spreads the falling tears across my face. Overcome by it all, I can't stand up straight. We arrive at the altar, he embraces me, and I grab him as if I am falling off a cliff. I feel him let go; then my heart free-falls. His bride walks down the aisle; her beauty is overwhelming. Soon, they stand face-to-face, hand in hand, under God's blessing, while the sun engulfs them into a silhouette. Holy words ride the breeze as his bride's golden hair floats in ribbons of light. Her chiffon dress, the color of a tender pearl, the fabric as smooth as angels' wings. I have never seen or felt anything more beautiful.

Over prayers and promises, the mountains, birds, and trees celebrate this union. As the sun fades, the sky unveils late-day stars. Strokes of vivid purple, orange, and pink brush across the sky. I feel God's presence so completely; I thank him with all that I am or ever will be for the chance to be here and for the road that brought us to this glory.

SIMPLE KIND OF MAN

After the ceremony, we make our way to the glass-walled barn. I adjust my scarf and give my lipstick another go. The space is transformed—we are welcomed by photos of Blake and Sontia, the smell of fresh flowers, hearty food, and a real wood fire. The tables are decorated with sprays of fresh greens, winter citrus, and dozens of glass votive candles nestled and shimmering. The black Steinway piano anchors the center of the room.

It is time for Blake to play for Sontia. She sits behind him in a chair, her hair now undone and falling in a river of white gold. He plays his love for her, and I am overcome once again. The playing continues as his teacher and each of his piano virtuoso friends bring forth an offering.

Afterward, an area is quickly cleared to create a dance floor in front of the massive stone fireplace. It is time to surprise Blake with our mother-son dance. Weeks earlier, Sontia helped me craft a plan to ambush Blake. It was she who had asked if I wanted a mother-son dance. I reached out to my best friend's son, Nick, an accomplished singer/musician, and he agreed to turn the rock ballad "Simple Man" into a more tender version by using just his voice and an acoustic guitar. The song, simply stated, is advice from a mother to a son, and it would speak for me tonight.

I walk across the floor, feeling the smoothness of my blue dress against my legs. As I stop at the microphone, everyone dials down to silence. I let Blake and our guests in on the surprise and invite Blake to join me. Nick begins to strum his guitar. I have not had my hand in my son's hand for some time, and at this moment, my promise to not let go until he was grown is realized. My peripheral vision no longer exists. Blake looks at me as he never has before; his eyes pour out love, forgiveness, and understanding. Everything I ever wanted for him has come true. He has just married someone with character, heart, grace, faith, and boundless beauty. He is on a right and virtuous path of faith, focus, and moral structure.

The rest of the night is filled with dancing, laughing, and celebration. In the middle of it all, I stop and excuse myself. I take off my shoes and run up the stairs until I reach the balcony. Crouching down in my blue dress, I hold the railing. What I see below is carved into my heart forever, a symphony perfectly orchestrated. Life has never given me permission to take anything for granted, and tonight is no exception. I am simultaneously as empty and as full as I have ever been—feeling the duality of my existence and how grief punctures joy, making each more vivid. My son was my reason. *Now what do I do?* My happiness for him and grief of letting go are equally matched.

ON THE ROAD AGAIN

It's 7 a.m., and I gather my blue dress that is slumped over a chair. My lips are still stained from my fancy lipstick. A winter storm is rolling in. We're in a frenzy about leaving. When I hang my dress on the hanger, a hint of sweetness from the Versace perfume lingers. I grab my mean shoes and stripped pajamas, along with other female trappings, and shove them into my suitcase. In blistering wind, I walk from our cabin to get a coffee from the lodge. The glass barn shows little evidence of the wedding except for a few burned votives in a box and a pile of wilting greens on a table. The piano is closed, quiet, and alone. My hands are painfully cold.

The coffee welcomes me with warmth. I burn my mouth with impatience. I drink anyway. Angry walls of gray clouds come in low and intimidating. We have to leave soon. Yesterday's leftover makeup will do for now. I am hoping my twenty-four-hour deodorant will keep its promise.

As we pull away, I see the barn. I want to turn around, I want to live that day again, I don't want Blake to go, I don't want my sister to fly home, I don't want to face myself, and I don't want to be in this car driving down this road. The wedding would have been a perfect ending to my life. I was already dressed and looking fine; they could just find me in repose. But *nope*, apparently, my time here isn't done. Taking up knitting is not going to fix this! Nothing will ever fill the void. I must face everything I have been avoiding, neglecting, and ignoring. Snowflakes surround us, and the world becomes white. I close my eyes and try to feel my baby in my arms again.

LETTING GO

Blake was my first genetic mirror, the first blood relative I ever met, my only child, my only son—the human I have so fiercely attached to and focused on for over two decades. Now I see my six-foot-tall, broad-shouldered, blue-green-eyed, handsome son—a man with deep character, who turned out well despite me. Now three years later, Blake will be heading off to medical school in a few short months. They are also expecting a baby girl, who will be named Daya Lily. This is the big let go . . . faced with the same dread, exhilaration, and irrational fear of abandonment.

My son—flesh of my flesh, bone of my bone, my eyes in yours. The day you were born, I was introduced to miracles. My hand now rests in the strength of yours.

CHAPTER 10
SIMPLE KIND OF MAN

THEME 10: THE GENDERING OF MOTHERING AND MUSIC AND THE RETURN TO SELF

Alysa Zalma, MD

On the topic of mothering, Heidi writes about her son.

There is a softness in considering that my flaws may have strengthened his character.

One of my patients, a forty-five-year-old physician adoptee, discussed his regret and hope about parenting his ten-year-old twins, a boy and a girl. His wife was discharged from the ICU about three months before, after a supposed accidental overdose of her regular medications combined with alcohol. She was presently clean and sober for three months. In his psychotherapy with me, he was struck by some parallels to his childhood—namely, how his adoptive mother abused drugs and alcohol and died at forty-five—the same age as he is now. He wondered if it would have been better for him and his brother if his father had left the marriage. He wondered if he should stay with his wife and let his children deal with "similar trauma," something akin to his experiences growing up. We concluded that the uncanniness of the similarity was a way for him to have a "second chance" as an adult, to give his children a chance at a loving, stable household that he did not have.

He understood his desire to "right the wrongs of the generation past." The epiphany of the "second chance" phenomenon gave him validation that he had this chance with his children and awareness to use this information to help himself and his family.

He and his wife now have a more communicative marriage and want their children to remember their family of origin differently than he did.

This "second chance" phenomenon is one of the central themes of this chapter.

Heidi had previously understood her mothering as *damaged*. Whatever mothering attributes she felt she lacked seemed to be made right by Blake's interest and talent with the piano, the spinet that was her grandmother's. The piano became the conduit and container for the mothering that Heidi had experienced with her grandmother. She felt she lacked the ability to create the holding environment of her grandmother and saw the spinet as a transitional object by which Blake could be offered that quality of mothering.

Heidi took solace, comfort, and pride as Blake's interest, talent, and connection with the piano continued to grow and flourish. Through Blake's adolescence, the piano, representing Heidi's grandmother and all the essences of successful mothering, was his "safe container." This concept of the mother/container as part of normal infant development originated with the influential British psychoanalyst Wilfred Bion, as discussed in his theories of containment. Ease in understanding the Bionian concept of container as one that is a dynamic process between container and contained is discussed by Bionian scholar Thomas Ogden (Ogden 2004, 11356-7). The piano, as it relates to the interplay of the dynamic between Heidi and Blake, may be considered a Bionian container for the child-mother relationship.

Despite Heidi's intermittent retreat into maternal inadequacy, she continually felt motherly pride and adoration for Blake's aptitude at the piano. Through his talent and love of music, he inadvertently helped Heidi "right the wrongs" of the nurturing limitations of her adoptive parents. He helped her step into her role of a more capable, accepting, and loving mother, finding ways through the container of the piano to help her overcome her limitations, step up, and do the job of mothering.

Heidi identifies the piano with a more decidedly female gender and says that Blake "understands her." She personifies the piano as she feels it relates to how she would like herself to be.

. . . like most women, she [the piano] is full of infinite possibilities if she is cared for.

She may identify the piano as female because she has identified her grandmother as her most capable parent. To Heidi, Wongee was the one who could mother so expansively and unconditionally as to create a secure sense of being loved and a deep permission to be oneself.

In Heidi's personification of the piano as a protector and container for Blake, it was also an anthropomorphic representation of herself. She describes how he played the piano, highlighting the true nature of their relationship.

The piano always knew how to translate his heart, and together, they were one cohesive unit.

At fifteen, when Blake asked Heidi to teach him how to "play the piano," this may be interpreted as him asking her to find her confidence as his capable and loving mother. She attributes qualities to the piano that she always had in her power to offer him.

Heidi says of her Blake's piano playing,

I know what true love sounds like, and it is magnificent.

Because music has an ineffable and unfathomable quality that defies and eclipses human language, it explains the inexplicable and indescribable. Through the container of the mothering piano, Heidi can merge the concept of music, love, and personal experiences of what it is like to be mothered in a secure and healthy way.

Within the normal process of adolescence, the adolescent-mother relationship was accurate in Heidi's description of Blake's relationship with the piano (herself):

He fell in love with the piano without provocation and hated her with equal vigor.

The piano has also been esteemed within pop music as the embodiment of the Jungian archetype of mother. Concepts on the gender-ness of mother continue to be rethought and questioned with more awareness and acceptance of the full spectrum of how everyone chooses to express the complexities of their experience of gender.

Billy Joel partly earned his fame by becoming the broader and rethought mother/container in his famous ballad "Piano Man." Through the lyrics, he describes himself as the container/mother for anyone coming "to forget about life for a while."

It's a pretty good crowd for a Saturday
And the manager gives me a smile
'Cause he knows that it's me they've been comin' to see
To forget about life for a while
. . .
Sing us a song, you're the piano man
Sing us a song tonight
Well, we're all in the mood for a melody
And you got us feelin' alright.
—Billy Joel, "Piano Man," 1974

The "second chance" phenomenon of parenthood is realized when a parent witnesses their child successfully grow through adolescence and into adulthood to start the next generation.

Heidi poignantly says of this portion of parenthood,

This is the big let go ... faced with the same dread, exhilaration, and irrational fear of abandonment.

This may also be the experience of adoptees as adults, as they see their own biological or adoptive children grow into adulthood. This time of life, the time of "letting go," despite its potential grief, may be the second chance to mother/parent oneself, to return to the love affair with oneself, and to deeply find one's more complete sense of self.

CHAPTER 11
SUN-TE-UH (SONTIA), THE QUIET FINNISH QUEEN

*"I thought she was a princess, but she was a queen reserving her power, my son on bended knee, taking diamonds from the sky and scattering them in her eyes.
Their love will know eternity."*
—Heidi Marble

DID IT HURT?

It was as if a Finnish angel fell from Heaven onto our driveway to come for an interview to work on my food cart, not a mark on her crisp white shirt. A luminescence outlined her shape, sheets of wheat-gold hair swaying as she made her way to our front door. I grabbed my phone and sent my son a text message: *Your wife-to-be just drove up.*

I knew, like lightning knows thunder, that this angelic creature was my son's girl; the feeling overtook my cells as they buzzed in glee. I greeted this Finnish queen and asked her to join me at our round oak kitchen table, smothered in cookbooks, menus, and purchase orders. My mobile food cart business was going full blast, and I was hanging on by a culinary thread, my hands a mess of cuts, burns, callouses, and splitting skin. My dream of owning a café had turned, through a series of unfortunate events, into a food cart catering business nightmare. The Rolling Pin Eatery specialized in creative comfort food. The actual cart, a shiny black beast, sat just outside the house, its muscled tires bulging, an intimidating reminder of the hundreds of people I needed to feed. Demand was so great that we found ourselves at a seemingly unending series of major concert arenas, wineries, breweries, weddings, and festivals. It was becoming clear that I wasn't cut out for the relentless work of chef/owner. Now a culinary godsend sat before me, one who came for a job, not a mother-in-law.

I dusted the flour off my apron, pushed aside the mess on the table, and attempted to focus on my interview questions. Her wide, emerald-green eyes looked at me curiously as I tried to pronounce her name (Sun-tea-uh) Sontia. She handed me her résumé. The front page could have been a most-wanted poster, and I would have hired her anyway. As I dreamed of blond grandbabies, her essence filled the space. Her energy felt regal, and I could tell that her heart was crowned in a way she couldn't see. But the important thing that day was that she agreed to join our culinary battle so we could win over the hungry masses.

TRUCK-DRAWN CARRIAGE

Sontia started working for The Rolling Pin Eatery right away. She brought a sense of calm and order, as any queen should. I learned that she hailed from a large Finnish family of ten children, five girls and five boys, including adopted triplet boys. They were a family who practiced an exclusive religion, rarely marrying outside of their faith. My hopes about her becoming my son's wife were quickly dashed. Aside from that disappointment, it was time to focus. There was a kingdom to feed and a truck-drawn carriage to zig and zag across the land.

Sontia had a strong culinary background and stealthy kitchen skills. It felt like she just quietly appeared. Her precision contrasted with my freestyle approach. I was creating culinary bombs on the counters, floors, and my apron. We bonded over our love of ice cream, peanut butter, family recipe cards, and all things food. It wasn't long until our culinary dance swirled across the stainless-steel diamond-plated floor. We moved to the music of sizzling, slicing, frying, braising, and clanking until our hungry guests were pleased.

GAME OF THRONES — RED WOMEN

I had no idea that her beautiful Finnish mother would leave their father and take her children, including Sontia, with her only a few months after I met her. They would leave their riches and their friends and sacrifice all measures of security for a chance of emancipation. In that leaving, though, a space opened for Blake to have a shot at romance and for me to matchmake.

CROSSROADS

We were doing an event at Crossroads nondenominational church. It was Halloween night, and the food cart was poppin'. Hundreds of people were dressed in costumes, and lines of people wrapped around us. I was dressed like a box of donuts, literally, one dozen to be exact, with one that would not stay Velcroed, which was testing my last nerve. It was the first time I would meet some of Sontia's siblings, including the adorable triplet boys who were dressed as cops and firemen. We were serving lemon mousse with raspberry sauce, decadent chocolate cake with Halloween candy bark, gooey grilled cheese, and bubbling flatbreads. I remember looking out the window at their smiling faces as Sontia proudly handed them our plated yumminess.

For the month leading up to this night, I had seen my chance and worked hard to make sure Blake and Sontia worked together as much as possible. Among their shared tasks were cutting twelve million lemons, stripping fresh corn, and making more crepes than I would ever be able to use.

Blake had decided to run off to Iceland for a vacation, upending my plan for spark ignition, and on this crazy night, in the middle of our Halloween food service, I had to pick him up from the airport. I drove through night traffic, trying not to smash my donuts with the strap of the seatbelt. He ran up to the car and didn't even mention that I was in costume. As he jumped in and flung his overstuffed backpack in the back seat, he said, "Is my wife working tonight?"

My donut-boxed self almost burst into a cloud of powdered sugar and sprinkles. When we arrived back at the church, I could barely keep up with Blake's pace as he approached the food cart. I jumped in to help with the rush as Blake leaned against the stainless fridge, rummaging in his backpack for souvenirs that he had brought for everyone. When all the church bellies were full and the rush stopped, Blake handed out gifts from Viking land. When it was Sontia's turn, she blushed as he gave her a purple bracelet with heart beads, a magnifying glass, mini-jams, chocolates, and a ceramic bowl. It was clear she was the favorite. In the fire of her cheeks, I saw a flame rise, and it wasn't coming from the stove. I was as filled with happiness and gooey feelings as any good donut should be.

HER KING

And so, their love story began on the edge of autumn. It was as if Sontia and Blake emerged from another time and place and carved out a love story that was as chivalrous as it was equitable, respectful, adventurous, and honoring. My son knew that glass slippers and promises of a fairy tale life would not win this queen over; it would have to be his character. Their romance intersected at a time in her life when everything she knew was falling away. But instead of allowing that experience to close her heart, she remained open, curious, and brave. Blake was fearlessly in love with Sontia. They walked side by side as her world imploded, and they gradually built a life of unshakable love. I had a front-row seat to this beauty and pain, watching Sontia turn Blake into a man and watching Blake turn Sontia into a woman.

GOD EXISTS

Having dabbled in many belief systems, I have become a self-proclaimed religious mutt. I never latched onto anything solid during Blake's growing years, and among my regrets is not giving him a solid foundation of faith. Sontia brought not only my son but our whole family to the feet of God. Her existence was an answered prayer. Among my greatest heartaches was not being able to have a big family. I had religiously prayed that God would find a way to fill our lives with precious people. And with her, he answered.

In what felt like a parade of Finnish supermodels, Sontia introduced us to the rest of her family—her beautiful mother, her sisters, and her brothers. Every single one of them has movie-star looks, perfect features, beautiful smiles—and they are kind and loving. Sontia and her family showed us what walking your faith out really looks like; God is their father. Their trust, their belief, and their devotion made me ashamed of my wishy-washy relationship with our higher power. They anchor each day in prayer, reflection, and study, and to this moment, there has not been one occurrence that has caused them to veer off a faith-driven life. It is more than thick wooden crosses, leather Bibles, and showing up to sing pretty worship music; it is the pure love of God that lives in their darkest moments.

I saw this so clearly during the divorce that was both heart-opening and heartbreaking, when our home became for them a place to transition, a place for God to show his mighty grace. Our families meshed. I found myself happily grabbing extra chairs. We became adept at smashing people around the dinner table and eating with our arms pinned to our sides while praying, giving thanks for our blessings. Over four years, we have shared hundreds of meals and celebrated holidays and birthdays. We have enjoyed water balloon fights, swim parties, *Sponge Bob* marathons, pie making, cookie decorating, kitchen picnics, interpretive dance in pink tutus, giant bubblies, soccer balls, skateboards, volleyball games, fireplace and fire-pit hangs, trips near and far, outdoor church, swimming, trail making, garden planting, blanket forts, pianos, drums, guitars, and a lot of guacamole. Sontia not only brought her love; she brought a sense of family. It was as if God, in his provision, purposefully knitted us together at a time when we needed each other the most.

PEANUT BUTTER REBELLION

As the family's divorce proceeded, an emotionally bloody war of custody between mother and father played out in the courts. With defiance, Sontia went on her own sacrificial strike—she gave up peanut butter. She vowed that she would only eat it when they were around.

This simple act of giving up something that she loved so much was her quiet way of sharing the suffering.

I loved the weekends when the children came around, and peanut butter was allowed. The siblings were together. But on Sunday evenings, six o'clock always came too quickly. The house sulked as their giggles evaporated into nothing.

CROWNED JEWEL

I have a lavish three-drawered stashing station where I keep an assortment of family treasures: my dad's police badge and rodeo buckles, my birth father's fishing flies, my brother's coin ring, and Wongee's wedding rings. When I got wind that Blake wanted to propose to Sontia, I knew that it was time to share something special. As he stood above me one afternoon, I opened the drawer and placed both of Wongee's wedding rings on my pinky. I smiled, remembering how the ring always fell to the side of Wongee's finger, the ring that represented the truest kind of love. I showed them to Blake. The late daylight made the diamond come alive. I asked if he would like to give this ring to Sontia. He held the ring, smiled, and said, "She will love this, Mom."

Sontia was well versed on all things Wongee. The first time we met on that fateful afternoon, I had told her that Wongee was the inspiration behind the name for The Rolling Pin Eatery. In the grand scheme of divine planning, Wongee had inspired my love of cooking, which led to a food cart, which led to Sontia. On that day, I could see Wongee juggling the stars and tickling the clouds with delight.

SONTIA CHRISTOPHER, WILL YOU?

Mt. Saint Helens is twenty-nine miles from our home. Blake found a perfect spot on a flat promontory. Layers of mountain ranges stretched as far as the eye could see. The sky was full of sparse clouds, the ground covered in wild poppies. I had made a picnic, with recipes from their favorite restaurant, and we had carefully placed Wongee's ring in a small navy-blue Limoges box.

Blake dropped to one knee, pulled the smooth box out of his pocket, opened it, and said, "It's time. Sontia Christopher, will you marry me?"

DAUGHTER-IN-LOVE

Sontia, Sontantina, Sun-tea-Uh. My daughter-in-love has taken my heart, given me a daughter to love, given me the glory of seeing my son with an incredible partner, given us a new introduction to faith, and given our lives many full dinner tables. Not to mention that she makes the most divine homemade bread, brings her Zen wherever she goes, and encourages every crazy idea I've ever had. She can pull off amazing one-liners, combine the strangest spices, eat ghost peppers and crickets, dance ballet, and sing like a bird. She is dangerous in all the ways that are beautiful. This Finnish queen looks stunning in red. Her heart holds pain that most will never know. I watch as she holds the sacrifice of brave women standing in quiet strength. By the grace of all that is, I cannot wait to see my blond grandbabies, the ones I imagined on that first day as we sat at the kitchen table. I hope then to see all the siblings, the grandbabies, and my wrinkly self together—all crammed around our table, with mouths full of peanut butter.

CHAPTER 11
SUN-TE-UH (SONTIA) THE QUIET FINNISH QUEEN

THEME 11: ARCHETYPES

Alysa Zalma, MD

Erik Erikson, one of the most prominent twentieth-century developmental psychologists and psychoanalysts, is best known for his psychosocial stages of development, which have become the landmark stages for "normal" childhood, adolescent, and adult development. Despite her many challenges and traumas as an adoptee, Heidi has been able to create resiliency to cultivate and sustain generativity (Erikson's stage 7, *Generativity vs. Stagnation*) and allow space for her son to cultivate an adult romantic relationship (Erikson's stage 6, *Intimacy vs. Isolation*) with her daughter-in-law (Erikson 1963, 263-68).

This chapter provides hope to adoptees that, despite a challenged development, they can find ways to heal their developmental traumas as adults. One of the many ways Heidi could traverse her traumas was through her understanding of archetypes and the collective unconscious as discussed by the Swiss psychiatrist and psychoanalyst Carl Jung.

According to Carl Jung, the collective unconscious is a universally shared human experience independent of culture, race, and time. The experience of the collective unconscious is, according to Jung, expressed in archetypes, which are prototypical examples of human experience (Jung, 2011, 3-5).

As Heidi successfully demonstrates, connecting the self to the collective unconscious and its archetypes is a healing experience for people who feel disconnected from their biological roots and original culture/people.

Heidi's daughter-in-love, Sontia, personifies Jung's archetype of the Angel. This archetype has been expressed by an ineffable spirituality—the experience of "being saved" by a force greater than oneself.

> Why am I standing on a cloud
> Every time you're around?
> . . .
> Ooh, you're an angel
> Ooh, you're an angel
> Ooh, you're an angel
> In disguise, I can see it
> in your eyes
> Madonna, "Angel," Nov. 12, 1984

Heidi describes Sontia as

> **. . . a Finnish angel [who] fell from Heaven onto our driveway . . . not a mark on her crisp white shirt.**

The archetype of the Angel brings joy and magic upon Sontia's arrival. There is a path of light that spins from whence she walks (or cooks). She is the elevated being who banishes all evil and allows all good to come wherever she lands and stays. She brings healing, kindness, prosperity, and safety everywhere. There is no question of her love, intentions, and motives behind anything she does. Her love is always unconditional, and she is as beautiful as she is good. She is calm, brings peace, and represents complete faith and trust. She allows others an easier entrance into their own truest selves.

Heidi depicts the humorous juxtaposition of divine and mundane in Sontia, the angel who "crashes" into the realities of everyday human life. She describes herself wearing a donut costume, trying to run her mobile restaurant, The Rolling Pin Eatery, while Sontia is depicted as the Angel.

> **A luminescence outlined her shape, sheets of wheat-gold hair swaying as she made her way to our front door.**

Heidi feels immediately redeemed by Angel Sontia, who knows how to save the mobile catering business in her own brazen (yet angelic) way, with her stealth precision when handling eggs and lemon rounds.

Heidi notes that Sontia also represents the archetype of the Queen, a female figure of authority and wisdom, with the power to command reverence and respect (*Wonder Woman Magazine*, 2023). Heidi connects this to her need for a guiding force of this nature. Of Sontia, she writes,

> **I thought she was a princess, but she was a queen reserving her power, my son on bended knee, taking diamonds from the sky and scattering them in her eyes. Their love will know eternity.**

Heidi understands Sontia as regal, loyal, and powerful. The Queen also has the reproductive power to create a nation/society. She is capable of mature relationships, with the power to mystify, create, calm, and incite natural forces. This may be particularly important to adoptees. They may resonate with this archetype as the force needed to create a nation/family with utmost interest and importance.

Heidi moves into darker territory with Sontia's mother, eventually paying homage to Jung's archetype of the Shadow. Through her initial encounter with Sontia's mother, who left her husband, Heidi starts to understand the Shadow—the more inward and potentially "unacceptable" self. These are the experiences of the unspoken, the misunderstood, and the qualities of defiance and rebellion.

Through exploration her Shadow archetype, Heidi continues to heal from the universal human conflict of yearning for attachment and connection versus the desire for individuality and freedom.

Heidi initially says of Sontia's mother,

> **I had no idea that her beautiful Finnish mother would leave their father and take her children, including Sontia, with her only a few months after I met her. They would leave their riches and their friends and sacrifice all measures of security for a chance of emancipation.**

Here, Heidi explores why Sontia's mother would leave her marriage. She starts to understand the divergence of what are "acceptable" and "unacceptable" pieces of self. Jung understood that the pieces of self that one shows to the outside world are a mask/"public self" (another archetype called the Persona), and the more inward and potentially "unacceptable" self is the Shadow archetype. A deeper look into this archetype gives us perspective on how these qualities of ourselves offer us more potential to live more fulfilled lives (Perry, 2023).

Heidi interprets the Shadow archetype as the piece of self that Sontia's mother had to embrace to defy her public persona/mask to belong and stay connected to what Heidi described as her "paternalistic culture and religion." Through her understanding of this piece of Sontia's mother, Heidi was able to work through the purpose of the Shadow archetype, which is, according to Jung, the challenge in each person's life; *the Self* (another archetype) must realize it to become "whole" or "true to oneself" (Jung, 2013, 31). This is a universal process that each person must go through.

Heidi references *Game of Thrones*. By no coincidence, the red woman, Melisandre, of the original series gives birth to a shadow "son," who is depicted as the Shadow self of Melidsandre's lover, Stannis.

The Finnish Shadow/Red women, according to Heidi, must make the most difficult and painful choices in life. As Jung describes, they must grapple with the discrepancies of their persona and shadow selves. Heidi understands that these women must either submit to what society tells them (face an inner, symbolic death) or leave (and face an actual threat of physical death).

During the Finnish Civil War, these women had to submit to join the Red Army or defy/"betray" the system and join the resistance. As an adoptee who wanted to find her biological family, Heidi was once caught in the crossfire of betrayal by her adopted family (public self/mask persona) and her desire to acknowledge her "unacceptable" pieces of self to find her biological family (her shadow self). Adoptees may relate to this juxtaposition of internal experiences.

When the rules are broken, when we identify with our shadow self, we are no longer pulled by the root. We all, by recognizing the shadow in ourselves, see the potential for freedom and living our lives the way we wish. Free choice and free will are part of being human.

Cilia Conway's *The Intuitive Tarot*, a Jungian-inspired tarot deck, depicts many of the Jungian archetypes discussed in this chapter and invites the viewer to "read" into the cards to discover an understanding of the various archetypes and what roles these archetypes play in their lives (Conway, 2004, 11).

Conway depicts card VI as *the lovers*. The more "traditional" name of this card is *choice* (Conway, 2004, 44). In *Intuitive Tarot*, card VI is a picture of two lovers fused at the shoulder, portraying the tension between keeping the status quo (being pulled by the root) or choosing to change (pulling by the root). It invites the choice between stagnation or forward motion, status quo, or change. For the lovers, the choice of "pulling *by* the root" is an active process. It is accomplishing the Eriksonian task of normal development, feeling safe enough to choose one's lover/mate "over" their parents. For adoptees, this may represent the lack of safety to seek out their biological families actively.

To "choose" stagnation is a passive choice. As adults, we may feel that we are doomed to repeat these passive "choices." Many events in life may feel like a reenactment of earlier traumas. In the tension and conflict presented by card VI, one may feel that something is being done *to* them, without their permission and beyond their control, and feel that they do not have permission to make a more active choice. This is part of the complex experience of adoption.

Once we realize that we have *any* choice, we begin to break the intergenerational cycle of trauma and move into richer and more authentic lives.

The title of *daughter-in-love* is a comment on the dichotomy between active and passive choices. It is a departure from the traditional term—"daughter-in-law"—which implies that the "choice" of the daughter is made by the son/partner marrying the daughter.

Will adoptees be doomed to repeat the patterns of the past? Heidi has learned the Finnish word "Sisu" from Sontia, which she understands as a mixture of courage, ferocity, and tenacity. It also means having sovereignty over one's experience and being true to one's best and most true self. By choosing to heal and grow, Heidi understands Sontia's plight more deeply. She describes,

> **. . . everything she knew was falling away. But instead of allowing that experience to close her heart, she remained open, curious, and brave.**

By recognizing Sontia's family's traumas as universal conflicts similar to hers, Heidi could free herself from the bondage of what was meant to hold her adoptive family together.

Pulled by the Root implies initial passivity in adoption. Someone else has decided for the adoptee, who did not have a choice. By understanding one's archetypes more deeply and feeling more connected to the universal human "family" described in Jung's collective unconscious, adoptees may find it empowering to experience their lives as a more active process.

CHAPTER 12
A BOY NAMED AMY

"Children born to another woman call me 'mother'.
The magnitude of that tragedy and the depth of that
privilege are not lost on me."
—Jody Candas

IF I "ONLY" KNEW

After my horrendous bout with cancer, I was left to navigate a world that had stripped me of my fertility and blunted my future. On the rusty blade of survival, I stumbled through a graveyard of deceased hopes; my arms reached to the heavens, asking (begging) for another child, specifically a girl child. I could not sort out how God might possibly agree to such a request. Bringing another human into a situation where my life expectancy was tenuous at best felt like a big ask. I am sure God was up above saying, "Don't be greedy; you are alive, and stop asking for more." Nonetheless, my annoying prayers continued in the hope that God would find a way to keep Blake from having to deal with his parents alone. If only I had known then how my prayers would be answered. God, in his infinite humor, wheeled a fifteen-year-old into our lives, a longhaired skater boy named Amy.

RAIN HAS A TEMPER

Thirteen-year-old Blake was dressed in his signature beanie, his blond curls peeking out from the rim. He was wearing a PacSun T-shirt layered with an unbuttoned flannel shirt. It's likely that he had a few chin zits at the time. To lure him home from his new love, the Battle Ground Skate Park, Troy and I built a half-pipe in our 3,000 square-foot shop so everyone could drop in—literally and figuratively. It was obvious that the drug scene was alive and unwell among the skaters at our local skatepark. I thought that spying from 300 feet away, in my parked car, was going unnoticed until Blake sent me a text message saying he could see my hair—I had no idea my eighties' styling could be seen from such a distance.

Despite my cover being blown, though, our bait worked. On this rainy night, Blake's friends were drawn to our home to skate, and that included Becky, Amy's little sister, who would soon become the bridge to a lifelong friendship. Blake thought highly of Becky, and so did all the other wheeled boys. He also thought highly of Amy, idolizing his skating abilities. He often sat on the sidelines at the skate park so he could study Amy's moves. Amy had seen Blake plenty of times, but he thought Blake was a "poser" and wanted nothing to do with the boy who sat it out. When Becky FaceTimed Amy to show him the indoor half-pipe she had discovered, Amy asked, "Who's house are you at?" When she turned the camera toward Blake, Amy replied, "What? *That kid?*"

Before we knew what was happening, Blake's skating idol had hitched a ride and was on his way to "drop in." As soon as Blake learned that Amy was coming, he jumped on the pipe and started skating to impress. Amy walked into the shop through a curtain of rain, and he couldn't believe his eyes—the wood smell, the massive half-pipe, a dozen high-tech speakers pulsing rock music, and Blake grinding along the coping, swooshing down fearlessly, doing air outs, hand plants, and my favorite, the "disaster." Amy confessed that he was blown away by Blake's hidden skills and felt bad for having made an uninformed judgment.

When the skating burned out that evening, the rawboned kids made their way into the main house. I was having pizza with some friends when Amy walked through our front door for the first time. He was cocky from the get-go. His "I am cooler than anyone who has ever existed" attitude came through in the way he glanced around quickly and threw an abrasive hello at us. His greenish-brown eyes were full of light and deep pain. I knew he was in trouble. From that point forward, he started showing up without warning, just in time for dinner. And no matter how many times we offered to pick him up, he would run, walk, skateboard, or (underage) drive himself to our home. So much was unspoken; my questions were met with an "It's okay—no one cares." I got used to trying to piece together why this child didn't want to be at home. I knew he needed to be with us, and I didn't want to push him away with interrogation. I just wanted him to feel safe.

SWELL BOWS

When Amy came into our lives, all my hopes of pink rooms and prom dresses went by the wayside. There would be no pedicures or hair braiding for me—although Amy's hair was long enough for that. God wanted us to parent this boy. I relented and became a "skater mom." Well equipped with first aid, snacks, and a fully charged phone, I led the charge to every skate park in Oregon and Washington, with a load of skinny boys packed into the car like greasy sardines. Spending most of my time doing verbal pat downs, sobriety checks, or safety-gear enforcement, and cheering on breathtaking skating tricks or being there to grab ice for "swell bows"—those are elbows that look like aliens from the impact of falls—I provided enough Band-Aids to cover an entire two-story building. I listened to more rap music than Snoop Dog and provided many party-of-ten restaurant meals, early morning McDonalds runs, and gas station stops for Red Bull, corn nuts, and candy bars.

Before I could comprehend what was really happening, our home smelled of well-worn Van's shoes, pizza boxes, shoe glue, and Axe body spray. I secretly found myself starting to enjoy the culture, the individualism, the X-games, and the skating videos of Tony Hawk and Pedros Barros. The rasp and clickety clack of ball bearings and polyurethane wheels, the shrieks of scrapes, and the slap of skin on concrete became a soundtrack on repeat.

But I drew one clear line. I knew a few of the kids smoked pot, but they soon learned that I have the olfactory senses of a bloodhound; swell bows would have been the least of their concerns if I had caught anyone with a joint. If they wanted food, parks, and my protection, there were *no drugs allowed.*

UNTOLD STORIES

To this day, he cannot give me a reason why people call him Amy. Maybe so God could do more stand-up? After an investigation worthy of a top-notch FBI agent, I discovered that Amy was Romanian, from a wealthy family of six children: two older brothers, two sisters, one younger and one older, and a sweet baby who had passed away at six months. His story would unfold slowly over the next ten years, and what I learned in glimpses broke my heart. The story was too much for him to tell all at once. Out of respect for him, I will not get into the gritty details. The core of my abandonment drew me to help this young man, our pain well acquainted.

MOVING DAY

We had anticipated that maybe one day Amy might want to officially move in. He was already at our home most of the time. Blake was excited about the idea of getting an unexpected brother, especially one he admired so much. A routine set in—meals around the table, homework, games, and family time. Amy also gave Blake heavy doses of big-brother behavior: bouts of ignoring, plenty of put-downs, lots of one-upping, and plenty of locked-door ice-outs. For sure, Blake was learning firsthand about the sacrifices he was required to make—sharing his parents, his home, his friends, and his stuff. As hard as it was to watch, I knew it was strengthening both of them.

One golden glow afternoon, the sun halfway to sleep, Amy pulled up to his usual parking spot in front of the house. His energy came through the door before he did. He was disturbed and anxious, and when he brushed off Hound's excited, slobber-filled greeting, her head sank in disappointment. As Amy entered the kitchen, he felt smaller to me, his shoulders curled in, his hazel eyes glassy, and his skin pale. I asked him what was wrong. He told us his family was going to move into a more elaborate home, in a more elaborate neighborhood, fifteen miles away. To which I said but didn't feel, "You must be so excited, Amy?"

He looked down at his antsy feet and said, "I don't want to go with them. I want to move in with you guys."

His eyes slowly rose to meet mine and then Troy's. Luckily, we both had an enthusiastic reply. "Absolutely! As long as it's okay with your parents. We don't want to cause any problems."

With that, it was shoulders back and smile on; he raced off to talk to them. His parents' answer quickly became evident when his dad pulled up in a truck with Amy's mattress and a few other furnishings.

I knew that how I responded in that moment would matter. By the grace of my humorous God, I remembered Amy telling me how much he wanted to decorate his own room one day. I ran back into the house, grabbed my keys, loaded Amy into the car, and drove to Home Depot to buy paint so he could make his room his own. In those huge moments of transition, I watched Amy wander through the colorfully labeled paint cans and thumb through paper samples. With pure joy, he picked out blood-red and pitch-black. I took a heavy gulp and paid, and before I knew it, the bedroom and Amy were the colors of a giant ladybug. In a two-day storm of hammers, nails, paintbrushes, drill motors, and hanging and banging, Amy created his teenage version of a nursery.

I'M NOT IMPREZA'D

Amy was settling in nicely. We were closing in on his sixteenth birthday. He managed to talk his mother into buying him a Subaru Impreza that was so low to the ground that it almost created sparks when it moved. For reasons I am not mechanical enough to explain, the large exhaust pipes created a loud, deep rumble that you could hear from the other side of the world. It seemed like nothing we could afford could ever compare to this silver Subaru Impreza until I learned that Amy had *never* had a birthday party. Then, I was off to the races.

Who knew an Angry Bird party could spread so much happiness? In short order, we gathered all his handsome nerd and skater-boy friends to join in this monumental celebration. I brought a cake with bright-red and yellow icing to represent Angry Bird and carefully pushed down the right number of candles into the vanilla sponge. Everyone gathered in their elastic-strapped, pointy, red, grumpy, bird-faced hats while bird plates, napkins, and cups cluttered the counter. Under the glow of sixteen candles and the sound of awful singing, Amy blew out a tiny forest of flames. As he made his wish, smoke curled around his smiling face as love curled around my heart.

CALIFORNIA SCREAMING

We were the all-in, over-the-top parents that most people roll their eyes at. And quite frankly, we don't care that our shop has gone through more transformations than Lady Gaga. We were determined to remain in the house where everyone gathered. I had an open-door policy and plenty of home-cooked meals to keep 'em coming. Soon, our cub crew of teenagers and young adults formed.

As we learned more about Amy, we discovered that he had not traveled anywhere outside of our state. We could not wait to show him the world. California seemed an obvious place to start, with its skate parks, sun, and beaches. So, we planned a spring break trip. For some insane reason, I thought we would be able to relax, but *nope*. The trip became a mission to keep Blake and Amy from dying.

Watching Amy and Blake skate was nerve-racking enough. Add the excitement of world-class skate parks and pretty girls, and these wheeled birds, with their flannel wings, tested the limits of my cardiovascular system. When we went to Venus Beach, all was going smoothly as my boy birds started doing their skateboarding thing. Then I noticed Blake step out of the concrete bowl as if something scared him. I sensed danger, and as I came closer, I saw Amy rise out of the concrete bowl into the air, reach superhuman heights, and fall flat (right on his back), his skateboard zipping to a still. He got up and did it again and again, and with each thud, I would scream, "Stop, stop!" He was possessed. It was like all the hurt and anger accumulated in him was being purged. Everyone who was watching felt the danger—the flying, the falling, the blood on his elbows, the fire-red of his face. His shirt stuck to him like wet skin. Just as I was crawling over the concrete barrier to physically try to block him, he edged the coping and flipped the board into his hand. The crowd roared as he brushed past me. His arms streaked in drying blood, he left some of his pain behind him.

HARD TO OPEN

There was so much pain tightly packed in Amy's heart, especially when he first came to live with us. Over time, he unpacked slowly, in unexpected ways. When I would see this unfolding, I would pay attention. Trust came gradually; his vibrant defense mechanisms were always at the ready. He only wept in front of me once; it was the kind of weeping that sounds like a thousand souls moaning. The privilege of being his witness during that hour meant everything to me. His modus operandi was to work out pain through skating, listening to music, driving fast, working on his car, perfecting his schoolwork, and keeping his personal items in pristine condition. As quickly as he opened, he would shut and go back to the "nothing bothers me; I'm a tough guy" stance.

But gradually, he allowed us in. He showed his caring heart—by helping pick my sick mother up off the floor and petting the dog when he thought I wasn't looking. His heart was willing to be seen despite what he had been through.

FAMILY RULES

Anyone who knows me accepts that I am tolerant until I am not. I front-load my trust, and there's a road to Hell and back if you break it. For the kiddos in our lives, the following three were nonnegotiable:

1. Clean up after yourself; don't make extra work for anyone else (me).
2. No underage drinking, drugs, or R-rated nonsense.
3. No opposite-sex sleepovers. Period. Exclamation point!

Amy decided he would test our boundaries on all three. Shall we start with rule 1? For someone as ambitious as Amy, taking out the bathroom trash and wiping down the sink seemed to escape him. Despite the demos that I so lovingly provided, it never happened.

As for rule 2, Amy prided himself on being anti-drugs and anti-drinking, which made our lives easier—until "that night," the night we went out for dinner and came home to find him intoxicated and passed out on the hound dog's bed. I was so angry; I gave that problem to Troy.

As for rule 3, it was obvious that it was disregarded when his girlfriend walked out of his bedroom one morning. After she left, I asked him to leave for twenty-four hours and told him not to return unless he could respect the rules. We gave him a specific time to come home. If he didn't show up on time, we had made up our minds that we would stand our ground and ask him to go back to his house. When the time came, with military precision, I heard the distant rumble of his Subaru. My heart smiled, but I kept my game face as the rumble of his car grew louder. He entered the house and made his way to the fireplace, where we were sitting. He had just showered and was dressed smartly, carrying two large rectangular, hastily wrapped packages.

After he pulled up a dining room chair and apologized for being disrespectful, he handed us his gifts. I eagerly unwrapped mine to find a plaque that had a set of biblical family rules on its face. On the back, he had handwritten a note in black Sharpie. Troy's plaque said, *KEEP CALM AND DRINK BEER*, and it also had a handwritten note on the back. We shed tears and shared hugs, and we told him to go to his room and stay forever. At that point, I couldn't have given a load of butt nuggets what he did wrong; we loved him too much to let him go.

WATCHING HIM FLY

A few weeks ago, when I interviewed twenty-seven-year-old Amy for this chapter, I took time to remind him that he helped us as much as we helped him, that he completed our family.

That was never more evident than at Blake's wedding, when Amy stood by him as his best man. When I asked Amy to tell his version of the truth about his time with us, expecting some hard responses, this is what he said: "I loved every minute of being with you and Troy and Blake. I chose you, and you chose me. You guys are my home. I wouldn't change the good or the bad. I loved it all."

Amy moved away almost three years ago. He graduated from Oregon State University with a civil engineering degree. He now lives in a high-rise apartment in Vancouver, Canada, working as an engineer for Kiewit. Every few weeks, he sends me a song he likes, and I send one back to him. I have repainted his room, but I have left the sign on his door that says, *Amy's Room*. His drawers are still full; his closet has a smattering of items. It is as if he left it that way to remind himself and us that he belongs to this family. Whether it's a noisy Subaru, on a skateboard, or with his bare feet—I hope he always finds his way home. He is ours, and we are his. I thank God every day for the son who grew in our hearts.

CHAPTER 12
A BOY NAMED AMY

THEME 12: THE EPIPHANY OF NOT KNOWING
Alysa Zalma, MD

Amy's lack of history, lineage, and information is startling and disturbing; the reader is left to wonder. We can't help but think, *Why was he relinquished so easily to the Marble family?* We wonder why, after his initial bravado and indifference, he was so quick to want to become part of the Marble family when they offered it. The reader is not invited into heavy details of Amy's story with his biological parents. The story took years for Heidi to unfold; she does not disclose all the information and protects Amy's privacy. Even though she did not know the details in the earlier stages of their relationship, Heidi felt a kinship and an understanding between them. This kinship stemmed from experiences of abandonment that many children of adoption face. Amy was still in the home of his biological parents, but he felt psychologically abandoned.

> **To this day, he cannot give me a reason why people call him Amy. The core of my abandonment drew me to help this young man, our pain well acquainted.**

Heidi and Amy had an immediate connection because of their shared abandonment. The traumas of adoption continued into Heidi's adulthood, and she had a chance to right some wrongs. Healing from trauma has been referenced in previous chapters—how to transcend abandonment and challenge the belief systems of brokenness and unworthiness.

In this situation, Heidi must come to terms with disappointments regarding her health that left her unable to have more biological children. She used her relationship with Amy to help heal her abandonment as an adoptee and challenge her belief systems.

As a child of adoption, her experience and insight afforded her more finesse when offering Amy an opportunity to be adopted. Although it was legally unofficial, Amy's biological parents agreed that he would live with the Marble family. This adoption brought altered allegiances and losses. Ultimately, creating these new strong family bonds was healing for both Heidi and Amy.

Due to their brisk permission for Amy's absorption into the Marble family, it seems that Amy had already been psychologically relinquished by his biological family. When he joined them at age sixteen, Heidi did not want to ask him too many invasive questions.

The readers' not knowing how, why, or what happened to Amy—gives us a portal into the horrors and the protective nature of the imagination of adopted children.

Heidi admits this from the beginning—readers will not know why. Amy's family rapidly agreed to the offer that Amy live with them.

His parents' answer quickly became evident when his dad pulled up in a truck with Amy's mattress and a few other furnishings.

This information further seduces the reader to ask *why*.

Why was Amy not included in his family's home? Or was he? Why just a mattress? Was his mattress strewn on the floor of their house somewhere, unsettled? Did he have a room that felt "settled"? Why did his parents quickly drive his mattress to another family's driveway? Did they not love him? Did he not love them, or did he feel somehow unworthy of their love? Why did they deem him unlovable? Why did this happen?

From Amy's point of view, these questions may look like this:

Why did they drop off my mattress so quickly? Do my parents not love me enough? Why do they deem me so unlovable that they would be willing to drop off my mattress so easily and quickly?

In previous chapters, Heidi got relief and validation around questions concerning her "un-lovability" and embraced belonging with her biological family. However, as many adoptees will relate and concur, Heidi had to pay a tragic price for those answers to her questions.

The answers damaged her relationship with her adoptive mother, who felt betrayed by Heidi's need to find and know her biological mother and sister.

Amy may have had anxieties about betraying his biological family to live with the Marbles. It is a valid concern for many adoptees, as allegiances, betrayals, and the question of lovability are the core issues many adoptees face.

It is unclear what the statistics are for adoptees who adopt children of their own. Perhaps there are ways for our system to concretize better and offer this valuable information in more available and systematic ways. In this way, adoptees who go on to adopt children of their own may offer their insight into the experience of "not knowing" that is highlighted in this chapter to agencies that aid in the adoption process. This is also of particular interest to the biological and adoptive families of the adoptees. It would also help the communities that interface with the adoption community, such as the educators and the mental health professionals who are of service to adoptees.

Heidi adopting Amy into their family speaks to the depth of her understanding of the opportunities she could offer as an adoptee. She has immediate kinship and empathy; she understands the vicissitudes of abandonment that many adoptees feel.

She also understands that adoptees may feel torn by allegiances to their adoptive and biological families. They may feel that they should not/don't deserve to know their biological families. She understands that they may feel horrified but compelled to know why they feel that they were unlovable and relinquished. Heidi had personally grappled with why her biological parents would relinquish her. In the readers' not knowing about Amy, we are left only to wonder if Amy thought this way, too.

For the adoptee, the question of *why* is a fantasy, and not knowing may be protective. To think their biological parents were "right" or "wrong" to relinquish them keeps the adoptee's fantasy alive. It protects against other realities—fearing their biological parent may be dead or unable to care for them.

One example of this fantasy that returns the child's locus of control to them is the thought, *If I am a better child, my adoptive parents will not relinquish me, or maybe my other parents will come back and get me.* It also allows the adoptee to make the biological parents into whoever they want. They entertain the idea that their biological parents may "change their mind" and return for them.

The reader is left wondering who Amy's biological parents are from a psychological perspective. Maybe it would be easier for us to put them in a favorable light and not lay blame on either Amy's presumed unlovability or the presumed tragedy of his biological parents' shortsighted character.

> Maybe far away,
> Or maybe real near by.
> He may be pouring her coffee.
> She may be straightening his tie.
> Maybe in a house,
> All hidden by a hill.
> She's sitting playing piano.
> He's sitting paying a bill.
> Bet you they're young.
> Bet you they're smart.
> Bet they collect things like ash trays and art.
> Bet you they're good.
> Why shouldn't they be?

Their one mistake was giving up me . . .
So . . . maybe now it's time
And maybe when I wake
They'll be there calling me baby
Maybe . . .

Annie, written by Thomas Mehan, produced by Martin Charnin, Mike Nichols, and Arielle Tepper Madover. The Alvin Theatre, debuted April 21, 1977.

There are as many impossible costs for keeping the fantasies alive as there are for knowing the answers. Knowing may not dispel some of the illogical yet intrinsically felt unworthiness many adoptees hold. Readers may not know the answers, but because we will not know, we may further understand the adoptee's experience. Our not knowing may also offer us insights into how we may be able to understand some of these unavoidable conflicts that can erode the adoptee's experience of their best self.

CHAPTER 13
COUNSEL

"Out of suffering can emerge the strongest souls. The most massive characters are seared with scars."
—Kahlil Gibran

"I came to you with hope I didn't know I had. You helped me feel my way out of the darkness."
—H. Marble

HEAL/LEAN

It feels right to end this book with the reality of healing. The statistics on suicide and mental health issues amongst adopted people are four times greater than the general population. To heal we need to lean, lean into each other, ourselves and the professionals who can help us navigate complex trauma. These three great counselors gave me insights and practical ways to move from shadow to the light. They met me where I was and understood what my pain was about. They gave me the right nudges, the right words, and the right guidance to enable me to begin healing. They helped in my quest to come to terms with my adoption, my identity, and my longing for peace. Their guidance helped me address two significant parallel events—my own awakening during my adoptive mom's dying process. This writing is a tribute to them and the life-changing work counselors/therapists do in the world.

THE BLUE CHAIR

The afternoon I met bereavement counselor Lynette Ramirez, I was in crisis, driving down a busy road, in my black car, with my huge black Tom Ford sunglasses, wearing black clothes, closely clutching my black mood. The only thing that wasn't black was my coffee. The trauma covered me like skin. Emotionally hungover, I was averse to bright lights and sharp sounds. My eyelids were half shut, and my upper lip was snarled. The blinker pounded my head with its vicious *clink, clink*. I pulled into a parking spot under the scattered shade of gnarled oak.

Before getting out of the car, I grabbed my iridescent three-ring binder, filled with musings, poems, and questionable tree drawings. Its lively colors caught the light, a moving rainbow in my cold hands. How dare everything be so bright? I shoved the notebook in my black bag and entered the three-story building—looking as if I were headed for a funeral.

The sign for bereavement counseling pointed toward the basement, of course. I thought to myself, *A basement makes so much sense right now. At least it will be dark.*

The overly padded stairs made my steps feel as if they were marshmallow fluff. Inside the lobby, offensively hopeful artwork contrasted the dark corridors of my mind. A kind receptionist greeted me, the flicker of her computer screen animating her glasses. I stared at the business cards of the qualified people while she checked me in. I decided not to warn her that there wasn't a degree on those cards that was gonna touch this situation. She invited me to sit down to wait for my appointment with Lynette. I looked at the assortment of chairs. When the crushed blue velvet one caught my eye, among a wave of black ones, I sat down. It was very possibly my level of insanity, but the chair instantly supported the emotional weight I was carrying; it was strong and soft, giving me a moment of rest. I pulled my notebook out and read a few of my poems in silence.

I took a deep breath when, abruptly, my reading trance was broken by Lynette's warm greeting. Her eyes were not quite brown, not quite green; her smile and hand were reaching out for me. I followed her down a wide hallway into a room with a round table and a chair in the corner holding a slumped-over teddy bear. I placed my notebook and a few pens on the table. Lynette closed the door, sat down, folded her hands, leaned in, and said, "How can I help you?"

My eyelids opened all the way. I felt a few knots of tension release; my soul peeked out to see what we were looking at. No one had asked how they could help me in a very long time. My emotions were boiling over, and I could no longer hold onto them. In that first hour, she heard my whole life.

My mom probably had the longest hospice stay known to man. Her nurse was always in awe of her gradual decline. Her stubbornness in life made her death equally as stubborn. I wanted the suffering to end. I couldn't handle any more of her rebukes. I thought the heartbreak of our torn relationship and her torturous death would do me in first. At the time, I was halfway to crazy, partway to sane.

Over the next two-plus years, Lynette helped me navigate the rough terrain of dying and living. What I learned from Lynette is worth repeating, and it starts with these simple questions.

ASK YOURSELF EVERY DAY

1. What things can I change? = (Strength)
2. What things can I change but don't? = (Hopelessness, depression, anxiety)
3. What things can't I change but try to? = (Ceaseless striving, exhaustion)
4. What things can't I change and choose to release? = (Peace/acceptance)
5. What is true today? What is enough for today? (Peace/acceptance)

DRIVING BY BRAIL

Lynette's drawing was as questionable as mine, but she was able to sketch a series of very tall, pointy mountains, representing the larger problems I had to conquer. She wasn't bad at drawing roadways and cars to show how emotional regulation relates to driving. These visual examples helped me understand important points and gave me something to put in my pretty notebook. I still reference my notes, her drawings, and her emails to remind myself that we can only drive one car at a time, and we can only climb a mountain one step at a time.

Here is an email thread I would like to share:

Good morning, Heidi,
You are on a road moving toward health and peace. As you go down this road, you sometimes try to drive three cars, but you are continuing to grow. As you slow down, you are able to hear, see, and respond to voices that communicate a fork in the road that is important to look at. You are not on that road alone; you have to support people in your life. It might be a road worth driving down because it can release you to take care of issues or release you from hiding from issues. Either way, it is healthy and wise to have faith that you have enough to make whatever part of your journey is for today. Not tomorrow's journey but today's. Muse about what you are seeing on the road today . . . not what you can't see but what you can see. You *aren't* a fortune teller; it costs you so much [to worry].

SEATED

That blue chair became my symbol of help when navigating the crisis of losing my adoptive mom to a slow death. My time with Lynette gave me just enough strength to take the next step, road, breath, or bite, or more accurately, to make the next choice. A few months before my mom passed, Lynette took another job. She had helped strengthen me, but I was shattered to see her go. I thought I would never see her again. Then, twenty-four hours before my mom passed, we found our way to each other on this seemingly endless road. I was holding my mom's smooth, cold hand, sitting on her forest-green recliner, with its waterproof pad, a box of mismatched photos at my feet, when

Lynette arrived at the care home. I had just spent an hour showing and telling, getting excited over the slightest movement in my mom's eyes or mouth. An electric candle stood on her dresser on the advice of her caregiver, Michelle, so her soul could find its way when it left her body. The plastic flicker was making a strange clicking noise. A box of uneaten chocolates was growing soft in the sunlight.

Lynette entered the room. Her hands and eyes reached for me, and then she greeted my mom with a tender grasp, whispering, "It's nice to finally meet you!" Then she and I walked into the empty bedroom next door. At that point, I was twenty-seven days into watching my mom actively die. Everything about me was disheveled. We pulled up two chairs, knee to knee. I reached into my bag for my iridescent binder and read Lynette my last entry—with an auctioneer's speaking pace. Lynette asked me to slow down and start over. I poured out everything I had left in me. When I finished, she put on her coat and gathered her bag. I felt the enormity of our work together.

On the one-year anniversary of my mom's death, I called the bereavement center and asked if I could buy the blue chair. They said no but agreed to send me a photo, which I treasure. In retrospect, the chair was never for me; its job was to continue to give comfort and provide a safe place for whoever must cope with great loss.

SOUL WOUNDS
Cheryl Butler, counselor, MA, LMHC, and Minor Miracle Counseling

Our lives intersected during an intense period of pain, when I was trying to heal my relationship with my adopted mom. I felt desperately alone, scared, angry, and exasperated. My counseling sessions with Cheryl helped me sort through the pain and realize the significance of soul wounds, attachment wounds, and healing. She also helped me realize that the child in me was running the show from a very immature place, adding to my suffering.

Here's an email from Cheryl, July 26, 2011:

> Heidi,
>
> I'm thinking about attachment wounds...
>
> If you could know that a significant part of your anxiety in relationships comes from the way you attached as a child, it would help you in the healing process to understand that because of that soul wound, you enter relationships and interact in relationships with some trepidation and fear. People's responses have huge impacts because of the insecurity of your early attachments. Knowing this means that you can understand at a deep level the intensity of your emotional response when you open your heart to share and others don't respond the way you hope, need, or want. Now that you have brought yourself home, you can care for yourself. You can reassure yourself that no matter how others respond, you are secure. The rejection or rebuke from others doesn't mean you will not survive; it doesn't mean that you are not lovable or okay. It simply means the other person had an emotional response that you need to seek understanding about. You are attached to yourself and God, and the deeper you understand this, the greater the space in the soul for healing and the greater freedom others have to respond–and the greater your freedom of response back. You will not feel too threatened, and you will have a greater ability to set limits and boundaries over others' manipulative and abusive behaviors.

Another email from Cheryl, July 25, 2011:

> Light
>
> May this speak to every cell in your body and bless your day. It is powerful.

"Now to him who is able to do immeasurably more than all we ask or imagine, according to his power that is at work within us" (Ephesians 3:20).

Bringing light, healing, and hope to all our relationships and most desperate situations, holding your thoughts captive to the truth, bringing light to them, and challenging them will change your life. The more practice you get in doing this, the less time you will spend in the darkness. The light is always just a thought away, shifting focus from lies to truth. The wounds are real, they are deep, and they need healing *one at a time*; real work is learning how to grieve, getting really good at it, and forgiving.

Phrases from Cheryl:
- I am capable of feeling negative emotions. I welcome those feelings as being part of who I am. I give myself permission to feel fully.
- I am free; I am not responsible for fixing anyone's problems.
- Others are not my source of approval.
- I am the master of my thoughts.
- Forgiving means canceling the debt.
- Thinking it doesn't mean it's true; feeling it doesn't mean it's true.
- Set boundaries to protect yourself.
- Take your eyes off others' responses.
- I am enough. Who I was created to be is good enough. I have worth and value. I have a right to be here.

GO TO THE WONGEE TREE

The gray clouds seem oddly comforting, the misty rain coating my black eyeglasses. I am ready to take on my "*ass*"ignment.

Go to the wongee tree where you sprinkled half of your mom's ashes and talk to her. Ask her to forgive you. *Me forgive her? Seriously? Shit, shit,*

SHIT, that is what needs to happen. My latest counselor, Carolyn DeLeon, asked me to do this a few days ago, and my mouth went dry. As she firmly stated, my lack of forgiveness toward myself and my mother is a boulder blocking the road to healing. With great reluctance, I meandered across the rain-soaked driveway. The tree was standing tall, with bare branches, and a concrete angel covered in bird poop leaned against the trunk. Winter was deep. My eyes closed shut on a memory of reaching into the black box, pulling out her remains, and scattering them. I looked for any sign of her ashes on the ground; three years since her death, long since taken by the earth. Through the roots, she has become part of the tree, and I was there to make my peace.

I spoke out loud. "Mom, I want to go back and have you sit with me on the edge of my bed, like you did whenever I was hurting. On the edge, we could talk it out, and I always felt better. You were such a good listener and advisor; you were everything to me. When you retracted your love, the last part of my innocence died. I could never find my way back to your heart. At first, I was devastated; then, I became resentful, a martyr. You never looked at me the same way again. I felt the rejection in every cell of my body for decades. Can you forgive me for turning on you? For not being 'really' there when you were sick and vulnerable? I went through the motions enough to keep my guilt from overtaking me. Can you forgive me for wanting you to go so the hurt would 'stop'? The problem is it hasn't. All I ever wanted was for you to love every part of me, to understand that I am the daughter of two mothers. We missed our chance at twenty extra years of love, and that crushes me. Can you forgive me for never letting you back into my heart? You were my best friend. I loved everything about you. What I wouldn't do to see your gold eyes shine with love for me, to feel the smoothness of your hand on my brow. I am sorry our collective unhealed pain caused us to die to each other. In the fire and wonder, in the singe of coming out of the fog, my soul twirled into madness. I felt the leaving, and then I left myself, which is the worst loss of all. I hope you are proud that I have written my truth;

that is how you raised me. We also have a global podcast called *Pulled by the Root* that creates a safe space for people to share their experiences regarding adoption loss. I hope you know I am working toward healing like a ravenous animal. I am grounding my tangled roots into the soil of self-worth. When everything falls away, I pray our spirits can meet on the edge of heaven's bed, where only love matters."

PULLED BY THE ROOT

Daughter of two mothers,
Pulled by the root.
Mud and earth blot out my soul,
Hallow in my bones.
I have looked around, under, through to find peace,
Holding my broken heart like an axe,
Splitting, shattering.
We belong to the night sky, the stardust, the suns amber glow,
The holes we dig, the holes we cover on this snarled path.
So much cannot be undone.
If I can forgive you, then I can forgive me.
I place myself firmly on the ground of redemption.
Naked feet mired in rich soil,
My roots sink in and hold onto everything that is still beautiful.

CHAPTER 13
COUNSEL

THEME 13: THE TRANSFERENCE-COUNTERTRANSFERENCE RELATIONSHIP
Alysa Zalma, MD

This chapter is about transference, the phenomenon between doctor and patient, where the patient "transfers" the relationships of their past and its associated unconscious processes to the psychiatrist or therapist. This phenomenon and the relationship that occurs as a result of it is the crux of psychotherapy treatment. The role of transference has as its genesis Josef Breuer and Sigmund Freud's study of the hypnotic treatment of hysteria, but it was more formally defined with Freud's description of his analysis with his patient Dora (Freud 1963, 137-8). Since then, transference continues to be studied for its clinical significance in contemporary psychiatry and psychodynamic psychotherapy (Ilkmen, 2019 408).

Heidi discusses her experiences with two therapists at pivotal times in her life, both when she needed mothering but was simultaneously defiant. One of these experiences began with her perhaps experiencing the role of "abandonee" in her mother-daughter relationship as she pulled her car into the first counseling center parking lot.

Her ambivalence in her relationship with her mother immediately finds its stark polarities as she enters the center's waiting room. She, in her black sunglasses, "clutching her black mood," discovers a beautiful soft blue velvet chair, seemingly placed there just for her.

Heidi had an appointment with Lynette, a therapist at the center.

Despite her inconsolable fury, there was ambivalence. She didn't want help. Yet she did. She wanted mothering from a therapist she had not yet met.

Heidi sat down.

> **. . . the chair [therapist/mother] instantly supported the emotional weight I was carrying; it [therapist/mother] was strong and soft, giving me a moment of rest.**

Transference is a significant tool in psychotherapy. Because it carries access to unconscious material of patients' past relationships and repetitions, it continues to be considered one of the most effective means to treat patients within a psychoanalytic framework (Bourdin, 2023).

Heidi brings the fury of her relationship with her adoptive mother to the blue chair, symbolizing the therapist/mother, a metaphor for the transference relationship. When she sits on it, she is soothed. When she and her therapist meet, the transference relationship has already begun. As the transference relationship with her therapist was so compelling during her treatment, Heidi tries to purchase the chair from the counseling center after her therapeutic relationship ended.

Part of the captivating nature of the transference relationship is that it offers the patient a "second chance" to replay what happened in the original relationship. For Heidi, in her relationship with her adoptive mother, feelings of abandonment, rage, confusion, and betrayal surface immediately in the transference relationship even before she has met the therapist.

Because the therapist is not the original transference object, meaning that the therapist is not actually Heidi's mother, the transference relationship affords the opportunity to "redo" the relationship in a more healing way as the unconscious material becomes more conscious while the transference relationship develops. Through this relationship is the unique opportunity to heal the traumas that occurred in the original relationship.

When her therapist leaves the transference relationship (takes another job), Heidi does not feel abandoned with the same ire and despair as in the original mother-daughter relationship. Heidi feels that she has been able to process her mother's death more humanely.

As a psychiatrist and frequent partner in transference relationships with patients, I sometimes explain to them the phenomenon between us as "the past alive in the present." Unless a relationship feels "live" (happening now) for the therapist and patient, there is less hope for progress and healing. In my clinical experience, it is more powerful for patients to "live the past in the present" in the transference relationship than to simply recount the past and tell the therapist what happened.

The therapist must be aware of when they feel comfortable in the transference relationship with the patient and when they feel uncomfortable. This portion of the therapeutic relationship is called the countertransference. This more comprehensive view of the therapeutic relationship explains the therapist's unique responses to the patient's therapeutic material based on their own unconscious experiences and their own memories that are separate from the patient's. The effective therapist learns to use and harness these unique and notable experiences of their own as windows into the patient's inner psychic world for which the patient may yet have no language (Jacobs 1991, 132). The power to heal a patient's prior relationships occurs most robustly within this transference-countertransference relationship.

In this relationship, Heidi describes her therapist and their meeting for the first time.

> **Her eyes not quite brown not quite green, her smile and hand reaching out for me, the blue chair released my weight.**

Within the early therapeutic relationship, in all its complexities, Heidi says,

> **. . . the atrophy in my body loosened, my soul peeked out to see what we were looking at.**

Janet Malcolm, noted journalist and author of *Psychoanalysis: The Impossible Profession*, writes candidly about the profession and describes her firsthand experience of transference with analyst Aaron Green, whom she interviewed to discuss psychoanalysis. As in the case of both Malcolm and Heidi, the transference relationship occurs quickly, either upon the initial meeting or before. For Malcolm, the phenomenon of transference happens to her even though she will not see Green for psychotherapy but for an interview. This is part of the compelling yet controversial thesis on transference that Malcolm brings forward.

Malcolm remembers the day she met Green. She comments on her experience of the transference relationship at their first meeting. "I remember that the day was freezing because I remember the agreeable warmth of the low-ceilinged, dimly lit room in which he received me; I felt as if I had come out of a bleak, harsh woods into a cozy lair. This feeling of comfort and relaxation, I now suspect, derived from something besides abundant steam heat" (Malcolm 1981, 5).

Malcolm, however, has some gloomier comments about the transference relationship. After much research, she echoed what Freud himself believed: that every relationship is a transference relationship, and thus, every relationship is an invention according to each individual's early blueprints of all of their prior relationships. She writes somewhat fatalistically that this "at once destroys faith in personal relations and explains why they are tragic: We cannot know each other. We must grope around for each other through a dense thicket of absent others. We cannot see each other plain. A horrible kind of predestination hovers over each new attachment we form" (Malcolm 1980).

Despite Malcom's masterful yet ambivalent account of her experience in a relationship with Aaron Green that approached the transference/countertransference relationship between therapist and patient, Heidi's experience with this phenomenon has had a profound healing effect. It has helped her develop her identity as an adoptee such that she has been able to lead a life based on a more active process of determining and discovering her truest and most authentic self.

If transference exists in every relationship, this may allow us more opportunities than restrictions. Like Heidi, we may use the power of transference to understand ourselves more deeply and completely. This may allow us to enter into more meaningful relationships with this new ability to be our best selves.

If we all have transference experiences with everyone, it may stand to reason that we also have countertransference responses to everyone based on our past that is separate from the pasts of others. We can choose to allow the acknowledgment of transference and countertransference to limit us or to help and enlighten us. This amplifies the choice between a passive and active process of life. As adoptees, as members of a collective unconscious "family" of humanity, the thesis of *Pulled by the Root* is to turn the experience of passivity and the inability to choose one's destiny into one where choices, actions, and free will determine one's most comprehensive and truest identity. They are well within one's reach.

ACKNOWLEDGMENTS
(HEIDI MARBLE)

The acknowledgments could be a novel in and of itself. It must start with parents both known and unknown; the lessons their absence and presence taught me built my soul. Thank you to my dedicated husband, Troy, my incredible son, Blake, and his beautiful wife, Sontia, who supported the evolution of this book. To my siblings Justin Jon, Jennifer Louise and Jeffy/ "Pangy" my gratitude for bringing so much joy to my life. To my Grand Nugget Daya Lily for allowing me to experience love in its purest form.

My coauthor and dynamic friend, Alysa Zalma, MD, tirelessly walked with me through this process, giving years of devotion to this work. To her husband Stephen Back for supporting our effort without hesitation. Our *Pulled by the Root* team, Stephanie Joy Pipes, creative director, Sean Farley, musician/sound engineer, Alex Mazurkevich, video/audio, Jon Betz, film consultant, and initial editor Jim Newcomer. Without their help, *Pulled by the Root* would not exist. To Amy Hansen and Elle Klassen my thanks for taking over the podcast when I needed time to heal. The love these amazing humans funneled into my life gave me the strength to share my truth. I thank the pain that helped me find the deepest roots of the human experience.

ACKNOWLEDGMENTS
(ALYSA ZALMA, MD)

Now that *Pulled by the Root has* been written, my gratitude to all of my nature and nurture families takes on a completely new meaning and depth to me. Thank you to my wonderful husband, Stephen, my soulmate and karma twin, who continues no matter what to tend the garden of my soul and teach me about miracles. Thank you to my beautiful daughters, Ariel and Shandra, who are my infinite source of joy and purpose, whom I love and who love me in a way that teach me there is no ceiling to how magnificent life can be. Thank you to my son-in-law, Matt; in the depth of his ability to love, I see the promise of hope and joy in the next generation. Thank you to my benevolent brother, Adam, my sister-in-law, Melinda, and my nephew, Nathan, and my niece, Sophia, who all are the strength, promise, and bedrock of my family. Thank you to my brilliant parents, Ralph and Terry, my beacons of pure light, my beautiful and worthy biology, my inspiration, and my true loves.

I thank my radiant soul sister, Heidi, who has taught me that I also have family beyond my biology, who has taught me the power of community and the sharing of the gifts of talent and love, who brought me to know and love Troy, Blake, Sontia, "Grandnugget" Daya, Steph, Sean, Alex, and all of her other cubs. Our friendship and work together has changed my life.

BIBLIOGRAPHY

CHAPTER 1

Greenberg, Jay R. and Stephen A. Mitchell. 1983. *Object Relations in Psychoanalytic Theory.* Cambridge, Massachusetts and London, England: Harvard University Press.

Hulett, Kim J., and S.P. Heiney. 2021. "Forgiveness and Health Outcomes in Cancer Survivorship: A Scoping Review." *Cancer Nursing.* Jul-Aug 01;44(4):E181-E192. doi: 10.1097/NCC.0000000000000809

Ingerman, Sandra. 1991. *Soul Retrieval — Mending the Fragmented Self.* New York: HarperCollins Publishers.

Klein, Melanie. 1975. *The Writings of Melanie Klein Volume 1. Love, Guilt and Reparation and Other Works 1921-1945.* New York: The Free Press, Macmillan, Inc.

Maynard PG, van Kessel K, Feather JS. 2023. "Self-forgiveness, self-compassion and psychological health: A qualitative exploration of change during compassion focused therapy groups." *Psychology and Psychotherapy: Theory Research and Practice.* Jun;96(2):265-280. doi: 10.1111/papt.12435.

Toussaint LL, Shields, GS, Slavich GM. 2016. "Forgiveness, Stress and Health: a 5-Week Dynamic Parallel Process Study." *Annals of Behavioral Medicine* 2016, Oct:50(5) 727-735. doi: 10.1007/s12160-016-9796-6.

Worthington Everett L., Witvliet, Charlotte van Oyen, Lerner Andrea J., and Michael Scherer. 2005. "Forgiveness in Health Research and Medical Practice." *Explore (NY).* May;1(3):169-76. doi: 10.1016/j.explore.2005.02.012.

CHAPTER 2

Bettelheim, Bruno. 1977. *The Uses of Enchantment.* New York; Vintage Books.

Brinich, Paul M. 1990. "Adoption from the Inside Out: A Psychoanalytic Perspective." In *The Psychology of Adoption*, edited by David Brodzinsky and Marshall D. Schechter. 42-61. New York, Oxford; Oxford University Press, 1990.

Brody, Jane. 2018, "What Twins Can Teach us about Nature vs. Nurture." *The New York Times,* Aug. 20, 2018. https://www.nytimes.com/2018/08/20/well/family/what-twins-can-teach-us-about-nature-vs nurture.html#:~:text=The%20studies%20of%20reared%2Dapart,percent%20influenced%20by%20the"20en'ironment

Brodzinsky, David M. 1990. "A Stress and Coping Model of Adoption Adjustment." In *The Psychology of Adoption*, edited by David Brodzinsky and Marshall D. Schechter. 3-24. New York, Oxford; Oxford University Press, 1990.

Cardno, AG, Marshall, EJ, Coid, B, Macdonald, AM, Ribchester, TR, Davies, NJ, Venturi, P A Jones, A, Lewis, SW, Sham, PC, Gottesman, I, Farmer, AE, McGuffin, P Reveley, AM Murray, RN. 1999. "Heritability Estimates For Psychotic Disorders: The Maudsley Twin Psychosis Series." *Archives of General Psychiatry* Feb;56(2):162-8. doi: 10.1001/archpsyc.56.2.162. https://pubmed.ncbi.nlm.nih.gov/10025441/

Center for Disease Control and Prevention (CDC) Genomics and Precision Health, August 2020) National Center on Birth Defects and Developmental Disabilities, Public Health Genomics Branch in the Division of Blood Disorders and Public Health Genomics https://www.cdc.gov/genomics/disease/epigenetics.htm#:~:text=Epigenetics%20is%20the%20study%20of,body%20reads%20a%20DNA%20sequence.

Freud, Sigmund. 1923. *The Ego and the Id. The Standard Edition of the Complete Psychological Works of Sigmund Freud, Volume XIX (1923-1925): The Ego and the Id and Other Works, (1-66).* https://www.sas.upenn.edu/~cavitch/pdf-library/Freud_SE_Ego_Id_complete.pdf.

Greenberg, Jay R. and Stephen A. Mitchell. 1983. *Object Relations in Psychoanalytic Theory.* Cambridge, Massachusetts and London, England: Harvard University Press.

Johnson D, Barclay R, Mergener K, Weiss G, Konig T, Beck J, and NT Potter. 2014. "Plasma Septin9 Versus Fecal Immunochemical Testing for Colorectal Cancer Screening: A Prospective Multicenter Study." *PLoS One* 2014; Jun 5;9(6):e98238 doi:10.1371/journal.pone.0098238.

McCartney D, Stevenson A, Hillary R, Walker R, Bermingham M, Morris, S, Clarke T, Campbell A, Murray, A, Whalley H, and David J Porteous. 2018. "Epigenetic signatures of starting and stopping smoking" *EBioMedicine, The Lancet* 2018; 37:214-220.

Tang Q, Cheng J, Cao X, Surowy, H and Barbara Burwinkel. 2016. "Blood-based DNA methylation as biomarker for breast cancer: a systematic reviewexternal icon." *Clinical Epigenetics* 8: 115 (2016). https://doi.org/10.1186/s13148-016-0282-6.

CHAPTER 3

Byrne, Peter. 2008. "The Many Worlds of Hugh Everett." In *Scientific American*, October 21, 2008.

Engels-Smith, Jan. 2021. Soul Retrieval Class, Lightsong School of 21st Shamanism and Energy Medicine.

Hoffman, Stefan, PhD, Grossman, Paul and Devon E. Hinton. 2011. "Loving-Kindness and Compassion Meditation: Potential for Psychological Interventions." *Clinical Psychology Review.* Nov;31(7): 1126-1132. doi: 10.1016/j.cpr.2011.07.003 https://doi.org/10.1016/j.cpr.2011.07.003

Tegmark, Max 2003. "From Quantum to Cosmos." In *Science and Ultimate Reality; From Quantum to Cosmos*. Edited by Barrow, J.D., Davies P.C..W, and C.L. Harper, 1-18. London, Cambridge University Press. https://space.mit.edu/home/tegmark/multiverse.pdf.

Vilenkin, Alexander and, and Max Tegmark. 2011. "The Case for Parallel Universes ("Why the Multiverse, Crazy As it Sounds, is a Solid Scientific Idea"). *Scientific American*. July 19, 2011.

CHAPTER 4

Buddhaghosa, Bhadantacariya 1975. *Path of Purification*. Translated by Bhikku Nanamoli Kandy, Sri Lanka, Buddhist Publication Society.

Grace and Lightness, 2023. https://graceandlightness.com/hooponopono-for-forgiveness/ January 1, 2023.

Hanh, Tich Nhat. 1975. *The Miracle of Mindfulness*. Translated by Mobi Ho. Boston, Beacon Press.

Ho, JMC, Chan, ASW, Ching, YL, Tang, MKT, 2021. "Book Review: The Body Keeps the Score: Brain, Mind, and Body in the Healing of Trauma" *Frontiers in Psychology (12): 1-2*. https://doi: 10.3389/fpsyg.2021.704974

CHAPTER 5

Adhikari, Srijanee, 2017. "Androgyny in Renaissance Art." Intro819.wordpress.com/2017/11/12/androgyny-in-renaissance-art/

Hamburger, W.W. 1997. "Emotional Aspects of Obesity." *Obesity Research*, 5 (2): 162-171. https://doi.org/10.1002/j.1550-8528.1997.tb00658.x

CHAPTER 6

Ogden, Thomas. 1997. *Reverie and Interpretation*. Jason Aronson, Inc. New Jersey, London. Jason Aronson, Inc.

Winnicott, D.W. 1953. "Transitional Object and Transitional Phenomena – A Study of the First Not-Me Possession." *The*

International Journal of Psychoanalysis, 34: (89-97).

Winnicott, D.W. 1960. "The Theory of the Parent-Infant Relationship." *The International Journal of Psychoanalysis,* 41: (585-95).

UK Essays.com. "Holding and Containing – Winnicott (1960)." www. https://ukessays.com/essays/psychology/holding-and-containing-winnicott.php#

CHAPTER 8

Freud, Sigmund. 1965. *The Interpretation of Dreams*. James Strachey, ed. New York, Basic Books.

Ingerman. Sandra (1991). *Soul Retrieval — Mending the Fragmented Self.* Harper San Francisco, 1991.

Markin, Daphne. 2006. "Sometimes a Bag Is Not Just a Bag,." *The New York Times Magazine*. Feb. 26, 2006. nytimes.com/2006/02/26/style/tmagazine/sometimes-a-bag-is-not-just-a-bag.html.

Rogers, Carl. 1957. "The Necessary and Sufficient Conditions of the Therapeutic Personality Change." *Journal of Consulting Psychology*, 21(2), 95-103. https://doi.org/10.1037/h0045357.

CHAPTER 9

Anthony, Rebecca E., Paine, Amy L., and Katherine H. Shelton. 2019. "Adverse Childhood Experiences of Children Adopted from Care: The Importance of Adoptive Parental Warmth for Future Child Adjustment." *International Journal of Environmental Research and Public Health* Jun; 16(12): 2212. 2019 Jun; 16(12): 2212. doi: 10.3390/ijerph16122212

Harlow, H. F. (1958). "The Nature of Love." *American Psychologist, 13(12), 673. https://doi.org/10.1037/h0047884*

CHAPTER 10

Ogden, Thomas. 2004. "On Holding and Containing, Being and Dreaming." *The International Journal of Psychoanalysis.* 85:1349-64.

CHAPTER 11

Conway, Cilla. 2004. *The Intuitive Tarot—Unlock the Power of Your Creative Subconscious,* London: St. Martin's Press.

Erikson, Erik H. 1963 Second Edition. *Childhood and Society.* New York. W.W. Norton and Co.

Jung, C.G. 2011. *Four Achetypes from The Collected Works of C.G. Jung Volume 9, Part 1 Bollingen Series XX.* Translated by R.F.C. Hull. Princeton and Oxford: Princeton University. Press.

Jung, 2013. *Aion; Researches into the Phenomenology of the Self from The Collected Works of C.G Jung, Volume 9 Part II.* Translated by R.F.C. Hull. Princeton and Oxford: Princeton University. https://ia600606.us.archive.org/11/items/collectedworksof92cgju/collectedworksof92cgju.pdf

Perry Christopher. 2015. "The Jungian Shadow." *The Jungian Society of Analytical Psychology,* August 12, 2015. https://www.thesap.org.uk/articles-on-jungian-psychology-2/about-analysis-and-therapy/the-shadow/

Wonder Woman Magazine. May 11, 2023. "What is The Queen Archetype and How to Embody Her in Your Daily Life." https://www.wonderwomanmag.com/what-is-the-queen-archetype-how-to-emody-her-in-your-daily-life/.

CHAPTER 13

Bourdin, Dominique. 2023. "On the Analytic Transference." *International Journal of Psychoanalysis.* Aug;104(4):691-700. doi: 10.1080/00207578.2023.2230771.

Freud, Sigmund. 1963. "Dora: An Analysis of a Case of Hysteria." Reiff, Philip, Ed. New York: McMillian Publishing Company.

Ilkmen, Yasemin S and Sibel Halfon. 2019. "Transference Interpretations as Predictors of Increased Insight and Affect Expression in a Single Case of Long-Term Psychoanalysis." *Research in Psychotherapy*. Dec 19; 22(3): 408. doi: 10/4081/ripppo.2019.408.

Jacobs, Theodore. 1991 *The Use of the Self, Countertransference and Communication in the Analytic Situation*. Madison: International Universities Press, Inc.

Malcolm, Janet. 1981. *The Impossible Profession*. New York: Alfred A. Knopf, Inc.

Malcom, Janet. 1980. "The Impossible Profession - II" *The New Yorker Magazine*, November 23, 1980. https://newyorker.com/magazine/1980/12/01/the-impossible-profession-ii.

www.ingramcontent.com/pod-product-compliance
Lightning Source LLC
LaVergne TN
LVHW091720070526
838199LV00050B/2485